AF709295

Doenitz at Nuremberg: A Reappraisal

War Crimes and the Military Professional

Doenitz at Nuremberg: A Reappraisal

War Crimes and the Military Professional

H. K. Thompson, Jr.
Henry Strutz
co-editors

Amber Publishing Corp. New York City

ISBN 0-916788-01-6 (trade edition)
ISBN 0-916788-02-4 (limited signed edition)
Library of Congress Card No. 75-26202
Printed in the United States of America
Copyright© 1976 by Amber Publishing Corp.
21 Hudson Street, New York City 10013

To Karl Doenitz

a naval officer of unexcelled ability and unequalled courage who, in his nation's darkest hour, offered his person and sacrificed his future to save the lives of many thousands of people.

EDITORS' INTRODUCTION

The project from which this book stems was begun by the co-editors in 1956, on the occasion of the release of Grand Admiral Doenitz from Spandau. The purpose was a sampling of up-dated qualified opinion on the Nuremberg and related "war crimes trials" of Axis personnel conducted by the Allies just after World War II, with emphasis on the trial of Doenitz. The initial results encouraged us to proceed further, which we have done, slowly and methodically, over a period of almost 20 years.

A variety of responses was received, not all of them by any means favorable to our basic position. Among those who continued to support the trials, there were several categories: (1) a hard core who still maintained the legality of the proceedings, consisting in large measure of persons who had in some way participated in the "trials"; (2) those who while admitting that the proceedings were illegal, felt that they were necessary as an instrument of political policy; and (3) those who felt that the trials were an attempt to establish a new body of international law aimed at limiting future "aggressive wars"; nevertheless many in this category were disturbed at the *ex post facto* application of this newly created "law." Since the arguments advanced by proponents of the trials are still prevalent officially and in the media, we have felt no compulsion to give them further voice in this work. Statistically they represented an extremely small percentage of the responses received by us.

In deciding which contributions to include in this book, it was necessary to read, evaluate and categorize many thousands of letters, briefs, and manuscripts, varying in length from a single sentence to 30 pages. We were concerned with selecting a cross-section of the arguments advanced, containing as little duplication as possible, and a reasonable representation of contributors by rank or position, nationality, and field of endeavor. Thus the reader will find, in addition to the military, representative opinions from clerics, authors, diplomats, journalists, lawyers, publishers, jurists, statesmen of every description, and even theatrical personalities. For the convenience of readers, an alphabetical listing of contributors appears at the back of the book.

The authors appear in this work without preconceived order of any kind. In fact it might be said that the last shall be the first. More attention was paid to design and typographical balance than to the contents of any statement or rank of the writer. Photographs (where obtainable with the cooperation of the subjects) and facsimile signatures were used to add visual interest and emphasis. Most (but not all) of the contributors are now retired from public life, as might be expected with the passage of years. In our identification of personalities, we have merely indicated branch of service or occupation. Retirement by 1976 must in most cases be assumed as all of our contributors were either exercising commands of importance or were determining policy during the World War II era. As such, they are best qualified to evaluate it now. A word of caution. In extremely few instances has any one contributor seen the work of any other. Each has expressed his own views in his own way, and cannot be held responsible for the views of others, including the editors. Some addressed themselves only to the Doenitz case, others only to the general question of Nuremberg, still others to a combination of the two.

Many potentially useful opinions received were not, for a variety of technical and practical reasons, used in this book. We saw no point in reproducing, over and over again, the same arguments expressed in almost identical language, merely to produce a book of great length. Then there was the problem of obtaining reprint permission in some cases, as well as locating estates and next-of-kin. To mention but a few opinions which do not appear in this book: Dean Douglas Horton of the Harvard Divinity School expressed the view that our arguments are incontrovertible. General Walter Bedell Smith (Chief of Staff, A.E.F. in Europe, 1944-1945; Ambassador to the Soviet Union, 1946-1949; Director of the Central Intelligence Agency, 1950-1953, and Under Secretary of State, 1953-1954), commented that his indirect connection with the Nuremberg trials had been on his conscience for many years. Vice Admiral Emory Scott Land (Chairman of the U. S. Maritime Commission, 1938-1946, and head of the War Shipping Administration, 1942-1945) found himself in general agreement with the views of Admiral Gallery (see Prologue). Attorney Joseph N. Welch (counsel for the U. S. Army in the famous McCarthy hearings) expressed his disapproval of the Nuremberg trials, holding them to have been a mistake. And, on the lighter side, the famous Hollywood show dog, Rin Tin Tin, sent us a message for Admiral Doenitz over the signature of owner and dog-trainer, Lee Duncan, but bearing an authentic paw print of the canine star. Ultimately, all of the papers and research materials used (and unused) in connection with this book will be available to scholars in the H.K. Thompson Collection at the Hoover Library on War, Revolution and Peace, Stamford University.

During our research for this book, we obtained access to some original unpublished source material. As the readers are no doubt aware, one of the great errors of the Nuremberg and related proceedings was to deny to Axis personnel the defense of having complied with orders of duly constituted higher authority. This particular "heritage" of Nuremberg has left us with a situation where any official in any chain of command must evaluate orders received in terms of his own code of personal morals or ethics and the implied moral or ethical codes of others, rejecting those orders which he feels unsuitable. The obnoxious doctrine has been carried over into civilian life, undermining for example — the American educational system. Applied in the military, the results can only be total chaos. Our research led us to a pertinent original letter in our possession. Jefferson Davis (West Point graduate, U.S. Secretary of War, and President of the Confederacy) wrote on Jan. 18, 1883, to General C.J. Wright, that he had, "...no hesitation in answering your inquiry as to whether an officer on the field of battle may exercise his discretion as to whether he will obey an order of his Chief. Nothing certainly could be more destructive of success than such confusion and disturbance in the plan of battle as would result. Though an officer should see plainly that to obey the order of his Chief would be to sacrifice his command, he has no right to question the purpose for which the order was given, but should rather assume that it was essential to the success of the Army of which he was only a part, and like a patriot give himself as a willing offering on the altar of his country." Similarly, President Dwight D. Eisenhower held *(New*

York Times, May 13, 1954) that, "The obedience of an officer must be absolute and is not subject to private moral scruples. The very being of an Army consists in the execution of the commands of the leaders and the laws of the Government without hesitation, the responsibility for which rests alone upon the Commander-in-Chief...In the Army, as especially in State Service, the oath of allegiance obliges obedience to those in command and their orders. Not for one second would I ever suffer disobedience or insubordination."

In "Bitter April," an excellent article in *Shipmate* (published by the U.S. Naval Academy Alumni Association), April, 1959, the naval historian Rear Admiral John D. Hayes, discussed the dilemma faced by Southern naval officers at the outbreak of the Civil War in 1861, and their various fates after the Union victory in 1865. Admiral Hayes notes, "After more than a decade, Americans are again hearing and reading the term 'war criminal.' This time it is applied not to former enemies but to officers of an army which up to a few months ago was under the tutelage of a U.S. Military Mission. At the same time, a campaign is now under way to remove the appellation 'war criminal' from the record of Grand Admiral Karl Doenitz, recently released from Spandau Prison in Berlin. Many distinguished naval officers have given their blessing to this campaign, holding that the 'crime' for which Doenitz was convicted was, in reality, the effective professional direction of the wartime navy of his country, a 'criminal standard' under which any career military or naval officer could be convicted..." After discussing the cases of American naval officers of Southern birth in the Civil War, Admiral Hayes concludes, "The only case of reprisal was against Raphael Semmes of *Alabama* fame...Welles [Gideon Welles, secretary of the Navy] dared not bring Semmes to trial before a naval court martial and President Johnson would not allow the case to come before a civil court. After three months of imprisonment, Semmes was allowed to go free. The similarity between the action against Semmes and against Doenitz is readily apparent. The difference in the outcomes does not reflect credit on another generation of Americans."[1]

Direct and indirect applications of Nuremberg doctrines took place in the years following World War II, notably over incidents and policies in Korea, Cuba, Vietnam, and Cambodia. Even in the 1956 Anglo-French-Israeli venture in Suez, some editorial opinion held Anthony Eden, English prime minister, to be a "war criminal" in the Nuremberg sense, but no international tribunal chose to pry into that can of worms. In Korea, the essential issues were the question of aggression by North Korea versus the counter-claims of provocation, and the matter of the authority of the U.S. President to order troops to foreign battlefields without Congressional consent, the latter of course a domestic question. No "International Tribunal," military or otherwise, was convened by anyone, and the whole Korean affair was swept under a United Nations rug, *ex post facto* of course, by its stamp of approval on the essentially unilateral American action. Cuba was another matter, capably summed up in the "Capitol Stuff" column of the *N.Y. Daily News* on Jan. 26, 1959, "The State Department, itching to protest in the name of humanity the con-

1. Excerpted with permission of the author and the U.S. Naval Academy Association.

tinued slaughter of members of the Cuban army and Batista's police by Fidel Castro's conquering rebels, has discovered itself neatly gagged by our own America's example. As Castro pointed out, it was we Americans who first thought up the idea of 'unconditional surrender' and 'death for war criminals.' And if we considered this correct against the defeated Germans back in 1946 what is wrong, he asks, about the Cubans applying the same judicial process to their fellow enemy Cubans in 1959?...Castro is on solid ground. We showed him how to do it...The original idea — strictly unconstitutional — was that of former President Franklin D. Roosevelt. It squared up with his other decree — equally distasteful to military personnel — that of 'unconditional surrender'...We have set the course; Castro only follows it. With us, Roosevelt issued the decree and the late Justice of the Supreme Court Robert Jackson, with other war-inflamed members of the bench, were his assistants in the injustice. They forgot, or overlooked in their Nuremberg procedure, a small but important part of the American Constitution which reads: *Article One, Section 9 — No bill of attainder or ex post facto law shall be passed...*"[2]

The Vietnamese adventure, with Cambodia thrown in, divided the United States and raised Nuremberg-like issues galore, with the unfortunate precedents created by the so-called International Military Tribunal invoked by draft-card burners and every manner of dissidents. Lord Bertrand Russell was instrumental in convening an international "war crimes tribunal," based on Nuremberg and sitting in Sweden, to indict the U.S., not in a legal sense since the tribunal was legally incompetent, but to bring the issues before a "court" of world opinion. Again the Nuremberg chickens came home to roost.

Telford Taylor, U.S. chief counsel and one of the major proponents of the Nuremberg, Tokyo and related proceedings, has made some concessions in his book, *Nuremberg and Vietnam: An American Tragedy* (Quadrangle Books, Inc., A New York Times Company, 1970). On page 86 of that work, he notes that, "...Karl Doenitz was only a commodore and commander of the small U-boat arm when the war began; the Tribunal found that he had neither been present at Hitler's conferences nor informed about his plans, and based the conviction on the fact that Doenitz 'waged' aggressive war because his submarines were 'fully prepared to wage war.' On that basis every commander of combat troops or ships would have been equally guilty, but the Tribunal's opinion showed no awareness of these far-reaching implications. Inferentially though not explicitly the judgment on Doenitz was repudiated by a later Nuremberg court that acquitted on the same charge commanders of much higher rank than Doenitz on the ground that they were not at the 'policy level'..."[3] That *inferential but non-explicit* repudiation of the Doenitz conviction was of no aid to Admiral Doenitz, and the "Tribunal" permitted him to serve ten long years of confinement in the Spandau Prison under conditions which resembled those alleged against prison-

---

2. Excerpted with permission of the *N.Y. Daily News.*

3. © 1970 by The New York Times Company. Reprinted by permission of Quadrangle/The New York Times Book Co. from *Nuremberg and Vietnam: An American Tragedy*, by Telford Taylor.

keepers of Axis regimes. And to this patent injustice, the U.S. Government placed its seal of approval.

Mr. Telford Taylor also, in 1965 he relates, ultimately became a critic of U.S. involvement in Vietnam, which he terms in his book (page 207), "the most costly and tragic national blunder in American history." He sums it up as follows, "...And so it has come to this: that the anti-aggression spirit of Nuremberg and the United Nations Charter is invoked to justify our venture in Vietnam, where we have smashed the country to bits, and will not even take the trouble to clean up the blood and rubble. None there will ever thank us; few elsewhere that do not now see our America as a sort of Steinbeckian 'Lennie,' gigantic and powerful, but prone to shatter what we try to save. Somehow we failed ourselves to learn the lessons we undertook to teach at Nuremberg, and that failure is today's American tragedy."[3] Viewed somewhat differently, Mr. Taylor stands hoisted by his own petard, and the United States trapped again by its endorsement of and participation in the Nuremberg proceedings.

Among the many inconsistencies and inequities which serve to invalidate the Nuremberg and related trials was their failure to deal with the subject of aerial bombardment. Instead, the Doenitz submarine service was singled out for condemnation, as if there were any substantial difference between a tordepo from below and a bomb from above; the matter of "warning" might be about equal, but aerial bombs generally carried substantially heavier loads. Instead, the Tribunal realized that such Allied acts as the bombing of Dresden and the unleashing of the atomic bomb upon Japan would be, by the Tribunal's own definition, such as it was, "war crimes" *par excellence,* and therefore must be swept under the Nuremberg rug. The defense which would have inevitably been offered in aerial bombardment cases, that such bombings "shortened the war," could easily have been overcome. It was clearly the incredibly stupid Allied policy of "unconditional surrender" which prolonged the war and, "stiffened the enemy resistance to the cost of uncounted American and Allied lives" (John O'Donnell in the *N.Y. Daily News,* Jan. 26, 1959).[2] Justice Robert H. Jackson stated at the Nuremberg trials, "...if it [the Nuremberg proceeding] is to serve any useful purpose, it must condemn aggression by any other nations, including those which sit here now in judgment." This was *not* done. "Judges" do not sit in judgment on themselves, as Justice Jackson well knew.

One might ask why, in view of the extent of U.S. involvement in the Nuremberg proceedings and the participation of U.S. prosecuting personnel, the basic unconstitutionality of the process did not cause a review in U.S. courts by writ of *habeas corpus* despite the provisions of Article 26 of the Charter annexed to the London Agreement providing that "The judgment of the Tribunal shall be final and not subject to review." Article 26 was intended to get the political officialdom of the U.S., England, and France "off the hook" at home because of the obvious legal repugnance of the Nuremberg proceedings. Counsel for various defendants in Nuremberg and related trials did indeed petition the U.S. Supreme Court, but these petitions were first dodged on the grounds of "no original jurisdiction." On December 20, 1948, the petitions were finally denied, the Supreme Court taking the interesting position that,

"We are satisfied that the Tribunal sentencing these prisoners is not a tribunal of the United States." Then why, one might ask, were U.S. citizens and government officials serving as prosecutors and judges, and why has the U.S. government participated in and endorsed an alien tribunal which does not accord to defendants the same rights which American defendants would receive before U.S. courts at home?

Finally, on June 5, 1950, the U.S. Supreme Court had to face the issues, defense counsel having secured a ruling from the Court of Appeals of the District of Columbia holding that, "if a person has a right to a writ of *habeas corpus*, he cannot be deprived of the privilege by an omission in a federal jurisdictional statute." Stripped away by this ruling was all the hokus about the "international" character of the Nuremberg and other such tribunals. Pressed to find a way out, the U.S. Supreme Court mustered its legal courage and insight with the final side-stepping ruling that, "A non-resident enemy alien, especially one who has remained in the service of the enemy, does not even have qualified access to our courts." *That* was how it resolved the legal issues. Justice Hugo L. Black, in his dissent, exposed the utter hypocrisy of the Supreme Court decision. Justice Black wrote: "The Court cannot, and despite its rhetoric on the point does not deny that if they [the defendants] were imprisoned in the United States our courts would clearly have jurisdiction to hear their *habeas corpus* complaints. Does a prisoner's right to test the legality of a sentence then depend on where the government chooses to imprison him?...We ask only whether the Military Tribunal was legally constituted and whether it has jurisdiction to impose punishment for the conduct charged. Such limited *habeas corpus* review is the right of every citizen of the United States, civilian or soldier...Any contention that a similarly limited use of the *habeas corpus* for these prisoners would somehow give them a preferred position in the law cannot be taken seriously..."[4]

U. S. Supreme Court Justice Wm. O. Douglas held (in Hirota vs. MacArthur, 338 U.S. 197, Dec. 1948) that, "The fact that the tribunal has been set up by the Allied Powers should not of itself preclude our inquiry. Our inquiry is directed not to the conduct of the Allied Powers but to the conduct of our own officials. Our writ would run not to an official of an Allied Power but to our own official. We would want to know not what authority our Allies had to do what they did but what authority our officials had. If an American General holds a prisoner, our process can reach him wherever he is. To that extent at least, the Constitution follows the flag. It is no defense for him to say that he acts for the Allied Powers. He is an American citizen who is performing functions for our government. It is our Constitution which he supports and defends. If there is evasion or violation of its obligations, it is no defense that he acts for another nation. There is at present no group or confederation to which an official of this Nation owes a higher obligation than he owes to us. I assume that we have no authority to review the judgment of an international tribunal. But if as a result of unlawful action, one of our Generals holds a prisoner in his custody, the writ of *habeas corpus* can effect a release from that custody. It is the historic function of the writ to examine into

4. Frederick Williams in *American Mercury*, August, 1957

the cause of restraint of liberty. We should not allow that inquiry to be thwarted merely because the jailer acts not only for the United States but for other nations as well." Today, in 1976, there sits in Spandau Prison in West Berlin one solitary prisoner, Rudolf Hess, now upwards of 80 years of age, who has been incarcerated by the Allies since his ill-fated peace mission to England in 1941. This prison is maintained, in rotation, by four powers, the U.S., Great Britain, France, and the Soviet Union. Needless to say, the cost, in large measure, is met by U.S. taxpayers and without their knowledge and approval. The three Western powers have long ago agreed to support the release of this solitary prisoner on humanitarian grounds alone, but they are blocked by the Soviet Union, which is anxious to maintain a military garrison in West Berlin. One wonders what might result if, during a period when the Spandau garrison was under command of the U.S. military unit, a *habeas corpus* action were to be brought against the commanding officer thereof, bringing Hess before a U.S. District Court which could inquire into the unconstitutionality of the *ex post facto* considerations which brought about his incarceration?

The conduct of the American judges at Nuremberg was, to say the very least, of the most questionable propriety. One of the judges, Francis Biddle, reveals in his article on Nuremberg in *American Heritage*, Vol. XIII, No. 5, August, 1962, that the U.S. judges knowingly permitted the Soviet prosecutor to admit false evidence against the defendants (page 70). Further, Justice Jackson hosted a party for visiting Andrei Vishinsky (notorious Soviet prosecutor in the bloody Stalin purges), at which party the American judges joined in a toast by Vishinsky, "To the German prisoners, may they all be hanged!" (page 71). By any ethical standards of any bar association in the western world, such "judges" should have been disqualified and themselves charged.

War is a political weapon of sovereign powers. It has always existed in the history of mankind and, however much an idealistic condition of perpetual peace and harmony is to be desired and striven for, human nature and the state of the world today give every indication that war will continue to exist. It appears that Isaiah's day when the nations shall not make war any more will unfortunately be a long time in dawning. In the interim, to plan for the contingency of "aggressive war" is the duty of all general staffs and to be prepared to conduct "aggressive war" is the duty of all military commanders. Nothing else makes any sense. What is left to us in the wake of the more and more widely discredited Nuremberg proceedings is the fact that a staff which seeks to defend its nation under all contingencies stands guilty of a "crime against peace" and a military commander who maintains his troops or vessels at battle readiness stands guilty of "conspiring to wage aggressive war." The remedy is to destroy the Nuremberg "principles" and put them to rest for all time. But there is no machinery for this, no courts to which to appeal, no body of law to invoke. Historians can continue to chip away at Nuremberg, to try to set the record straight, but this is of little comfort to the professional military officer — and the professional civil servant — who must do his duty, who must continue to comply with the directives of legally-constituted higher authority. To ease the burdens placed upon those dedicated men and women is one of the objectives of this book. Contained herein is a wealth of fact, of argument, of legal and other opinion which can be cited and used, time and time again, in the continuing struggle against Nuremberg and its works.

H. K. Thompson, Jr.
Henry Strutz

New York City
June, 1976

ACKNOWLEDGMENTS AND CREDITS

No work of this nature could be undertaken without incurring an enormous debt of gratitude to a large number of persons. Particular thanks are due to each and every contributor, including those whose views we were not able—solely because of space limitations and publishing considerations—to include in this volume. Very special thanks are due to Admiral Thomas C. Hart and Vice Admiral Charles A. Lockwood, guiding mentors without whose valuable and active assistance this project could not have been successful. Similar thanks are owing to a senior and highly respected submariner whose active duty status entitles him to anonymity. Other acknowledgments are made to Mrs. Janis Eisenhower Causin, Mrs. Bettina Byrd Iwersen (executrix of the Estate of Frank L. Beals), Frederick Williams, Rear Admiral Chester W. Nimitz, Jr., Mr. Sidney Linder (for his typography), and to General Matthew B. Ridgway for his helpful suggestions. A large debt of gratitude is owing to pioneer authors in this field, particularly F.J.P. Veale (for his *Advance to Barbarism,* and *Crimes Discreetly Veiled),* to Rear Admiral Dan V. Gallery (for his *Twenty Million Tons Under the Sea),* to Viscount Maugham (for his *U.N.O. and War Crimes),* to Hon. R.T. Paget (for his *Manstein),* to Montgomery Belgion (for his *Epitaph on Nuremberg,* published in the U.S. as *Victors' Justice),* to Lord Hankey (for his *Politics: Trials and Errors),* to A. Frank Reel (for his *The Case of General Yamashita),* Peter Calvocoressi (for his *Nuremberg),* to Captain Russell Grenfell, R.N. (for his *Unconditional Hatred),* and to R.W. Cooper (for his *The Nuremberg Trial).* Most, if not all, of these works are out of print, and a number were published in England, but major libraries should have them. Lastly, thanks are due to the public information services of the U.S. Army, Navy, and Air Force, also to the U.S. Naval Academy Alumni Association, all of which were helpful and cooperative.

Photographic credits are hereby made to: Foto Mattern (Santiago), Muscella Studio (Chester, Pa.), Moulin Studio (San Francisco), Bassano Ltd. (London), Hay Wrightson (London), Stuckeys (Falls Church, Va.), Conway Studios Corp. (New York), Tunbridge (London), J. Russell & Sons (London), Victor Mitzakis (London), Photo Lab. of Terminal Island (Calif.), Photo Lab. (Fleet Op. Training Ctr., N.O.B., Norfolk), McGarraugh (Delaware), Albert R. Miller (Washington, D.C.), Cartagena Foto (Madrid), Foto Olimpia (Guayaquil), John Hearder Ltd. (Sydney, Australia), Alfonso (Madrid), Elliott & Fry Ltd. (London), Hayes Photo Service (New Hope, Pa.), Antoine (Beirut), Valdoy & Cia. (Valparaiso), Polyphoto (Helsinki), Foto Luxardo (Rome), Lafayette Ltd. (London), Swiss Military Photo Service, Photomaton (Paris), Aramco Photo (C.E. Wilkins), Martin (Valparaiso), the Imperial War Museum (London), Frederickson Studios (Pensacola, Florida), Fabian Bachrach, Arleen Tyrrell Richardson, Photo Lab. Kelly Field (Texas), Olavi Airaksinen (Finland), Photo Elite (La Haye), Lorens (Madrid), Adolphus Tear (Ipswich, England), Obergs Studio (Stockholm), S. Malmoodee (Karachi), Auto-Pose (Stockholm), Wm. Beal (Salt Lake City), Blank & Stoller Photo, Government of the Sudan, Arsley (Ankara), Frank T. Dobinson (Brighton, England), the Associated Press, Augusta Berns, Turk Fotograf, Ziegler Photo (Netherlands), Faber & Faber

Ltd. (London), the U.S. Army Signal Corps, the Chief of Naval Operations, and the official photo services of the U.S. Army, Navy, Air Force, and Marine Corps.

Finally, we acknowledge with thanks the reading of the manuscript and suggestions by attorney Jack N. Albert, the assistance of Mr. Fred Casoni, Mr. Eddie Sennefelder, and Rev. Dr. A. Busch, also the aid in research by the Library of Congress and the Law Library of Yale University.

The Editors

PREFACE

To identify myself, may I say that after completing my collegiate and legal education, I was engaged in the practice of law in the State of Ohio for more than forty years prior to 1939, when I was elected to a Judgeship on the Supreme Court of Ohio and served continuously on that court until January 2, 1957. I am now retired. For a period of over twenty years before I became a member of the Supreme Court, I lectured on International Law at Mount Union College of Alliance, Ohio.

In order to make my comments intelligible, it seems to me that a brief factual historical statement as to the origin of and the procedure carried out in the so-called "Nuremberg Trials" is necessary. The tribunal involved was created, and the crimes within its jurisdiction were designated and defined, by what is known as the London Charter entered into on August 8, 1945 by and between four nations — The United States, The Soviet Union, Great Britain and France — victor nations of World War II, for the purpose of designating and defining certain acts committed in the course of the war as war crimes and the prosecution of certain officials of conquered Germany charged with the commission of such crimes.

The Charter designated and defined three classes of crimes. Class "A" under which most of the defendants were charged and tried, defined the crime as follows: "The planning, preparation, initiation or waging of a war of aggression, or a war in violation of international treaties, agreements or assurances, or participation in a common plan or conspiracy for the accomplishment of any of the foregoing."

William L. Hart
Justice of The Supreme Court of Ohio
1939-1957

The so-called International Military Tribunal began its trial sessions on November 20, 1945, and concluded them on October 1, 1946. Twelve of the twenty-two defendants were convicted and sentenced to death by hanging; seven were convicted and sentenced to imprisonment for terms ranging from ten years to life; three were acquitted. Those sentenced to death were executed on October 16, 1946, with the exceptions of Martin Bormann who had not been found and never was before the court in person, and Hermann Goering who had committed suicide a few hours before the hour of execution.

During and following the trials, much criticism of them was expressed by legal authorities and by the press. The substance of such criticism was that morally the trials were unfair because instituted and carried out by the victors over the vanquished in a past war, and that the tribunal administered "political justice" based on a desire for vengeance, thus sacrificing "democratic" for "totalitarian" concepts.

Under the heading of "Aggressor Nations," the *Chicago Tribune*, under date of October 2, 1946, the next day after the sentences were imposed, carried an editorial which said: "The truth of the matter is that no one of the victors was free of the guilt which its judges attributed to the vanquished." Measured by the Code and standards applied in these trials, it is disturbing to contemplate how the officers of our American forces might have fared had they been tried for their conduct in letting loose the devastation which practically wiped out Hiroshima on August 6, 1945, and Nagasaki on August 9, 1945, the former two days before and the latter the next day after the adoption of the London Charter to which the United States was a party.

In my judgement, the procedure by which the Nuremberg Tribunal was created and the criminal trials thereunder conducted, was completely fraught with illegality. May I briefly state my reasons for this judgement. In the first place, American authorities have invariably taken the position that an individual forming a part of a nationally organized army or navy and acting under the authority of his government, cannot be held answerable as a private trespasser or criminal for acts committed under such authority. Such acts are considered acts of the state and not those of the individual.

In the case of Dow v. Johnson, 100 U.S. 158, 163, the Supreme Court of the United States held that an officer of the United States Army was not liable in a civil action for injuries resulting from acts ordered by him, in his military character while in the service of the United States in the enemy's country, and this doctrine has been consistently recognized in this country. The rationale of this case is consistent with and illustrates the application of the rule here discussed.

In connection with the famous McLeod Case (1840), Daniel Webster, then Secretary of State, wrote the British Minister as follows: "That an individual forming part of a public force and acting under the authority of his government is not to be held answerable as a private trespasser or malefactor, is a principle of public law sanctioned by all civilized nations, and which the Government of the United States has no inclination to dispute."

After World War I the Conference of Paris, engaged in formulating the peace treaty between Germany and the Allied enemy nations, proposed to make provision for the prosecution and punishment of the Kaiser for alleged war crimes, but the two American representatives at the Conference, Secretary Robert Lansing and Dr. James Brown Scott, the latter an eminent American authority on International Law, refused to go along with such a proposition. They took the position that: "If the former Kaiser was not, according to international law, subject to criminal prosecution for acts chargeable to him while the chief of a state, it is not apparent how any trial before a tribunal set up by the Allied and Associated Powers, and rendered competent to impose a penalty such as might be decreed in a criminal case, could take place without manifesting an abuse of power."

Charles Cherry Hyde, in his work on International Law, in commenting on the position of the American representatives to the Conference, on this subject says: (Volume II, page 850) "It is believed that the American position was sound. If the design of the Allied and Associated Governments was to inspire respect for international law by the foe which had violated it, there was solid reason to make no demands for the surrender of individuals to be punished criminally on account of acts which were not internationally illegal."

Furthermore, these four national powers instituting the Nuremberg Trials did not separately or jointly possess any sovereign power to create a special court to try alleged criminal offenses committed outside the territorial jurisdiction of any one of them — necessary under all systems of law to exercise authority over the life and liberty of its subjects within its territorial jurisdiction — or sovereign authority to convict officers of the German forces of so-called criminal offenses not committed within such jurisdiction. It is true that some claim was made that under international law there exists certain "common law" crimes, not specifically created by legal enactment, which crimes existed and were recognized and prosecuted by the Nuremberg Tribunal. But this position was belied by the fact that the powers in question deemed it necessary to specifically define the crime in the same joint charter which created the tribunal. The London Charter defined the offenses for which the defendants were tried in specific language heretofore quoted.

It has been generally conceded that there is no recognition of sovereign power which is the creation of or operates within the jurisdiction of international law. That none exists is to be inferred from the provisions of the Charter of the United Nations, Article 13, of which provides that the General Assembly may "initiate studies and make recommendations — for the purpose inter alia — of encouraging the progressive development of international law and its codification." The wording of the provision makes it clear that the Assembly itself is not empowered to create or codify international law, but to encourage the development and codification of such rules by the constituent nations or by international tribunals vet to be created.

There was also much valid criticism expressed in this country at the time of the trials, and since, to the effect that the nations involved in the prosecutions had seen fit to submit the matter of guilt and punishment to a make-shift court created by the prosecuting nations for the one special purpose and which went out of existence immediately upon securing the convictions for which it was organized. From a legal standpoint, there is no answer to this criticism. It was completely justified. The fact is that there does not exist and never has existed any international court or tribunal having jurisdiction to try offenses such as those named in the London Charter.

The designation and definition by the London Charter of the so-called crimes with which the defendants were charged, after such so-called offenses were committed, clearly violated the well-established rule against ex post facto legislation in criminal matters. The generally accepted doctrine is expressed in the adage: *"Nullum Crimen Sine Lege"* — a person cannot be sentenced to punishment for a crime unless he had infringed a law in force at the time he committed the offense and unless that law prescribed the penalty. Courts in passing on this proposition had declared that: "It is to be observed that this maxim is not a limitation of sovereignty, but is a general principle of justice adhered to by all civilized nations."

In my opinion, there was no legal justification for the trial, conviction or sentence of the so-called "war criminals" by the Nuremberg Tribunal. We have set a bad precedent. It should not be followed in the future.

PROLOGUE

(The following excerpts from the epilogue to Rear Admiral Dan V. Gallery's book, Twenty Million Tons Under the Sea, *© Dan V. Gallery 1957, are reprinted with his permission and with due acknowledgment to the publisher, Henry Regnery Co. of Chicago.)*

When the statesmen louse up *their* job so badly that they have to have the military men pull the chestnuts out of the fire for them, a lot of innocent bystanders are going to get hurt. When nations, by mutual consent, decide to ignore the commandment "Thou shalt not kill," it is very difficult for the military leaders to restrict the killing to just the right people.

You might think that since our submarines fought the same way the Germans did, we would sweep the question of Prize Warfare under the rug after the war and say no more about violation of the laws of war at sea. Our naval officers were perfectly willing to do this, but our statesmen and lawyers were vindictive. When the war was over, they insisted on trying the German Admirals Raeder and Doenitz at Nuremberg as war criminals for permitting their submarines to do exactly what ours did. A justice of our Supreme Court prosecuted them and tried to hang them. To our eternal shame, we convicted the German admirals of violating the laws of war at sea and sentenced them to long terms of imprisonment: Raeder to life; and Doenitz to ten years.

This kangaroo court at Nuremburg was officially known as the "International Military Tribunal." That name is a libel on the military profession. The tribunal was not a military one in any sense. The only military men among the judges were the Russians. Some military titles are listed on the staffs of the secretariat and prosecution counsel, but these belong to a lot of lawyers temporarily masquerading in uniform as military men.

Nuremberg was, in fact, a lawyers' tribunal, although I can readily un-

Dan V. Gallery
Rear Admiral, U.S.N. (Ret.)

derstand why the legal profession is ashamed to claim it, and deliberately stuck a false label on it.

I'm glad our real military men had nothing to do with the travesty on justice that the lawyers and "statesmen" conducted at Nuremberg. Raeder and Doenitz simply did their duty to *their* country in World War II, trying to straighten out the mess that their politicians got them into as all military men are sworn to do. Our politicians and lawyers set a rather stupid precedent when they tried these officers for carrying out the orders of their own misguided politicians.

Actually, the decision to court-martial the German military brass was on a par with the "unconditional surrender" blunder, which prolonged rather than shortened the war. From now on, Nuremberg gives enemy military leaders good reason for fighting to the last bullet and dying in the trenches rather than trying to negotiate surrender of a hopelessly lost cause. There certainly is no use in surrendering if you know you will be hauled up before a kangaroo court and hanged, as most defendants were at Nuremberg.

Even today, few people realize that the German Navy, in the last days of the war, evacuated several times as many refugees from East Prussia as the British Navy took out from Dunkirk. As soon as Doenitz got his people to safety in West Germany, he surrendered — but one of the charges on which our Supreme Court prosecutor tried to hang him was that he prolonged the war!

Had the German people seen fit to try their own military leaders for losing the war, I might go along with that. Or if our statesmen had insisted on hanging the Nazi politicians and had felt that a mock trial was necessary before doing it, I could see some logic in that. But our politicians and lawyers were undermining their own authority when they convicted the German generals and admirals. After all, one thing the much maligned military brass *must* do, in a democracy as well as a dictatorship, is to swallow their convictions, if any, and do as they are told by the politicians. . .

At Nuremberg, mankind and our present civilization were on trial, with men whose own hands were bloody sitting on the judges' seats. One of the judges came from the country which committed the Katyn Forest massacre and produced an array of witnesses to swear at Nuremberg that the Germans had done it. Maybe crimes of such magnitude as those charged at Nuremberg should be left to the Last Judgment for punishment.

The outstanding example of barefaced hypocrisy at Nuremberg was the trial of Admiral Doenitz. We tried him on three charges: (1) Conspiring to wage aggressive war; (2) Waging aggressive war; and (3) Violation of the laws of war at sea. Even the loaded court at Nuremberg acquitted him of the first charge, but convicted him of the other two. How in the name of common sense a military officer can wage any kind of war except an aggressive one without being a traitor to his country, I'll never know. I took an oath when I entered the U.S. Navy almost forty years ago, to defend the United States against all enemies — and there wasn't anything said about doing it in a non-aggressive manner. . . If the Nuremberg evidence had shown that Doenitz waged a non-aggressive war, the German people themselves would have been entitled to hang him.

Doenitz's conviction on charge three — violation of the laws of war at sea — was an insult to our own submariners. Admiral Doenitz requested early in the trial that our own Admiral Nimitz be summoned as a witness in his defense to testify about how our subs operated in the Pacific. Our Supreme Court prosecutor had to hem and haw and to back water fast when that hot potato was tossed at him. Admiral Nimitz (God bless him for the honest seafaring man that he was) finally submitted a sworn statement, answering questions put to him by Doenitz's counsel and said that our submarines in the Pacific waged unrestricted warfare the same as the Germans did in the Atlantic.

Despite this, we convicted Admiral Doenitz on the charge of violating the laws of war at sea. If the old gentleman ever gets out of jail, I hope I never meet him. I would have trouble looking him in the eye. The only crime he committed was that of almost beating us in a bloody but "legal" fight.

Doenitz's conviction for violating the laws of war in carrying out the orders of his government, raises a serious question. We have just promulgated a Code of Conduct for our fighting men, designed to steel them against brainwashing if captured, and thus to protect them from prosecution in our own courts for improper conduct while prisoners of war. Perhaps, to protect our soldiers from prosecution by tribunals like Nuremberg, we should amend the oath of allegiance they take when they enter the service. After what we did to Doenitz, maybe we should add a proviso to the oath saying, "Before carrying out the orders of my superior officers, I will check to insure that they are compatible with our international commitments, the Charter of the United Nations, etc., etc."

The only precedent set at Nuremberg in which I take any stock at all is that they didn't *hang* any admirals!

The Nuremberg trials placed a solemn stamp of approval on a code of war at sea which we not only didn't follow ourselves in World War II, but which may embarrass us in the future. We are, at present, busily engaged in building atomic submarines designed to remain submerged for weeks at a time. It is absurd to think that these submarines will expose themselves on the surface to follow the archaic code of sailing ships, which we confirmed as being the law of war at sea for the atomic age when we threw Doenitz in jail.

Lest there be any mistake about how I feel on this matter, I hasten to say I am *not* in favor of actually trying to follow Prize Rules with atomic submarines. I'm in favor of denouncing pacts which can't be followed in war time and of announcing what everybody knows anyway: that in case we are attacked, we will defend ourselves with every weapon in our arsenal.

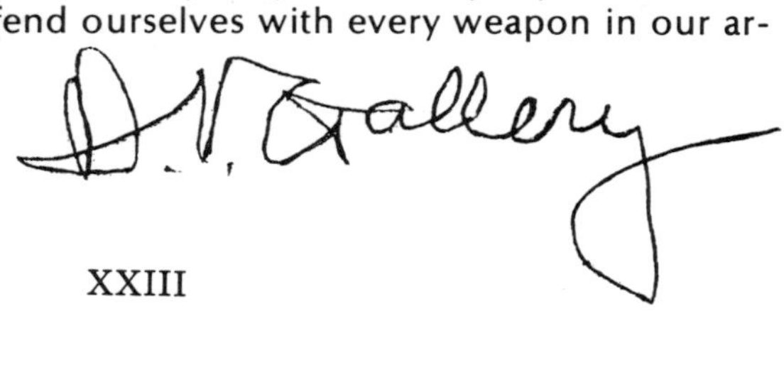

Excerpts from The Law and Custom of the Sea, *by H.A. Smith, D.C.L. (Oxon), Professor Emeritus of International Law in the University of London, Stevens & Sons Limited, London, 1954, second edition, pages 175-176, here published by permission of Sweet & Maxwell, Ltd.*

The future historian will probably regard it as a disaster of the first order that the doctrine of reprisals, after more than a century of desuetude, should have been revived early in the first world war. Its practical result has been to destroy the conception of an objective law of war, standing above both belligerents and providing an independent standard by which the whole world can judge the actions of each. The position to which we have now come is that each belligerent decides for himself which of the rules it will suit him to observe and fastens upon his adversary the responsibility for his own illegalities.

The resulting confusion can be illustrated from the judgment which the Nuremberg Tribunal pronounced in the case of Admiral Doenitz. Upon the count of the indictment which charged him with "crimes against peace" Doenitz was acquitted, but he was convicted upon the counts which alleged "war crimes" and "crimes against humanity" and sentenced to ten years' imprisonment. The prosecution charged him with responsibility for the German submarine warfare, particularly violation of the Protocol of 1936, which laid down that submarines, like surface ships, were forbidden to sink merchant vessels without making provision for the safety of those on board. Upon this point his main defense was founded upon the British Admiralty orders, which were described by the Tribunal in these words:—*Shortly after the outbreak of war the British Admiralty, in accordance with its Handbook of Instructions of 1938 to the Merchant Navy, armed its merchant vessels, in many cases convoyed them with armed escort, gave orders to send position reports upon sighting submarines, thus integrating merchant vessels into the warning system of naval intelligence. On October 1, 1939, the British Admiralty announced British merchant ships had been ordered to ram U-boats if possible. In the actual circumstances of this case the Tribunal is not prepared to hold Doenitz guilty for his conduct of submarine warfare against British merchant ships.*

In other words, these ships had been so far assimilated to warships by the Admiralty orders that they were no longer entitled to the protection of the Protocol. But the Tribunal went on to say that this defense did not apply to the sinking of *neutral* ships in the 'operational zones'—*The proclamation of operational zones and the sinking of neutral merchant vessels which enter those zones present a different question. This practice was employed in the war of 1914-1918 by Germany and adopted in retaliation by Great Britain. The Washington Conference of 1922, the London Naval Agreement of 1930, and the Protocol of 1936, were entered into with full knowledge that such zones had been employed in the first world war. Yet the Protocol made no exception for operational zones. The order of Doenitz to sink neutral ships without warning when found within these zones was, therefore, in the opinion of the Tribunal, a violation of the Protocol.*

The tribunal then went on to discuss the "no rescue" orders, the defense on this point being that under the conditions of modern warfare rescue was in fact impossible without putting the submarine herself in peril. The Tribunal refused to accept this plea, but at the same time found itself bound to recognize some rather embarrassing facts on the other side:—*In view of all the facts proved and in particular of an order of the British Admiralty announced on May 8, 1940, according to which all vessels should be sunk at sight in the Skagerrak, and the answers to interrogatories by Admiral Nimitz stating that unrestricted submarine warfare was carried on in the Pacific Ocean by the United States from the first day that nation entered the war, the sentence of Doenitz is not assessed on the ground of his breaches of the international law of submarine warfare.*

The clumsiness and obscurity of this language perhaps indicate the embarrassment which the members of the Tribunal felt in dealing with the case of Doenitz, and it is not easy to ascertain from the rest of the judgment the precise facts upon which he was condemned.

Herbert A. Smith, D.C.L.

Excerpts from pp. 215-219 of PROFILES IN COURAGE *by President John F. Kennedy, Copyright © 1956, 1961 by John F. Kennedy. By permission of Harper & Row, Publishers.*

In October of 1946, Senator Robert A. Taft of Ohio was the chief spokesman for the Republicans in Washington, the champion of his party in the national political arena and the likely Republican nominee for the Presidency in 1948. It was a time when even a Senator with such an established reputation for speaking his mind would have guarded his tongue, and particularly a Senator with so much at stake as Bob Taft...But Senator Taft was disturbed—and when he was disturbed it was his habit to speak out. He was disturbed by the War Crimes Trials of Axis leaders, then concluding in Germany and about to commence in Japan. The Nuremberg Trials...for "waging an aggressive war," had been popular throughout the world and particularly in the United States...But what kind of trial was this?...The Constitution of the United States was the gospel which guided the policy decisions of the Senator from Ohio. It was his source, his weapon and his salvation. And when the Constitution commanded no *"ex post facto* laws," Bob Taft accepted this precept as permanently wise and universally applicable. The Constitution was not a collection of loosely given political promises subject to broad interpretation. It was not a list of pleasing platitudes to be set lightly aside when expediency required it. It was the foundation of the American system of law and justice and he was repelled by the picture of his country discarding those Constitutional precepts in order to punish a vanquished enemy...

These conclusions are shared, I believe, by a substantial number of American citizens today. And they were shared, at least privately, by a goodly number in 1946. But no politician of consequence would speak out...none, that is, but Senator Taft...The Nuremberg Trials were at no time before the Congress for consideration. They were not in any sense an issue in the campaign...To speak out unnecessarily would be politically costly and clearly futile. But Bob Taft spoke out.

On October 6, 1946, Senator Taft appeared before a conference on our Anglo-American heritage, sponsored by Kenyon College in Ohio...titling his address "Equal Justice Under Law," Taft cast aside his general reluctance to embark upon startling novel and dramatic approaches. "The trial of the vanquished by the victors," he told an attentive if somewhat astonished audience, "cannot be impartial no matter how it is hedged about with the forms of justice...About this whole judgment there is the spirit of vengeance, and vengeance is seldom justice...In these trials we have accepted the Russian idea of the purpose of trials—government policy and not justice—with little relation to Anglo-Saxon heritage. By clothing policy in the forms of legal procedure, we may discredit the whole idea of justice in Europe for years to come. In the last analysis, even at the end of a frightful war, we should view the future with more hope if even our enemies believed that we had treated them justly in our English-speaking concept of law, in the provision of relief and in the final disposal of territory..."

Nuremberg, the Ohio Senator insisted, was a blot on American Constitutional history, and a serious departure from our Anglo-Saxon heritage of fair and equal treatment, a heritage which had rightly made this country respected throughout the world. "We can't even teach our own people the sound principles of liberty and justice," he concluded...

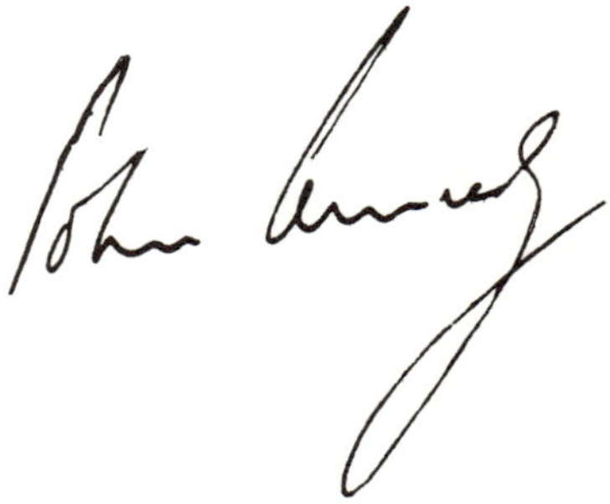

John F. Kennedy

Chicago Daily Tribune
THE WORLD'S GREATEST NEWSPAPER
FOUNDED JUNE 10, 1847
Sat., Oct. 6, 1956 H★ Part 1—Page 16

DOENITZ GOES FREE

Grand Adm. Karl Doenitz, commander of the German navy at the end of World War II, has completed his 10 year sentence as a "war criminal" and has been released from Spandau prison in Berlin. He was sentenced by an international tribunal at Nuernberg, acting under ex post facto "law" invented for the occasion. The penalties prescribed were never legislated by any lawmakers, but by representatives of the victor countries who then took over the prosecution.

The presence of Adm. Doenitz among the defendants presented the victors with an unforeseen embarrassment. He was charged with having conducted unrestricted submarine warfare. The tribunal reluctantly admitted that, in assessing this charge, an order of the British admiralty, dated May 8, 1940, directing that all vessels in the Skagerrak should be sunk without warning, could not be disregarded.

The tribunal was also obliged to take cognizance of the undisputed fact that the United States, from the first day of the war, had also waged unrestricted submarine warfare.

The laws governing submarine warfare were clearly and precisely defined in the London naval treaty of 1930, which specified that attacks were to be confined to unmistakable vessels of war, and then only after seeing to the safety of all hands. The American navy, in its official report on the submarine campaign against Japan, admitted an indiscriminate campaign in which nine out of every 10 Japanese ships sunk were noncombatant vessels. Of 276,000 Japanese drowned in these attacks, 105,000 were civilians.

Under the circumstances, the Nuernberg tribunal was in no position to work up a production against Adm. Doenitz on the same grounds. Its decision that its judgment must weigh similar acts on the part of the allies established a novel principle in jurisprudence—i. e., that whether a particular act was or was not a crime depended on whether the prosecution also had committed it. If the victors had committed it, it could not be a crime.

Nevertheless, the blanket charges against the defendants of planning, preparing, initiating, or conducting aggressive war were sufficiently broad to produce a finding that Adm. Doenitz was guilty of something — probably the crime of fighting, as a professional officer, in the service of his country. He got 10 years—a verdict proving once again that might makes right, and that hypocrisy can surmount all obstacles.

Doenitz as senior
lieutenant aboard
the *U-39,* 1917

Doenitz aboard the
cruiser *Emden*
in the South Atlantic, 1934

Doenitz (at left) in conference
on submarine strategy, 1940

Doenitz as
Grand Admiral,
1944

Doenitz
in 1975

Aumuehle, 1975

I consider this collection of letters historically valuable. The letter writers have courageously expressed their opinions. They have written in an independent manner of how they experienced or evaluated the events. I respect this, and am grateful to the contributors. My particular thanks are due to Mr. Keith Thompson and Professor Henry Strutz who were the initiators and compilers of this collection of opinions.

Grand Admiral

"I may, and do, say that I have always regarded the Nuremberg prosecutions as a step backward in international law, and a precedent that will prove embarrassing, if not disastrous, in the future."

Honorable Justice Learned Hand
U.S. District Judge, Southern District of N.Y., 1909-1924
U.S. Circuit Judge, Second Circuit, 1924-1951

"I have read Rear Admiral Dan Gallery's book, *Twenty Million Tons Under The Sea* and believe that he expresses the sentiments of the majority of U.S. Naval Officers in the Epilogue of his book, with regard to the Nuremberg trials. In this enlightened age, it is difficult to imagine how a professional naval officer in high command, could be tried by the conquerors of his country for: (1) conspiracy to wage aggressive war, (2) waging aggressive war and (3) violation of the laws of war at sea. Even politicians with but slight knowledge of submarine operations must know that the old laws of war (visit and search) were impossible conditions for submarines. Then why were the laws of war at sea not changed or the use of submarines outlawed? . . It does not appear that unrestricted submarine warfare is any more brutal than the bombing of undefended cities from the air."

Admiral Jesse B. Oldendorf, U.S.N.
Commander, Battleship Division 2, Pacific Fleet, 1944

"The sentence of Grand Admiral Doenitz, as well as that of Admiral Raeder, was a travesty of justice in being tried for what any loyal military officer is trained to do in time of war, and constitutes a dangerous precedent in the cases of military officers who are on the losing side in future conflicts."

H. E. Yarnell.

Admiral Harry E. Yarnell, U.S.N.
Commander-in-Chief, U.S. Asiatic Fleet

"My opinion on the trial of Grand Admiral Doenitz is that it was wholly unjustified and a disgrace to the national governments sanctioning it."

Rear Admiral Reginald R. Belknap, U.S.N.
Director, Mining and Mine-sweeping, U.S. Atlantic Fleet, 1915-1917

"In my opinion...the Allied post-war prosecutions were not in accordance with Justice...it is my fervent wish that Grand Admiral Karl Doenitz should know that he is regarded as a great naval officer, and if he suffered—which he did—it was for doing his duty."

Honorable William Cosgrave, LL.D.
President, Dail Eireann, 1922
President, Executive Council of Irish Free State, 1922-32
Minister of Finance, 1922-23; Minister of Defense, 1924
President, United Ireland Party, 1935-44

"I am glad that Admiral Karl Doenitz has been released. My only regret is that he was not released much earlier. I could never accept the Nuremberg Trials as representing a fair and just procedure. This is particularly true in this case of an old soldier who had to perform his duty to his country and obey the commands of his superiors."

Dr. Igor I. Sikorsky
Aircraft designer; invented the helicopter
Built and flew first multi-motored airplane

I. I. Sikorsky

[To Grand Admiral Doenitz]

"Permit me to express my admiration to you for your attainments as an outstanding wartime leader of your country's navy. Although we fought on opposite sides it is fitting to acknowledge your professional excellence in Naval Science. It is hoped that never again will our two great countries, Germany and the United States, be engaged in armed conflict against each other."

Admiral Joseph J. Clark, U.S.N.
Commander, Aircraft Carrier Divisions 3 and 4, 1948-1951

"Admiral Doenitz and other leaders who were imprisoned should be recompensed for their treatment...We can never adequately compensate the leaders punished by imprisonment or death...There are no generally accepted principles in international law under which they could have been tried and punished...And there is no international criminal tribunal. What we did in this case was to resort to private vengeance."

Dr. John L. Gillin
Emeritus Professor of Criminology, University of Wisconsin
Author and expert on crime

"I have been boiling mad for years over the 'war crimes trials,' which I think were despicable and contemptible, and smack more of ancient Rome's barbarism than of a so-called civilized country. Our country's hands are not free of blood and crime, in spite of our vaunted 'democracy' and 'noble aspirations,' etc., etc., ad nauseum. Not only were the 'war crimes trials' one of the blackest spots on our recent black (and Red) history, but the bombing of the only two Christian cities in Japan in August 1945 via the atomic bomb calls to high heaven for retribution...To say that the trial of Admiral Karl Doenitz is a 'barefaced hypocrisy,' as you state in your letter, is the understatement of all time. It is outrageous that a man serving his country in all honesty and patriotism should be considered a 'criminal' by a country which has its own share of criminals, and not honest and patriotic ones, either..."

Taylor Caldwell

Taylor Caldwell
American novelist

"The Nuremberg 'war crimes' trials convicted and imposed prison confinement on some senior officers of a defeated military force for the performance of duties and orders imposed upon them in the conduct of the war. When emotion subverts reason as a guide for legal codes and processes, a distortion of justice of this type becomes an almost certain product...I don't know that this observation will give much solace to Admiral Doenitz for the imprisonment that slanted justice imposed, but if it gives a little, I'll feel that this letter was worthwhile."

Major General Orvil A. Anderson, U.S.A.F.
Director, The Air Force Historical Foundation
Deputy Commander, 8th Air Force, 1944-1945
Senior Military Advisor, U.S. Strategic
Bombing Survey, 1945-1946

United States Senator William Langer
Former Governor of North Dakota

[To Grand Admiral Doenitz]

"I have always felt, and still feel that you were treated unfairly and adversely in the heat of the moment, and your conviction by the Nuremberg Military Tribunal was a miscarriage of justice. Even in your brief capacity as the head of the German Government you acted as a line officer who, in the words of an old soldier, 'tried to do his duty as God gave him light to see that duty.' All those who shared such feelings rejoice today in the fact that you are free and ready to return to an active and useful life."

"...it can be said that a military commander carries out the orders of his superiors, and that these orders are presumably in consonance with the national policies of his government...a military commander should not have to answer for the political and military decisions of his political leaders. It does not appear that Grand Admiral Karl Doenitz was guilty of anything more than carrying out directives which in the last analysis stemmed from Hitler. In this he acted as any loyal military man would have done. Therefore, his conviction at Nuremberg is, in my opinion, a grave injustice. Time brings many changes. Today Americans have an obvious friendship for the Germans and Japanese, and this friendship is reciprocated. It is interesting to speculate what the results would have been if it had been possible...to postpone the War Crimes Trials for ten years, even five. One thing is certain: calmness and objectivity would have been more evident and justice would have been better served."

Vice Admiral Marion E. Murphy, U.S.N.
Chief of Staff, Amphibious Force, Pacific Fleet
Director, Guided Missile Program
Asst. Chief, Bureau of Ordnance

"I must say that I agree as to the unjust and illegal procedures taken against Grand Admiral Karl Doenitz. Creating a special and unique trial outside of international laws to judge the acts of the chief who has done nothing but his duty, is to dictate beforehand and to command his sentence in a definite sense. The nation, nations or entities which followed such a procedure without restraint, rule or respect, which did not recognize the principle of obedience of orders, and which did not feel the authority of any law whatsoever, have descended to a low level. To respect and observe standing international laws — those laws that had not been imposed by the will of the winner but by the straight conscience of Humanity — should have been the method to follow. Respect for laws has always ruled in history, as it ruled in the evolution of power and authority. Without respect for law, no one is free. I am convinced that he who best accomplished his military duties is doing the best for his country. He who knows how to respect and recognize these same duties in the enemy, knows how to respect law and does something for the prestige of his country. Having created the Nuremberg Tribunal to judge a chief who has known how to carry out the responsibilities of his mission, constituted a monstrosity and a nameless injustice. It has been said that war has two phases, the human and the divine. The human phase is represented by the whole material mechanism. The divine phase is represented by the spirit which encourages the fighter. This spirit is the discipline which teaches him and prepares him from his childhood to suffer, to fight, to conquer, to die, and always under the respect and protection of international laws. It is in the name of this spirit, that the High Command calls for the use of the special weapon with which he is to defend his country. To carry on with these duties cannot be termed a crime, and if it was so considered, should not have been imitated by the U.S.A., which at the end surpassed in unrestricted submarine warfare, as Admiral Nimitz himself admits. If this type of war was justified by the Germans and Americans (both used it), we cannot explain how the winners would concentrate their anger on the conquered, creating special trials to condemn as a crime of war the *duty performed* and at the same time the *patriotic feeling,* setting a precedent that would bring up future fears tending to limit the military preparedness of their own nations. It is highly sensible that this campaign of professional rehabilitation of the person of Admiral Doenitz has come forth upon completion of his sentence. The distinguished Admiral Doenitz has been an unjust victim of an uncontrolled passion."

Admiral Thomas Pizarro,
Peruvian Navy

“The greater part of our troubles is the result of World War I and the bad treaties which ended it. That war was a great step backward in gentlemanly behavior, humanity and fairplay. The Nuremberg Trials were contrary to legal precepts. Grand Admiral Karl Doenitz is merely one more victim.”

Alfonso of Bourbon and Orleans
Infante of Spain
Great-grandson of Queen Victoria of England and King Louis Philippe of France
Divisionary General of Aviation

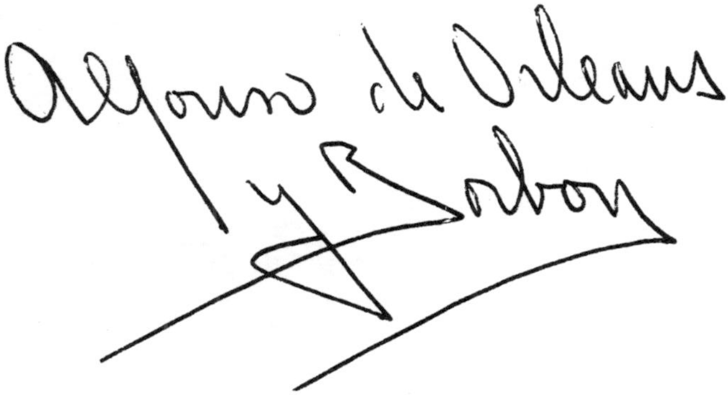

“It is not right to bring to trial officers or men who have acted under orders from higher authority...The most brutal act of the War was the dropping of the Atom Bombs on Japan...I consider it wrong to try Admirals, Generals, and Air Marshals for carrying out definite orders from the highest authority...the Allies were far from guiltless and should have taken that into fuller consideration.”

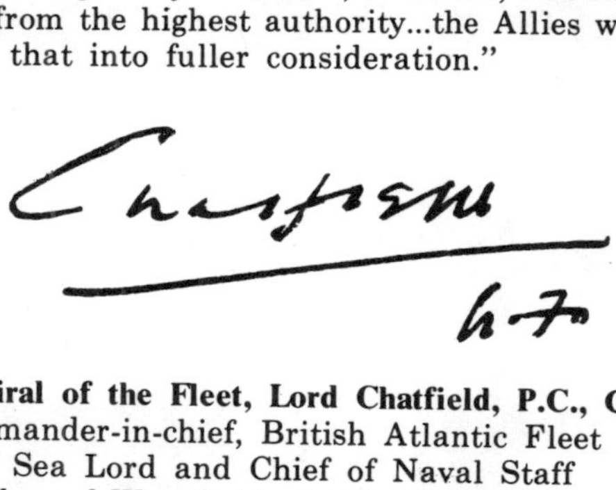

Admiral of the Fleet, Lord Chatfield, P.C., G.C.B.
Commander-in-chief, British Atlantic Fleet
First Sea Lord and Chief of Naval Staff
Member of War Cabinet, World War II

"I regard the Nuremberg 'war crimes trials' as one of the worst reflections upon enlightened leadership in world affairs as ever has been known. These trials by victor nations were for the purpose of punishing those of the opposite military forces for simply performing their duty which common honor required to be done. The trials really were a disgrace upon all who participated therein. Having no sympathy whatever with the defendants in their military objectives, yet I respected their duty to obey the orders issued to them by their country and its leaders. It is especially regretted that our country participated in the prosecution. It is hoped that such a situation will never be repeated. It is a stigma on American ideas of justice. As a former member of the Permanent Court of Arbitration at the Hague, I am deeply interested in the cause of peace. Peace can never be advanced by such methods as were developed during these alleged trials. Peace can only be made permanent under Law and not in defiance of Law."

Michael Francis Doyle

Michael Francis Doyle

Hon. Michael Francis Doyle, LL.D.
International lawyer, and Papal Chamberlain
Member, Permanent Court of Arbitration, The Hague
President, Electoral College of the U.S., 1945-1949

"My general feeling as historian...is adverse to setting up an international court to put on trial officers of a defeated nation for acts involved in the prosecution of their military or naval duties."

Charles Seymour

Charles Seymour, Ph.D., LL.D., Litt.D.
American historian and author
President Emeritus of Yale University

"I do feel that the trial of officers and even civilian officials was a most unfortunate and unjustified violation of international law. I am afraid our administration allowed itself to be led on by the Soviet's desire for vengence, and I am sure we will have cause to regret our participation both because it was inconsistent with our previous more generous and more gentlemanly attitude, and because it gave a precedent for the victor to revenge himself on individuals after any future war. Such action in violation of international law and purely to vent one's anger on individuals acting under orders is sure to come back and plague us in the future. I am glad to know that others appreciate this and that it may be brought to the attention of the American People at appropriate times."

Major General Ulysses S. Grant, III, U.S.A.
President, The American Peace Society

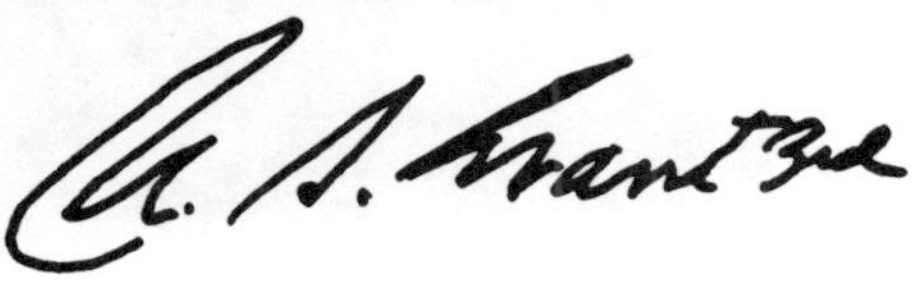

"I am happy to state that I have never regarded Admiral Doenitz as a 'war criminal.' As Grand Admiral of the German Navy his plain duty was to operate the forces under his command in that manner that would most effectively conduce to this country's success in the war. That is the duty of every Naval and Military officer of all countries. The idea of trying the leaders of defeated nations as 'war criminals' is but a first step toward the dark ages. It is a step that may affect the Naval, Military and Air Officers of any country if they are so unfortunate as to be defeated in war. I am very glad that Admiral Doenitz has been released and hope that his remaining days will be marked with the honor and affection of his country that he served so loyally and well during his long Naval career."

Vice Admiral John F. Shafroth, U.S.N.
Commander, South Pacific Area & South Pacific Force, 1943
Commander, Battleship Division 8, 1944

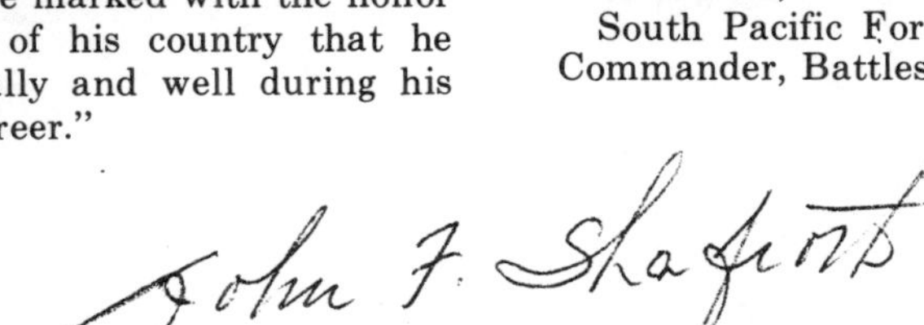

"Doenitz is no more guilty of a war crime than others on our side...The unrestricted submarine warfare directed by Admiral Doenitz against Allied shipping was no more of a crime than Allied mass bombing of German towns and cities...The excuse frequently offered that the towns and cities bombed contained military objectives will not hold water, as it could equally be applied to ships of which all, of any consequence, were making their voyages in furtherance of the Allied war effort...The Nuremberg Court cannot rightly be called a 'Military Tribunal' as political considerations were in prominence, to the exclusion of justice...It is my considered opinion that the Nuremberg Trials violated the reputation for justice so long held by the British and American peoples, and that many of the findings contravened our most sacred constitutional principles. It is true to say that when party politics are allowed to influence justice, the latter vanishes, and that is the picture which we see now — years after the event."

Air Vice-Marshal Hugh Champion de Crespigny, R.A.F., C.B., M.C., D.F.C.
Air Officer Commanding, No. 21 Group, 1943-1944
Allied Military Governor, Schleswig-Holstein, 1946-47

"I doubt both the justice and the wisdom of inflicting punishment upon those guilty of 'war crimes' committed under orders of a belligerent...Upon one point we must all agree, that when war is once over, patience and tolerance should be exerted to the end that the belligerents may resume normal peaceful relations."

Hon. Robert P. Skinner
U.S. Ambassador to Greece, Estonia, Latvia, Lithuania, Turkey and Abyssinia

"The Nuremberg Trials were a tragic mistake. They will haunt us always."

Major General James E. Chaney, U.S.A.F.

"I have never considered Karl Doenitz a war criminal in any sense of the term. He was merely a professional naval officer — and a mighty good one — doing his duty in the same way that Admiral Charles Lockwood commanding our Submarines, Pacific Fleet, did his duty. Our submarines engaged in unrestricted warfare, sinking any enemy ship they could without warning. Had the Japs won the war, I suppose Charlie Lockwood could have been found guilty of war crimes in the same way as was Karl Doenitz. I agree with Admiral Dan Gallery in calling all this a 'libel on the military profession'..."

Vice Admiral Hewlett Thebaud, U.S.N.
Commanded U.S.S. *Boise* in invasion of Italy
Commander, Cruiser Division 10, Pacific Fleet, 1943-1944
Director of Naval Intelligence, 1944-1945

[to Admiral Doenitz]
"Your unfortunate confinement has been a source of regret and shame to many Americans in all walks of life. You have been a professional military man and were merely serving your country. The Nuremberg Trials have created a deplorable precedent in international law."

Dr. Samuel T. Chambers
Professor of History, University of Baltimore

"I am glad to hear that Admiral Doenitz is free at last. The Nuremberg trials were a vindictive travesty of every canon of old military law. Doenitz was condemned for the acts that Admiral Fisher praised when von Tirpitz committed them upon British shipping."

Dr. Francis Neilson
American actor (with Wm. Gillette & Chas. Frohman Companies)
Playwright and poet; librettist for Victor Herbert
Author and historian

"I agree entirely with those who believe that the trial and conviction of Admiral Doenitz by the International Military Tribunal at Nuremberg are not in accord with the constitutional principles with which we are familiar. The trial of the so-called war criminals will, instead of advancing world peace, only deepen the wound caused by the war and kindle in the hearts of the defeated enemy the fire of revenge. We should profit from the wise counsel of Lord Stowell: 'A treaty of peace is, therefore, an agreement to waive all discussion concerning the respective rights of the parties, and to bury in oblivion all the original causes of war.' "

Honorable Bernabe Africa, LL.D.
Philippine diplomat and statesman
Commissioner of Foreign Relations
Acting Secretary for Foreign Affairs
Ambassador to Japan and Thailand
Delegate to S.E.A.T.O.

"Aside from the horrendous demand for 'Unconditional Surrender,' certainly the most stupid error of America's World War II policies was to sponsor and participate in the so-called Nuremberg Trials. From the standpoint of simple law and justice, these trials were a travesty on Anglo-Saxon traditions of jurisprudence. Equally significant, they set a precedent that may someday haunt our children when future wars take place. From the standpoint of bringing peace and reconciliation among the Western people of the world, the trials did nothing but harm. It is fortunate for the West that the German people have chosen to be charitable in their response to this tragic mistake. As a brave and patriotic officer, Admiral Doenitz deserves the respect of thinking people everywhere for the moral stamina he exhibited in answer to the attacks upon his devotion to duty and record of naval competence."

Honorable Howard Buffett
U.S. Congressman from Nebraska, 78th, 79th, 80th and 82nd Congresses; Lawyer

"If this case definitely will prevent any similar miscarriage of justice, then Grand Admiral Karl Doenitz will not have suffered in vain. That might be some slight compensation for him during the rest of his life."

Major General James I. Muir, U.S.A.
Commanded, 24th and 44th Divisions, World War II
Commanded 23rd Army Corps

"During the 'War Crimes Trials' in Tokyo, Colonel McCormack of the Chicago Tribune was in Japan for a visit with General MacArthur. I had the honor and pleasure of being the Colonel's host for three days in Osaka. My attitude towards the War Crimes Trials is epitomized in a terse reply by Colonel McCormack to my question concerning his possible attendance at the trials. He said: 'I will never lend my presence where legalized murder is imposed.' Thank you very much for permitting me to add my small bit to the condemnation of this aboriginal practice."

Major General Charles L. Mullins, Jr., U.S.A.
Commanded 25th Army Division, World War II
Deputy Commander, 2nd U.S. Army
Chairman, Armed Forces Delegation, Joint U.S.—Brazil Military Commission

"It seems to me only natural that all military personnel would abhor such procedures as the 'war crimes trials' and the various civilian and government agencies must be aware of such feelings. Therefore I feel we get nowhere in influencing public opinion in this matter until a great number of prominent civilians take a stand to prevent future trials of military personnel such as that of Grand Admiral Doenitz."

Vice Admiral Edmund W. Burrough, U.S.N.

"...When they [the Nuremberg Trials] were instituted, I felt that they were setting a very dangerous precedent...it seems to me that the victorious Allies, who admittedly indulged in the same practise (unrestricted submarine warfare), had no legal, logical, or ethical justification for prosecuting or condemning Admiral Doenitz. In doing so, they laid themselves open to a charge of hypocrisy and an abuse of the power which victory had placed in their hands. It does not seem to me an adequate answer for them to say that they prosecuted the Admiral because the Germans began the unrestricted warfare."

Honorable Frank A. W. Lucas
Judge of Appeal, High Commission Territories, Union of South Africa
Judge, Transvaal Division, Supreme Court of South Africa

"In regard to the trial of Grand Admiral Doenitz, I would like to be put on record as being in complete agreement with the views expressed by Admiral Gallery...My congratulations to you for your very commendable efforts to set the record straight."

Vice Admiral Frank W. Rockwell, U.S.N.
Commander, Amphibious Force Pacific, World War II

"I can only say that I agreed completely at the time with the views expressed by the late Senator Taft regarding the so-called 'war crimes trials'...I believe the trials in general were a travesty on justice."

Honorable Joseph H. Ball
United States Senator from Minnesota
Vice President, States Marine Lines

"I want to fully agree to the expressed opinion of Rear Admiral Daniel V. Gallery in his latest book, in which he calls the 'war crimes trials a libel on the military profession'. The dangerous precedent set at Nuremberg must be removed."

N. Wijkmark
Rear Admiral R.S.N.

Rear Admiral Nils Wijkmark,
Royal Swedish Navy
Squadron Commodore
Admiral-Superintendent
at Karlskrona, 1936-1944

"I have always considered the War Crimes Trials a great shame, the direct responsibility for which rests upon the legal fraternity of Great Britain and the United States. They were not only without sanction in International Law, but were directly in violation of our Anglo-Saxon Bill of Rights and Constitutional principles. The American Bar, to its great shame, failed to rally around the courageous efforts of Robert A. Taft to halt the infamous trials."

O. Glenn Saxon, LL.B., A.M.
Professor of Economics at Yale University from 1931
Commissioner of Finance and Control, State of Connecticut

"I am in full agreement with the sentiment expressed regarding the impropriety of the punishment meted out to professional soldiers following their conviction of war crimes at Nuremberg. I fully concur with Admiral Gallery's statement that the 'war crimes trials' are a 'libel on the military profession' and are a barefaced hypocrisy."

Major General William Church Davis, U.S.A.

"...you are perfectly right in branding the Nuremberg 'war crimes trials' in general as violating the common principles for civilized jurisdiction. There seems to be more of vengeance—'*vae victis*'—than of impartial justice. Especially from a military standpoint is the conviction of such men as Doenitz and Raeder as criminals revolting, and this can be a very dangerous precedent in the future. I think that the Nuremberg Trials did not honor the Western Powers. About unrestricted submarine warfare, I can't see any moral difference between this form of war and the dropping of bombs over undefended cities."

General Olof Gerhard Thornell, Royal Swedish Army
Commander-in-chief, Armed Forces of Sweden, 1940-1944
Chief of Military Staff to His Majesty, King Gustav V, 1944-1950

"I believe that Admiral Doenitz was unfairly persecuted. First, it is the duty of an officer of the Armed Services of any country to carry out the policies of his Government. His would be a sad country if he did otherwise. Furthermore, Doenitz was not tried by a military Court, but was sentenced by an International Tribunal under no law that existed during the hostilities of the war period. In my opinion, this was unjust. It was unprecedented."

Vice Admiral William W. Smith, U.S.N.
President, U.S. Naval Academy Alumni Association
Commander, Task Force, Aleutian Islands
Director, Naval Transportation Service
Chairman, U.S. Maritime Commission

"In general, I agreed with the unpopular opinion at the time of the late Senator Taft, against the trials."

Right Reverend Henry Knox Sherrill, D.D., D.L
Presiding Bishop of the
Protestant Episcopal Church

"Taking into consideration the sentence of Grand Admiral Karl Doenitz, commander of the German Navy, at the end of World War II, one should consider with disgust and sorrow this and similar deeds which are dishonorable not only for the winners but also for the development of the morals of humanity. Various events which we witnessed during the last two world wars showed us that humanity is not completely liberated from the spirit of the Middle Ages...And it is even possible to find noble gestures during the battles of the Middle Ages! The consideration and politeness shown by Alp Arslan, Emperor of the Seldjouks, toward the Emperor of Byzantium is a brilliant example. Although the cruelty and torments exercised upon the Turkish statesmen and military commanders during the First World War are somehow forgotten or ignored by humanity, I would like to state that, as a person who has seen and suffered some of these cruelties, the action directed against Grand Admiral Doenitz should be considered with sorrow and heartbreak. Unfortunately, humanity does not seem to have advanced beyond the motto, 'The winner is always right.' "

Lieutenant General Fahri Belen, Turkish Army
Chief of Staff of Turkish Army, 1941
Army Corps Commander, 1944-50
Member of Parliament since 1950
Minister of Public Works, 1950-51
Professor of Turkish War Academy, and author

"Intensely, I feel the conviction and imprisonment of Admiral Doenitz thoroughly unjust and completely outrageous."

Honorable George H. Earle, LL.D., D.C.L.
Governor of Pennsylvania, 1935-1939
U.S. Minister to Bulgaria and Turkey
Naval officer in World War II
Assistant Governor of Samoa, 1945

"I am strongly opposed to the trial, ex post facto or otherwise, of an officer for his performance of professional duties. It is my opinion that the trial of Admiral Doenitz was unwarranted, unjust and illegal."

Major General George L. Eberle, U.S.A.
Chairman, Joint Planning Staff, Allied Hq. Italy, 1944
Acting Chief of Staff, O. & T., War Dept.
Deputy Commandant, National War College, 1952-1954

"I always felt that the so-called 'war crimes trials' were unjust and were a reflection on the United States. I am glad that at least Admiral Doenitz, who was an honorable soldier, has been freed."

Brigadier General Robert E. Wood, U.S.A.
Acting Quartermaster General, U.S. Army, World War II
Chairman of the Board, Sears Roebuck & Co.

"As a soldier, the career, the trial, and the subsequent imprisonment of Admiral Karl Doenitz, World War II Commander-in-Chief of the German Navy, have always provoked my interest. It is also my opinion, that the name of Admiral Doenitz deserves a legitimate chapter in the annals of military science and history...We are all agreed that Germany was, before and in 1939, a defacto and a de jure state. That is to say, it had a legal personality. Admiral Doenitz was a regular officer in his country's service. In conducting the submarine warfare he was only an instrument of the state. This much could be said of any other officer whether allied or German. There was no substantial evidence to prove that Germany alone contravened the London Naval Treaty of 1930...Admiral Doenitz's responsibility in this case seemed to have been quite commensurate with the general behavior of the war. It is not for me however, to mention the particular nations which could have borne the same charge of unrestricted submarine warfare. It is rather paradoxical that the use of the atom-bomb, in Japan, which resulted in a terrible destruction to innocent lives and property seemed to have escaped the attention of the judges at the Nuremberg Trials. It was just as much the desire of the Allies to win the war as it was Germany's...Vengeance on the part of the Allies was the deciding factor. The world ought to have learnt a lesson from the aftermath of 1914-1918. Vengeance cannot be the means of establishing a lasting peace in this troubled world of ours. A more human approach to the problems must be the standard before the Statesmen of to-day. For certainty, a peace based on might cannot endure. Two wrongs can never make a right...one fails to see how a Commander of a fighting force could be individually guilty for the execution of war. The imprisonment of Admiral Doenitz is a flaw on the rules of Equity and Jurisprudence. One might venture to say it was a juridic hypocrisy...Grand Admiral Karl Doenitz was a great soldier, carrying out his duties in the normal course of his career. A fellow-soldier like myself can only wish that his name is cleared of the alleged criminal charge which, even to the layman, was vindictive and calculated to raise the arrogance of the victor and humiliate the honour of the vanquished. To clear his name of the charge, in my opinion, will be an expression of good will and human fellowship..."

Hon. Major General Mohamed Talaat Farid
Member, Supreme Council of the Republic of the Sudan
Minister of Information and Labor
Official Spokesman of the Republic of the Sudan

"I recall vividly the speech made by the Hon. Robert Taft at Gambier, Ohio, in which he condemned the ex-post facto laws under which the Nuremberg trials were being conducted. I agreed with him at the time, but such was the temper of the people that his speech was disregarded. I was also appalled to see Soviet Russia judging...when they themselves were...guilty. I am happy to join my name to those attempting to make amends to Admiral Doenitz."

Adolphe Menjou
American actor

"At the time the court was constituted for the Nuremberg war crimes trials I was impressed that somebody was tampering with dynamite. It occurred to me that if we had been the losers in World War II and Hitler and his allies the winners, and the winners had decided to proceed as we did, Roosevelt and Churchill would have been most likely on the way to the gallows. Looking at it from that standpoint it is discouraging. Anyway, it would take a lot of explaining to eliminate the barbaric atmosphere of the trial. What's the difference between Nuremberg and chaining the captured vanquished to the chariot of the victor to be dragged around an arena to the plaudits of the victor's henchmen?"

Hon. George Bell Timmerman, LL.D.
American jurist
Federal Judge, U.S. District Court, South Carolina
Member, House of Representatives of South Carolina

"The war crimes trials held in the heat of hatreds fresh in the minds of the judges, could not have been fair and impartial and therefore should not have been held at all. No military officers carrying out orders of their governments had any discretion and in no case should have been punished. Actual crimes should have been handled by their own governments and not by enemy governments."

Admiral Felix B. Stump, U.S.N.
Commander-in-chief, Pacific
Commander-in-chief, U.S.
Pacific Fleet
Commander Air Force,
Atlantic Fleet

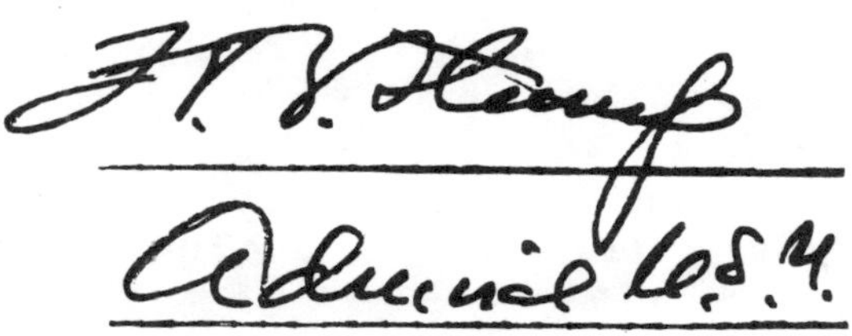

"...I have felt with my good friend, the late Senator Robert A. Taft, that the war crimes trials were a disgrace upon America and should never have taken place. Particularly incredible to me is the fact that the Communists should have been allowed to sit as judges in such cases."

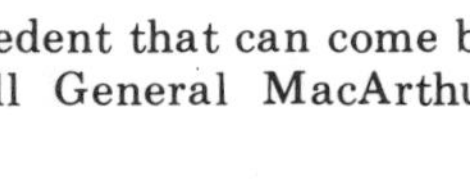

J. H. Gipson, Sr., Publisher
President, The Caxton Printers, Ltd.
Economist and author

"Our government has set a precedent that can come back to plague it sometime in the future. The Russians now call General MacArthur and General Marshall 'war criminals.' "

William R. Mathews
Editor and Publisher, *The Arizona Daily Star*

“...I can vouch that during the five years fighting of our Fleet, mostly attached to the British Fleet, I never heard any complaint of atrocities in submarine warfare which (including the Greek submarines) was unrestricted on both sides, nor anything against Grand Admiral Doenitz, who cannot be held responsible for individual transgression of his subordinates. He, therefore, cannot be guilty of ‘war crimes.’ But public opinion, no matter how honorary, does not annul the verdict. Only a proper revision of the trial by a judicial body would wipe out this injustice and perhaps others.”

E. Cawadias

Vice Admiral Epaminondas P. Cawadias, Royal Hellenic Navy
Commodore Commanding Submarine Flotilla, 1935-37
Commander-in-Chief, Greek Fleet, 1939-42
Minister of Marine, 1943-44
Principal A.D.C. to King Paul, 1947-51

“I can well remember, at the time of the Nuremberg Trials, my great uneasiness about the justice of placing senior, or indeed any officers, on trial for carrying out orders from higher authority.”

C. St. C. Cameron

Vice Admiral Cyril St. Clair Cameron, Royal Navy, C.B.E.
Director, Torpedo Division, British Naval Staff

“There was no justification in law or in fact for the trial, conviction and imprisonment of Admiral Doenitz by the international tribunal at Nuremberg. Admiral Doenitz conducted himself, his operations, his administrations, in the same manner, on the same level, as all honorable naval flag officers of the United States of America, Britain, Canada and Australia have in the past and did in World War II.”

Sincerely,
Allan E. Smith

Vice Admiral Allan E. Smith, U.S.N.
Commander, Task Force Aleutians and South Pacific, 1943-45
Commander Cruisers, Atlantic Fleet, 1948-50
Commander, U.N. Blockading Force in Korea, 1950-51

"As regards the War Crime Trials, I believe that I agree with most sober, considered thinking that they were a grave mistake and illegal — an item of war hysteria such as happens in every war. We should feel equally ashamed of our treatment of our West Coast citizens of Japanese extraction. To impose a civilian sentence upon a military leader for obeying orders is contrary to all of the rules governing the profession of arms down through the time of recorded history. Had the Germans been victorious, Patton could easily have been tried and sentenced for his aggressive tank action, and Spaatz for his bombing of Berlin and other German cities."

Major General Harry H. Vaughan, U.S. Army Reserve
Former Military Aide to the President of the U.S. (Harry S. Truman)
With U.S. Army Forces in Australia, 1942-43

"I do not hesitate to say that the war crimes trials of professional military officers by the victors of World War II was, in itself, one of the greatest, most unjust crimes ever committed by so-called civilized people...Undoubtedly military leaders of the so-called Allies, were just as guilty of the charges made against those who were tried, and the injustice of a court or courts, composed of the victors, in trying those who were defeated is something that no just and honorable man could possibly support."

Hon. J. Bracken Lee
Governor, State of Utah

"I consider that the Trials have done an immeasurable amount of harm. They have continued long into what should have been a period of constructive return to international co-operation and peace after the terrible brutality of the war. Insofar as these Trials reflect what may be future policy in relation to war, I consider that to perpetuate the idea of War Trials of Service Chiefs and Senior Commanding Officers can only serve to lengthen wars, because the loser will tend to fight to the last. Men may well prefer to be killed honorably on the field than to be hanged ignominiously later on. If Service personnel, at any rank, are thought to be guilty of specific criminal action, or action contrary to international law, it should be found possible to have them tried by their own Military Courts."

General Richard James Mulcahy of Ireland
Minister For Defense,
First Irish Cabinet, 1919, 1922-24
Commander-in-Chief, 1922-23
Minister For Local Government
and Public Health, 1927-32
Member of Dail Eireann, 1918-1948
President, United Ireland Party
since 1944
Minister For Education,
1948-51 and since 1954

"I applaud and endorse this effort to call attention to the injustice of the Nuremberg 'war crimes trials' and to the dangerous precedent created by them. The speech made by the late Senator Robert A. Taft on the subject completely expresses my opinion of and attitude regarding them."

Hon. Henry P. Fletcher, LL.D.
U.S. Undersecretary of State
Ambassador to Chile, Mexico, Belgium and Italy

"In my opinion, the trials of professional military men as for instance the Nuremberg Trials remind of the Barbarian days when prisoners of war were killed just because they had fought. This does not mean that trials of military men of the forces of *both parties,* who really acted against the laws and regulations of warfare will be excluded. On the contrary, but they have to be based on international law."

General Hendrik Johan Kruls, Royal Netherlands Army
Head of Department, War Ministry, London, 1941-44
Chief of General Staff of the Netherlands, 1945-51
President, Netherlands Joint Chiefs of Staff Council, 1948-51

"My opinion of the infamous Nuremberg Trials, expressed at the time, was that our country could never live down its participation in such a shameful travesty of justice. Today, my opinion remains the same, in spite of the specious attempts at justification by Justice Jackson and others connected with that dismal tragedy."

Major General John Shirley Wood, U.S.A.
Commanding General, 4th Armored Division, 1942-45

"I have noted that you are willing to add my own views to the collection of opinions related to the constitution, in the aftermath of World War II, of the International Military Tribunal at Nuremberg. I think that the 'war crimes trials,' as those involved in the proceedings of the Court of Nuremberg, the case of Grand Admiral Doenitz among others, is a controversial problem, the solution of which remains to be found in an agreement to be reached by the distinguished jurisconsultants who, as members of the Commission of International Law of the United Nations, have been entrusted with such a difficult task. I truly appreciate your courteous invitation to join the many personalities of the political and military world who have already expressed their opinion on the matter, and I avail myself of this opportunity..."

Paul E. Magloire
President of the Republic of Haiti, 1950-57

[to Grand Admiral Doenitz]
"...It would appear to me that you have been made the victim of your loyalty to your country and your determination to carry out the tasks assigned you by your government...In spite of the fact that forces under my command suffered thereby, I have always, as an officer, had respect and admiration for the highly effective manner in which you directed your submarine operations. And your conduct of the last difficult task which devolved upon you was beyond reproach."

Admiral H. Kent Hewitt, U.S.N.
Commander, U.S. Naval Forces in Europe, 1945-1946

"My opinion is that the 'war crimes trials' of career officers were the result of a hysteria on the part of those responsible and a failure to realize the changes in making war that were taking place. Many things contributed to these changes — Science, inventions, rapid communications, etc. It became evident in the First World War that the so-called romance in war was rapidly disappearing. War was to become an all-out effort and there were to be few or no non-combatants. The old rules, including 'restricted warfare' have, of necessity, disappeared. Therefore, to hold individual officers responsible merely because they were proficient enough to be placed in high positions of command is, as Admiral Gallery states, a 'libel on the military profession'. The case of Admiral Doenitz exemplifies the tragic results of such thinking."

Vice Admiral Glenn B. Davis, U.S.N.
Commander, Battleship Division 8, World War II
Commander, Potomac River Command and 6th Naval District

"This is an impressive list of names of distinguished men and women which you have gathered for the presentation and support of your attack upon the 'war crimes trials.' I am, of course, honored by your invitation for me to join this group of eminent public figures, and am glad to accept your invitation and thus add my name to theirs...I would like to say that I regard the 'war crimes trials' as a crime."

Rev. Dr. John Haynes Holmes
D.D. (Jewish Institute of Religion), L.D., Hum. D.
Vice Pres., and Director, N.A.A.C.P.
Director, American Civil Liberties Union

"...The trials had a very sad effect on me, and I had every sympathy towards those brave generals who were tried for carrying out their national duties and orders gallantly and honestly, the thing for which a soldier should normally be praised and rewarded. Would such court members accept or expect such treatment if they lost a war? In our old history and traditions, a leader when captured was treated honorably. To be a soldier and defend your country is a noble and honorable task and a prisoner of war is by law respected and properly treated. Why then should the defeated leaders be tried as criminals? It is a serious and most demoralizing precedent which is double-edged and may have the same effect on officers of both sides. I should say that it was not a lucky decision by those who made it."

Honorable Major General Ahmed Abdel Wahab, Republic of the Sudan
Minister of the Interior and Local Government, 1958-1959

"I am of opinion that the war crimes trials were illegal. If after each war, the victors establish a war crimes tribunal, the best men among the vanquished will be sacrificed at the altar of the thirst for blood of the victors. Why cannot the victors and the vanquished forget and forgive?"

Hon. W. Dahanayake
Prime Minister of Ceylon
Member of the Parliament of Ceylon
Minister of Defense, External Affairs, Agriculture

"In an old and simple adage it was said 'How could the adversary be an arbiter and the enemy be a judge?' That was what happened in the International Military Tribunal at Nuremberg, in the 20th Century with all the modern developement of International Law. The condemnation of the Grand Admiral Doenitz on *ex post facto* concepts was directly in violation of many constitutional principles and International Law. It was based on acts and orders by him not different from other acts and orders executed by Admirals and Governments in conducting the war. The principal weakness of the Nuremberg Tribunals was that their verdicts were given by representatives of the victors, thus applying the principle that 'Might Makes Right'. This tribunal should have been formed by representatives of neutral states who would have examined the conduct of the war from the point of view of both sides. A military profession is considered one of the most honorable professions. If the men who take up the responsibility of defending their country by accomplishing their duty were exposed to the inevitable justice of the victors, this renowned profession would become a most disgraceful one. This reminds us of the Dark Ages and proves that the spiritual developement of our World lags far behind the miraculous materialistic progress. Regarding the 'Unrestricted Submarine Warfare' or the unrestricted war in general, we can conclude that the two war parties were greatly alike in their actions. To end this letter, I would like to simply quote what one defendant stated during his trial at Nuremberg: 'Our one crime was that we were defeated.' "

N. Armanazi

Honorable Najeeb-Al-Armanazi, LL.D.
Secretary General of the Presidency of the Republic of Syria, 1932-1945
Syrian Ambassador to India, Turkey, Egypt, and the United Kingdom

"The precedent established by the Nuremberg Trials, in which officers of the armed services were charged before civil courts with criminal offenses, for acts which were normal wartime performance of duty, is certainly a dangerous threat to our own effectiveness...I do feel that Admiral Doenitz's case was a great miscarriage of Justice, and I heartily approve of the action you have undertaken to present those matters to him."

Frederick M. Trapnell

Vice Admiral Frederick M. Trapnell, U.S.N.
Commanding Officer, U.S.S. *Breton,* 1943-1944
Commander, Naval Air Test Center
Commander, U.S.S. *Coral Sea,* 1950-51

"My views in the matter of the War Criminal Trials, especially that of Admiral Doenitz, no doubt coincide with those of most professional Army, Navy and Air Force officers. War at sea was so swift in World War II, and more so now, that a submarine commander could not afford to jeopardize his mission (to destroy the enemy) or his ship. Often, the enemy consisted of several ships and aircraft. I have always felt that the 'War Crimes Trials' were the brain child of Stalin and sold to the U.S. and Britain. Stalin would have preferred to execute them. It was all done in a spirit of revenge, similar to the 'Unconditional Surrender' ultimatum instigated by Mr. Morgenthau. The purpose of war is victory and the soldier, sailor and airman should not be penalized if he carries out the orders of his civilian authority in an honorable manner. I am glad that Admiral Doenitz will have the opportunity of knowing the sentiments of U.S. professional service officers."

Commodore Carlos Augustus Bailey, U.S.N.
Commanded destroyers, World War II

[To Grand Admiral Doenitz]
"I am glad to be included among those privileged to salute you in this manner. Our profession is an uneasy one. And in carrying on the policies of our Governments we are frequently held responsible beyond the limits of our authority. You have paid a high price for such confusion. You may take satisfaction from the fact that you demonstrated superior skill and ability in your chosen field. The events of the past in no way lessen the respect in which you will complete, happily I hope, the remainder of your life."

Vice Admiral Gerald F. Bogan, U.S.N.
Commander Air Force, Atlantic Fleet
Commanded U.S.S. *Saratoga* and various Aircraft Carrier Divisions, World War II

"I agree with Admiral Gallery that the War Crimes Trials were a libel on the Military Profession and something which will definitely be used against our own Military and Naval Officers in the future should we be so unfortunate as to lose a war. There was no authorization or precedent in International Law for those trials and I consider the precedent set as that time to be most dangerous and an international disgrace."

Rear Admiral James D. Barner, U.S.N.
Aircraft manufacturing executive
Commanding officer, aircraft carriers, World War II

"Please add my name to those on the list to be presented to Admiral Doenitz. I certainly find the Nuremberg Trials a fantastic desecration of the ideals of a Western Civilization, and appalling miscarriage of justice, especially toward professional military officers and civil servants, and, in many instances, a misuse of evidence for vicious ends, all of which will someday be exposed as a shocking travesty of high legal and moral principles."

Henry M. Adams, Ph.D.
Professor of History, University of California
Military Police and Civil Affairs Officer in Italy, World War II
Executive Officer, Military Government Detachment, Saarland, 1945

"After World War II when Commander U.S. Naval Forces Germany (and Austria) a special staff group was organized by my office in Berlin to cover the naval phases of the Nuremberg trials (Doenitz and Raeder). On several occasions when these phases of the trial were in progress I attended the sittings as an observer when advised by General Mark Clark...Am quite certain that nothing was brought forth in the trials of both Admirals Raeder and Doenitz that reflected in any manner on their honorable conduct of the naval war."

Vice Admiral William Glassford, U.S.N.
Commander, Naval Forces, South Pacific, World War II
President Franklin D. Roosevelt's personal representative at Dakar

"I was and am against the War Crimes Trials in principle. Had a policy of no trials been adopted, exceptions could well have been made. The War Crimes Trials established a dangerous precedent which will someday back-fire. Matters such as Unconditional Surrender, War Crimes Trials and Balance of Power should not be considered and determined without looking far into the past, and well into the future, otherwise emotions of the moment will exert an undue influence."

Major General Orlando Ward, U.S.A.
Commanding General, 1st and 20th Armored Divisions, World War II
Commanding General, 5th Corps, 1946
Commanding General, 6th Division, Korea

"I feel strongly that the trial of Grand Admiral Doenitz and other military men who were 'guilty', if you may call it that, of nothing more than directing the operations of the military forces of their command in offensive or defensive operations were unjustly subjected to trial. War is not a humane operation and international treaties cannot be expected to hold sway when their disregard can mean the difference between victory and defeat."

Rear Admiral D.E. McKay, U.S. Coast Guard
Chief Communications Officer, Coast Guard Headquarters
Commander, 14th Coast Guard District

"I have always felt that the 'War Crimes Trials' as set and conducted—as a whole—were a serious mistake. They are very likely to set a bad precedent for any future unscrupulous victor in future wars for the trials of officers who are merely carrying out their normal duties. And from what I know of the case, it seems to me that my remarks apply with full force to Admiral Doenitz's case."

Major General Paul W. Baade, U.S.A.
Commanding General, 35th Infantry Division, 1943-1945
Military Governor of Hanover and Coblenz, 1945

"I believe that no sane person can approve what was done by the Nuremberg Tribunal, where all the norms of civilization were violated. The Tribunal acted both as plaintiff and judge. Indiscipline was fomented. Retroactive effect was given to laws conjured up for the purposes of the judges, whom they named from amongst themselves. The Tribunal punished patriotism—which demands obedience, particularly in a war, to the duly constituted government—and the saddest thing of all is the thought that several nations took part in it. Admiral Doenitz was a gentleman, an admirable and esteemed military man who defended his country as a person of honor ought to defend it, and the revision of his trial is imperative if we are to consider that Justice is the only road which will prevent the world from again falling into barbarism, to which it is unfortunately approaching ever nearer because of its compromises. Every person who has as a determining principle of behavior love for country, honor and self-respect, ought to imitate Admiral Doenitz."

Francisco Bastarreche

Admiral Don Francisco Bastarreche
Admiral of the Spanish Fleet
Member, Spanish Royal Council

"I believe that a military officer who is carrying out the commission or directive of his government...should not be accountable to any government other than his own...Certainly the support of his government's military policies or the execution of its military directives [by Admiral Doenitz] should not have made him subject to a so called 'Military Crime Trial.' "

B H Bieri

Vice Admiral Bernhard H. Bieri, U.S.N.
Commander, U.S. Naval Forces Mediterranean, 1946-1948
Representative, U.N. Military Staff Committee

[To Grand Admiral Doenitz]

"I am happy to know that your years of imprisonment have ended...Your name has always commanded respect from those of us who specialized in the use of the submarine as a weapon. No matter what the laws of war at sea may prescribe, any naval authority—any realist—is aware of the fact that submarine warfare cannot be conducted on a 'visit and search' basis...You were ordered to conduct 'unrestricted submarine warfare' as I was. We carried out our orders. Had we protested that such orders were illegal, others would have been appointed who would carry them out. Your loyalty and obedience cost you ten years imprisonment...Yet neither of us will ever regret our original decisions."

Charles A. Lockwood
Vice Adm. U.S.N.

Vice Admiral Charles A. Lockwood, U.S.N.
Commander, Submarines, Pacific Fleet, World War II

"This material confirms the adverse general opinion I have always had of the majority of these trials, as being illegal and travestic of justice, depending upon 'ex post facto' edicts that were not legislations or treaties. As to Grand Admiral Doenitz—as well as others—I consider he was most unjustly convicted and imprisoned for doing his duty in a way we should all respect. He has my best wishes. I greatly regret my country had anything to do with it."

Vice Admiral Walter S. Anderson, U.S.N.
Commanded battleships, Pacific Fleet
Commander, Cruiser Division 4, World War II
Director of Naval Intelligence

Walter S. Anderson

"...All I can say to Admiral Doenitz is that as an individual I deeply regret that my Country was a party to his imprisonment...In taking this step we have hurt ourselves more than those who were the victims. The quality of mercy has been forgotten. The only thing that we can do now is to say—'We have condemned you for things you did because you considered it your duty to your Country. For all such, forgive us. We were wrong.' "

J. W. Reeves Jr

Admiral John W. Reeves, Jr., U.S.N.
Commander, Aircraft Carrier Divisions, World War II

"The Nuremberg trials conducted by a so-called 'International *Military* Court'—which it was not—were a travesty of legality and violated the basic principles of justice which have been a treasured part of our heritage. They constituted a libel on the military profession. They robbed us of a moral victory and prestige which, after a long and costly war, should have been ours. In the light of our own practice throughout the war, to charge, and convict, Admiral Doenitz with violation of the laws of war—unrestricted submarine warfare—was simple and unadulterated hypocrisy. If after a war, professional military men are to be brought to trial—on trumped up charges—solely because of their prominence as military commanders...there is good reason to believe that they will fight to the bitter end with no thought of surrender. The ill-advised 'unconditional surrender' edict prolonged the war and prevented an early negotiated peace with the resultant saving in lives and treasure. These two blunders—'unconditional surrender' and the 'war criminal trials'—seem to have left out any consideration of what might be termed the characteristics of a successful war."

Thomas C. Kinkaid

Admiral Thomas C. Kinkaid, U.S.N.
Commander, Allied Naval Forces, S.W. Pacific, World War II

"I should be very glad to have my name appear with others who wish to show the respect with which they regard Grand Admiral Karl Doenitz. While I never knew Grand Admiral Karl Doenitz personally, as the Naval officer who had complete charge of the submarine campaign waged against the German submarines in the 1st World War, I would like to say a few words. When the 2nd World War was started the German submarines were much below a figure which could be said to be adequate to meet the needs of the German sea forces required in the 2nd war. Therefore what submarines were available were assigned in the attack of the convoys proceeding along the northern coast of Norway, bound for Murmansk and finally to Russia itself. By this time Russia was regarded as the arch foe that Germany would be forced to face. It is this particular part of the German attack system for which I express great admiration. No longer was the attack made as it had been in the 1st World War, but a new feature in the attack system was used. This system of attack resembled more the attack of destroyers under a smoke screen used by our Navy. It embodied the 3 point attack system used by our destroyers and the absence of a smoke screen to conceal the attacking forces was made up by attacks made at night in the darkest hours or when favorable weather obscured the attackers, and in this way differed from the attack system in use in the 1st World War. The success attendant on this new form of attack was phenomenal. All of the northern convoys suffered losses and one was almost completely destroyed.

"The Germans have been claimed to be cruel in their submarine warfare. Beyond what was deemed necessary for the country's good, the Germans were not as cruel as has been claimed. In the Pacific where a few of their raiders operated without opposition, they attacked freely a few ships. The ships captured may have been sunk or turned over for the raider's use but none of the passengers and crew were destroyed and were landed safely in southern ports. In contrast to this was the cruelty exercised by the Russians. During the Boxer Revolution in China I saw, in going up to Tientsin on the Peiho River, on one bank where the Russians went not a single thing was spared, men, women or children. On the other bank where the Japanese went up nothing was destroyed. The contrast was marked.

"For the reasons cited above I recognize in Grand Admiral Karl Doenitz the master technician that he was. I also recommend his system to the use of Americans in any sea warfare that might possibly develop...."

Admiral William V. Pratt, U.S.N.
Commander-in-Chief, U.S. Fleet, 1929
Chief of Naval Operations, 1930-1933
Naval Commentator for *Newsweek*, World War II

[To Grand Admiral Doenitz]

"As an officer of over 42 years of service in the Navy of my own country, I have always viewed your trial and sentence with extreme distaste. Your 'crime', as I see it, consisted in the giving of the major part of your life to effective and highly efficient service to the Navy of your country; so efficient in fact that you rose to the supreme command of that Navy in a great war. In the eyes of the Nuremberg trials court, that latter fact of your naval career seems to have been the greatest essence of your 'crime.' To me the Nuremberg trials have always been totally inexcusable and a horrible travesty on justice. This is especially true when such trials are used to punish the men of the military services who were directing those services in time of war, and thus giving nothing more than an expression of the basic purposes of their whole adult life. In the execution of their wartime duties, these officers naturally carried out, to the letter, the orders and directions which they received from the head of their government. If an officer...should ever, for one instant, consider disregard or disobedience to his government's orders, all cohesion in the military services would fail, from that moment, and the military services would fail in the one reason for their existence—the waging of successful war in the interests of their country...I hope that the years which stretch before you will serve, in some measure, to dull the memory of the ten years of illegal confinement to which you were subjected."

Rear Admiral Robert A. Theobald, U.S.N.
Commander, Northern Pacific Force, 1942-1943
Chief of Staff, U.S. Fleet
Author of *The Final Secret of Pearl Harbor* (1954)

"I consider the War Trials as one of the more disgraceful manifestations of the past war hysteria...I am confident that the trial of Admiral Doenitz was a gross miscarriage of justice..."

Vice Admiral Richard H. Cruzen, U.S.N.
Commander, Naval Forces, Philippines, 1951
Commander, Task Force, Byrd Antarctic Expedition

[To Grand Admiral Doenitz]
"I congratulate you upon having the health & equanimity to weather the vicissitudes of the period 1945-56 in Germany. This, to you was different but nerve-wracking, just the same as 1941-43 was to me. I was Comdr. Caribbean Sea Frontier when we bore the full pressure of your amazing submarine campaign in that area. Best wishes."

Admiral John Howard Hoover, U.S.N.
Commander, Marianas Islands,
World War II

[To Grand Admiral Doenitz]
"Unswerving obedience and loyalty have always been the requisite of a Naval Officer. These traits always are universally admired by all fighting men. It is my sincere opinion that you have the respect of all thinking fighting men, for your unswerving loyalty to your own country."

Carl Stockholm, President
The Navy League of the United States
("The Civilian Arm of the Navy")

"I feel very strongly on the basic principles involved in 'war crimes trials' and the flagrant travesty on justice resulting from such hypocrisy. It should be apparent from the record of the last decade that these trials of professional military officers have had no effect as a means of preventing wars or of lessening warlike attitudes and preparations for war by world nations. You may extend to...Admiral Doenitz my sympathy for any injustice suffered by him as a result of post-war mania and my personal congratulations for his excellent record of professional military accomplishment."

Rear Admiral James E. Arnold, U.S.N.R.
Commanding Officer, Advanced Amphibious Base, England, 1943-1944

[To Grand Admiral Doenitz]

"One of my first duties, when we entered the last war, was to pass to my Submarines our Navy Department's order to carry on 'unrestricted' war against Japan. As I recall the specifications of your so-called trial, the main charge against you was exactly that same thing. I did what I was ordered to do. You, my dear Admiral, have suffered over ten long years of imprisonment for likewise carrying out your Government's orders. Of course the action against you was grossly unjust; and it is a sorry blot on my Country's history. I could write much more along that line but I'll only express my one bit of satisfaction;—Despite some titles and uniforms worn by my own Countrymen in the Nuremberg affair, none of them were really Military or Naval men. Admiral, you have endured much. You may be very sure that at least your place in history will be of the best. You fought the kind of war that you were ordered to fight, over long difficult years, with great efficiency,—technically and as an inspired leader of men. Then, at the end, when charged with the full burden of your Nation's affairs, you also met that test superlatively well. You probably are far from wishing my sympathy but—may I salute you?"

Thos C. Hart

Admiral Thomas C. Hart, U.S.N.
Commander-in-Chief, Asiatic Fleet, World War II
U.S. Senator from Connecticut, 1945-1947

"I know of no charge against Admiral Doenitz which warranted his conviction and imprisonment. He occupied an important post during the war and, I believe, served his government faithfully. The war crimes trials were a reversion to the ancient practice of the savage extermination of a defeated enemy and particularly of its leaders. The precedent set by these trials will continue to plague their authors. Admiral Doenitz has my sympathy and best wishes."

Admiral Husband E. Kimmel, U.S.N.
Commander-in-Chief, U.S. Fleet, 1941

"The practice of castigating military leaders of belligerent nations merely because such leaders have performed the duty which denotes patriotic service to their respective homelands is atrocious and degrading to all persons who insist on such a practice. A military leader who performs his mission and service to his country with personal integrity and honor merits the approbation and respect of friend and foe alike. Fair play even towards one's enemy is a concept that has always dominated the spirit of America. All who have participated in any illegal award of sentence and imprisonment pursuant thereto in the case of Grand Admiral Karl Doenitz of the German Navy must be themselves condemned by conscientious people of any and all nations throughout the world."

Lieutenant General Edward M. Almond, U.S. Army
Commander 92nd Infantry Div., 1942-1945
Chief of Staff, Far Eastern Command, 1949-1950

[To Grand Admiral Doenitz]
"As a professional military man since 1 March 1910, I send greetings to you. May you enjoy life to its fullest during the remainder of your life. God will care for you and properly take care of those who unjustly confined you. God bless you."

Lieutenant General George E. Stratemeyer, U.S.A.F.
Commanding General, Eastern Air Command, Burma, World War II

"My opinion always has been that the Nuremberg War Crimes Trials were acts of vengeance. War is a political and not a legal act, and if at the termination of a war, should it be considered that certain of the enemy's leaders are politically too dangerous to be left at large, then, as Napoleon was, they should be banished to some island. To bring them to trial under *post facto* law, concocted to convict them, is a piece of hideous hypocrisy and humbug. When in September 1870, the *National Zeitung* complained of the considerate treatment accorded to the captive French emperor, Bismarck by no means shared this view. 'Popular feeling, public opinion,' he said, 'always takes that line. People insist that, in conflicts between States, the conqueror should sit in judgment upon the conquered, moral code in hand, and inflict punishment...This is an altogether unreasonable demand. Punishment and revenge have nothing to do with policy. Policy must not meddle with the calling of Nemesis, or aspire to exercise the judge's office...' Unfortunately for the world as a whole, the Western Allies could not produce a statesman of the caliber of Bismarck."

Major General J.F.C. Fuller, C.B., C.B.E., D.S.O.
British military historian and author

"...late on 7 December 1941, the Chief of Naval Operations in Washington by dispatch directed the Commanders-in-Chief, Pacific Fleet and Asiatic Fleet, and the naval coastal frontiers to 'Execute unrestricted air and submarine warfare against Japan...' In accordance with above orders it became general—and approved—practice not to attempt rescue of survivors of submarine attacks, unless such rescues could be made without prejudice to the execution of further warfare against Japan...The facts above stated were included in a deposition requested of me by Admiral Doenitz's defense attorneys, and were presumably used in his defense at the Nuremberg trials...It is my opinion that the American practice for unrestricted submarine warfare would be normal in future warfare."

Fleet Admiral Chester W. Nimitz, U.S.N.
Commanded 1st Battleship Division, 1938-1939
Chief, Bureau of Navigation, 1939-1941
Commander-in-Chief, U.S. Pacific Fleet, 1941-1945
Chief of Naval Operations, 1945-1947

"The war trials were a low level to which farce was connected, but I rejoice that Doenitz survived and is free. He was well liked by the American colony in Berlin and has many American friends. I send him my respects and good wishes."

Hon. Henry W. Shoemaker, Litt. D.
Colonel, Military Intelligence, U.S.A.R.
U.S. Minister to Bulgaria
Publisher, *Altoona (Pa.) Times Tribune*
Chairman, Pennsylvania Historical Commission

"...I do agree with Admiral Gallery's statement that the 'war crimes' trials were an illegal procedure and a 'barefaced hypocrisy.' I felt that way at the time of the trials and so stated."

Hon. Burton K. Wheeler
U.S. Senator from Montana, 1923-1947
Candidate for Vice-President
of the U.S., 1924
Attorney

[To Grand Admiral Doenitz]
"It was always my conviction that you and many of your comrades who were punished at the war crimes' trials at Nuremberg had only carried out your orders as professional military men and in the process that you had not committed offenses contrary or repugnant to international law or decency in human relations. I hope your remaining years will be attended by good health and happiness and as a former professional military man, I am sure you will strive to bring about better understanding between the peoples of your country and my own."

General A.C. Wedemeyer, U.S.A.
Commander, The China Theatre, 1944
Director, Axe Science and Electronics Corp.

"The press accounts of your recent release evoke in me the feeling of shame for my country which I felt during the travesty on justice known as the Nuremberg trials...I feel certain the vast majority of us were violently opposed to the proceedings, but were obliged to look on helplessly while honorable men who followed the honorable profession of arms in defense of their country, just as we did, were tried and found guilty of crimes that did not exist, by a prejudiced court composed of their enemies, under a code which no civilized country recognizes. The object of this letter, Sir, is to make my personal apologies to a distinguished and honorable man of war who has been crucified for the sin of fighting nobly for his country. We who fought honorably...salute you, Admiral Doenitz."

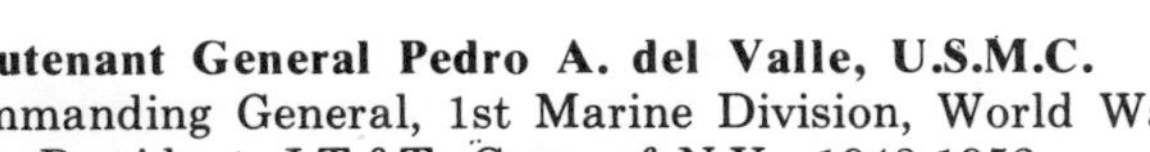

Lieutenant General Pedro A. del Valle, U.S.M.C.
Commanding General, 1st Marine Division, World War II
Vice President, I.T.&T. Corp. of N.Y., 1948-1952

"I was very happy to learn of the release of Admiral Doenitz from Spandau Prison...It is good to know that so many distinguished officers and civilians are to participate [in his testimonial]."

Hon. Joseph C. Grew
U.S. Ambassador to Japan, 1932-1941
U.S. Under-Secretary of State,
1924-1927, 1944-1945

"...The criminal trials of military leaders in Germany at the close of World War II were not in accordance with international law nor supported by legal authorization of any civilized country. The successful leaders of the German Army were picked out for punishment and the reason why they were tried at all was because their country lost the war...Admiral Doenitz was a courageous commander of the German Navy and did not deserve to be tried any more than did our Navy commander. Following this punitive, malicious and unauthorized doctrine, would our Navy commanders have been tried for their conduct had we lost the war?"

Hon. Usher L. Burdick
Lieutenant Governor of North Dakota
Member of Congress, 1934-1944, 1948-1954

"...I have always felt that the ex post facto nature, coupled with certain other aspects, of the Nuremberg trials, made them unjust and fundamentally wrong in principle."

Hon. Spruille Braden
U.S. Assistant Secretary of State
U.S. Ambassador to Argentina

"...with respect to the principle involved, that is, the trial of officers for carrying out competent orders in the conduct of a war, I must, of course, disagree."

Hon. James P. S. Devereux
Member of Congress
Brigadier General, U.S.M.C.
Defended Wake Island; taken as prisoner of war

"I have always regarded the Nuremberg Trials as a travesty upon justice and the farce was made even more noisome with Russia participating as one of the judges. I have followed your career with deep interest and high regard and I wish to extend to you my most cordial greetings."

Charles Callan Tansill, Ph.D.
Professor of History, Georgetown University
Author and historian
Advisor to U.S. Senate Committee on Foreign Relations

"During my period of Command in the Middle East and Mediterranean Theatres, there were no breaches of International Maritime Law by the Axis Powers reported to me. My own feelings on that matter were that those who had committed War Crimes should have been dealt with by Military Courts directly after the Armistice and that the Nuremberg Trials were staged as a political stunt."

Field Marshal Lord Henry Maitland Wilson of Libya
Commander-in-Chief, Middle East, 1943
Supreme Allied Commander, Mediterranean Theatre, 1944

[To Grand Admiral Doenitz]
"Please accept, with my greetings, my assurance that in the opinions of those professional naval officers of whose opinions I have knowledge, the war crimes trials of commanders-in-chief and their subordinates were in effect, to use the words of our Admiral Gallery, 'a libel on the military profession' and 'barefaced hypocrisy.' "

Vice Admiral Ralph Edward Jennings, U.S.N.
Commander, Aircraft Carrier Division 12, World War II
Assistant Deputy Chief of Naval Operations for Air

"...it always seemed to me to be grossly unfair that military commanders carrying out the legitimate orders of their Government should be branded as criminals."

General Sir Eric DeBurgh,
K.C.B., C.B., O.B.E., D.S.O.
Chief of General Staff, India,
World War II

"The war crimes trials were an abomination and will plague our people for centuries."

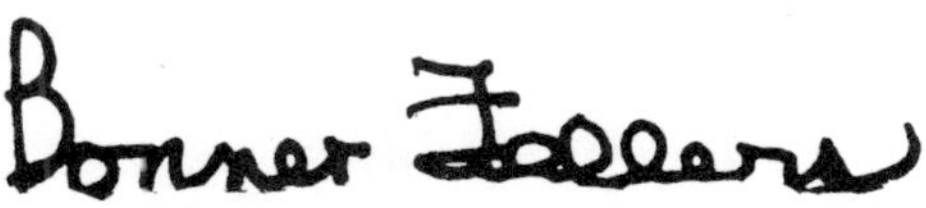

Brigadier General Bonner Fellers, U.S.A.
Member, Planning Group, O.S.S., World War II
Military Secretary to General of the Army Douglas MacArthur

"I am particularly glad...to participate in the messages of greetings and good wishes to Grand Admiral Doenitz. It so happened that I attended one of the sessions of the Nuremberg Trials and I felt then strongly that the conviction of professional military and naval officers was wholly improper and unjustified. Ever since, I have been greatly shocked and disturbed by this international action, committed in the height of passion."

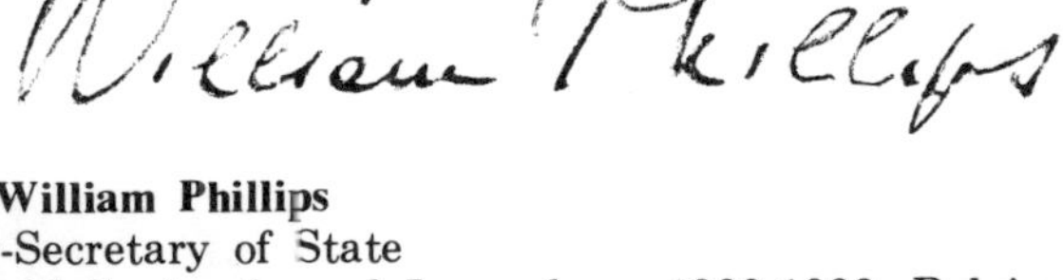

Honorable William Phillips
U.S. Under-Secretary of State
Minister to Netherlands and Luxemburg 1920-1922, Belgium 1924-1927, Canada 1927-1929, and Italy 1936-1941
Head, London Division, O.S.S., 1942
Personal Representative of President Roosevelt to India, 1942-1945
Political advisor to General Eisenhower, 1943-1944

"...I definitely feel that German officers and others who owed allegiance to their country and to their government and who had taken an oath of office to protect the German Government against its enemies were guilty of no crime in directing the fighting forces of Germany when war became a reality. This is, I think, particularly true of Grand Admiral Doenitz and Grand Admiral Erich Raeder and of the large majority of the Admirals and Generals in the German military services. For them to have pursued any other course would have amounted to flagrant treason against the German Government and the German People. Certainly any military man in any country is bound by his oath of office to fight for his country when that country becomes engaged in war. I consider that unrestricted submarine warfare is fully justifiable and that any German officer who engaged in such warfare was guilty of no crime."

Paul Hendren.

Vice Admiral Paul Hendren, U.S.N.
Commanding Officer, USS *Philadelphia,* 1940-1942
Commander, South Pacific Force, 1945-1946

"...I have a very long record of opposition to the holding of these trials, which began with speeches in the House of Lords during the war and has continued ever since...As I made, in conjunction with friends, a special effort to secure the earlier release of Admiral Doenitz, I gladly associate myself with your album, and especially with your hope that it will 'represent a milestone in the historical re-appraisal of the dangerous precedent set at Nuremberg,' and I would add, 'Tokyo.' "

Hankey

The Rt. Hon. Lord Hankey, P.C., G.C.B., G.C.M.G., G.C.V.O., LL.D.
Minister in War Cabinet, World War II
Member of Permanent Mandates Commission, Geneva, 1939

"...I was from the beginning very unhappy about the Nuremberg trials...the weak points of such trials are obvious: they are trials of the vanquished by the victors instead of by an impartial tribunal; furthermore the trials are only of the crimes committed by the vanquished, and the fact that the Katyn massacre of Polish officers was never properly investigated casts doubt on the conduct of such trials. The only tribunal that I can think of which could conduct such trials with propriety would be one representing the Vatican."

T.S. Eliot

T.S. Eliot
English poet and author

"Off Normandy and Provence it was necessary for our naval gunfire support groups to destroy villas, chateaux and, in one instance, a church. Possibly there were noncombatants killed by these actions. Our mission was to destroy enemy shore defenses—to facilitate the landing of our troops. We believed these buildings housed enemy machine guns and/or enemy fire control observers. *If* the Germans had won the war, would I have been placed on trial for prosecuting my particular part of the war to the best of my ability? I cannot imagine it! And would Admiral King have been placed on trial for his own or for my actions? It is impossible for me to picture! And yet it did happen in the case of Admiral Doenitz. I agree fully with Admiral Gallery's views regarding the trial of Admiral Doenitz and regret that those in power subjected him to such a humiliating experience."

C. F. Bryant

Vice Admiral Carleton F. Bryant, U.S.N.
Commander, Battleship Division 5, World War II

"I definitely believe that the trial and imprisonment of Admiral Karl Doenitz was a travesty of justice and has set a dangerous precedent for the future in which we, who have dedicated our lives to the Armed Services, will be considered and tried as criminals. My greetings to Admiral Doenitz and may he yet have a long and happy life."

Rear Admiral Joel W. Bunkley, U.S.N.
Supervisor of New York Harbor, 1942-46

"I have neither read nor followed the testimony concerned in the so-called 'War Crime Trials at Nuremberg' because the entire procedure, in my opinion, became a nauseating farce through the participation of Soviet 'judges.' The presence of these minions of a barbarous and mediaeval autocracy elevated this disgraceful episode to the stratosphere of hypocrisy."

Hon. James H.R. Cromwell
U.S. Minister to Canada, 1940
U.S. Advisor to President Syngman Rhee, Korea, 1941-45

"...it is my considered opinion that Admiral Doenitz suffered a grave injustice and a most dangerous precedent was established. In the unthinkable circumstances of the United States being placed in a similar situation by losing a war, every officer in a command position doing his professional duty would be subject to trial as a war criminal up to and including the commander-in-chief...There is neither logic nor justice in the assumption that unrestricted submarine warfare becomes a war crime only for the loser when used by all participants and unrestricted submarine warfare is unquestionably as much a part of war as atomic bombing. Every good wish to Admiral Doenitz."

Rear Admiral Edwin C. Parsons, U.S.N.R.
Pioneer pilot and World War I aviation ace

"...on Grand Admiral Doenitz's trial, I can assure you that I have been shocked with the idea that a career officer has been 'legimately' tried by his former enemies for 'atrocities' committed by him, relating to war operations carried out not for his own interest, but for the interest of his country. The precedent of the infamous Nuremberg trials constitutes an unparalleled blunder..."

Admiral Alexander E. Sakellariou, Royal Hellenic Navy
Commander-in-Chief, Greek Naval Forces, 1932-37; 1942-43
Deputy Prime Minister of Greece

"By the time an officer reaches the rank of high command as in the case of Admiral Doenitz he expects to accept and accepts the risks inherent in having tremendous responsibilities without commensurate authority. The authority rests with his government. In other words he accepts risks as in his line of duty in performing actions prescribed by his government regardless of what they may be...The average layman does not comprehend nor can he be expected to comprehend, the philosophical attitude underlying the professional military officer's dedication to his country, whatever country this may be."

Vice Admiral John B. Moss, U.S.N.
Naval aviator, 1925-1953
Assistant Chief, Bureau of Aeronautics

"I was in the Pacific during World War II and in the occupation of Japan for some years thereafter. I had no direct responsibility for the major trials in Tokyo but I was responsible for the Eighth Army Military Commission trials for war crimes which were held up until my departure from Japan in August, 1948...I had mental reservations concerning those who were tried for 'getting up a war.' "

Robert Eichelberger

General Robert L. Eichelberger, U.S.A.
Commander, 8th Army, World War II

"I agree that the trials of distinguished officers of the armed forces of Germany were entirely uncalled for and unjustified...I sincerely believe Admiral Doenitz has suffered unjustly and I sympathize with him for the long term of imprisonment he has suffered for his naval activities. I hope this will be of some help."

A. E. Montgomery

Vice Admiral Alfred E. Montgomery, U.S.N.
Commander, Aircraft Carrier Divisions 3 and 12, World War II
Commander, 5th Fleet, Pacific, 1946

"I am happy to add my few words of greetings and good wishes to Grand Admiral Karl Doenitz upon his return to freedom after those long years of confinement, to which he was so unjustly sentenced. Those war crimes trials of military and naval officers whose only 'crime' during World War II was effectively and efficiently leading the military and naval forces of their country were a lapse from present-day standards of civilization and justice...to the uncivilized ancient days of the Dark Ages. Let us fervently hope we have seen the last of such action."

E. G. Morsell

Vice Admiral Everett G. Morsell, S.C., U.S.N.
Senior Member, Phillippine Contract Settlement Commission, 1946

"That the barbaric *ex post facto* travesty of legality and morality represented by the Nuremberg Trials ***never represented the genuine attitude of even the heavily propagandized American public*** was made clear by protests like my own at the time of the outrage and subsequently. For myself, and I believe also for the majority of the American public, I apologize to Admiral Doenitz and the German People for what, done then in our name without our approval or consent, has resulted in such injury to everybody involved."

Professor Dr. Herbert C. Sanborn
Historian and author
Head of Dept., Philosophy and Psychology, Emeritus, Vanderbilt University

"...The essence of sovereignty is the sovereign's right to command his subjects and it is, therefore, the foundation stone of international law that no individual can be held either criminally or civilly responsible for obeying the command of his sovereign within the jurisdiction of that sovereign. This was precisely what those in the dock at Nuremberg were charged with having done...their trial struck at the very basis of international law. In future wars each side will be committed to calling its enemies criminals, and by placing their necks in a noose it becomes impossible either to limit or compromise. The only defence is victory, and we are back in the days of the barbarians...When we come to the sailors [at Nuremberg], I can find nothing in their record inconsistent with the highest traditions of a Service to which I was proud to belong. If I were to meet Admiral Doenitz I would feel that he was a man whose friendship would be an honour."

Rt. Hon. Reginald T. Paget, Queen's Counsel
Member of Parliament

"I am wholly in agreement as to the hypocrisy and illegality of the Nuremberg Trials...The basis of the trial was the definition, post facta, of the list of crimes. The constitution of the Court itself, reduced the trial morally, to a very cynical farce. The Nuremberg Trials set a dangerous precedent, and so must be exposed..."

Air Commodore G.S. Oddie, D.F.C., A.F.C.
Deputy Director, R.A.F. Flight Training, World War II

"I can state that I have felt from the very beginning, or the ending of World War II, that some of the actions of the Allied Powers with respect to many charged with 'war crimes' were determined by 'war passion' rather than reason. This especially applies to officers and men of the armed forces of our enemies in that war...I find it extremely difficult to agree with the course that was taken with respect to those officers and men of the field forces who simply carried out the orders of their responsible governments. If the commanders of our own armed forces should elect for themselves to decide whether the orders of our government were right or wrong, what assurance can our people have regarding their own freedom and security...our oath includes an unqualified statement to the effect that 'I will obey the orders of the President of the United States and of the officers appointed over me.' No mention is made of whether the orders are right or wrong, morally or spiritually, or whether they do or do not agree with international law. It leaves the service man no choice..."

Lieutenant General Reuben E. Jenkins, U.S.A.
Ass't. Chief of Staff, 6th Army Group, World War II
9th U.S. Corps, Korea
Ass't. Chief of Staff, G-3, U.S. Army

"I deem it a great privilege to express my esteem and admiration for a distinguished, talented and patriotic naval officer, Grand Admiral Karl Doenitz. As I have often told my classes in international law in Northwestern University, the conduct of Admiral Doenitz in the Second World War was exemplary, and his painful duty at the end of the war was performed with dignity of the highest order. The Nuremberg Trials were a disgrace to civilization, and, as a teacher of young men and women, I have deeply regretted that my country joined in this outrageous action. It was violation of international law, comity of nations and international morality. Whatever can be done to atone for it, should be done."

Kenneth Colegrove

Kenneth Colegrove, Ph.D.
Professor Emeritus of Political Science, Northwestern University
Consultant to General Douglas MacArthur during Occupation of Japan
Author

"I am not a submariner but I was a surface combat commander as a Rear Admiral in command of Task Groups in the South Pacific in 1942. All of our instructions in every media—air, surface, subsurface, were for unrestricted warfare. Many of our Battle Orders ended simply 'Kill Japs.' That meant any Jap and every Jap we could find except those who surrendered. So-called International Law was non-existent. Our job was to win as soon as possible. We—all of us—were guilty every day under the 'war crimes' criteria. But we could not have done otherwise even had we so desired. As professional military men we had a required job to do for which we had trained most of our lives. This was required, and expected of us by the U.S. Government. Had we disobeyed, a court-martial would have followed. Admiral Doenitz and many of the others tried were in positions identical to ours. They were without choice. There is not the slightest doubt in my mind that these trials were a 'libel on the military profession.' I was deeply sorry at the time for those fine professionals who were punished for doing their duty. Many of us said, 'But for the Grace of God, there go I.' It is not the military who criticize an opponent for doing his duty, for we understand. I hope this dangerous precedent is deflated before hysteria runs rampant another time. In the Doenitz case a respected admiral has paid an unjust debt. I am sorry."

M. S. Tisdale

Vice Admiral Mahlon S. Tisdale, U.S.N.
Commander, Destroyers, Pacific Fleet, World War II
Commander, Cruisers, Pacific Fleet, World War II

"I believe that the so-called 'War Crimes Trials' were an outrage against good morals, an absurdity in point of international law, and a deplorable error in policy. They set a precedent for what amounts to the legalized lynching of the leaders of the defeated side in any future war. Such feeble pretense to legality as they possessed was nullified by the fact that the so-called law under which they were held was ex post facto. The Germans could not have been expected to believe in their justice because they were conducted not by neutral and impartial judges but merely by a coalition of the victors. I'm glad to hear that Admiral Doenitz has been released and I hope that any so-called 'war criminals' who are still imprisoned will be released also."

Hoffman Nickerson
American author

"I have no doubt that the Nuremberg 'War Crimes Trials' were an instrument of revenge rather than of justice...Here we operated under a new law not in force when the alleged 'crimes' were committed, a law effected by a body incompetent to create 'laws.' I do not know under what adequate authority the 'International Military Tribunal' acted. Our own Supreme Court refused to review the Trials, nor is there any provision in our laws—certainly not in our Constitution—for the United States to participate in a punitive drumhead court gotten together without the benefit of Senate-approved treaties...about the German Navy and Admiral Karl Doenitz, I have seen nothing effectively to impugn his professional honor. I regret and I am ashamed that Admiral Doenitz should have been condemned and sentenced to serve ten years imprisonment at the hands of an illegal court in which our country illegally participated. As an American citizen, I apologize to Admiral Doenitz."

Colonel Ulius L. Amoss, U.S.A.F.
Deputy Chief of Staff, 9th Air Force, World War II
Operated international intelligence service

"As I myself have been carrying out the lawful orders of my superiors in the Navy for the past 50 years, I naturally feel that the sentence imposed on Admiral Doenitz was unjust...I have a copy of a general order issued by the Commander of our Naval Forces operating off the coast of California during the Mexican War in 1847-48. This order was addressed to the officers and men of the squadron in which my father was then serving. Some of the personnel of the squadron in the operations ashore evidently failed to carry out some of the tasks assigned them or were reluctant to carry out orders calling for the destruction of property or other uncharitable acts toward the native population, claiming that such orders were illegal. The squadron commander made it clear to them that it was not within the province of the recipient of an order to decide for himself whether the order was legal or not. The only point that concerned them was whether the order was issued by duly constituted legal authority. I agree that international law has no punitive provisions but rests entirely on comity."

Vice Admiral Alfred W. Johnson, U.S.N.
U.S. Naval Delegate, Inter-American Defense Board, 1942-1945

"I consider the 'war crimes trials' in general and the trial of Admiral Doenitz in particular, a matter of mass hypocrisy resulting from a war-bred hangover. True, politicians were responsible, but I recall few protests from the man in the street at the time. The military, who had a greater license to be angry, were opposed to it at the time—especially the 'professional' sailors and soldiers!"

Vice Admiral A. Stanton Merrill, U.S.N.
Commander, Cruiser Division 12, World War II

"As regards the legality of these trials, is there any question but that judged by previous standards they were illegal? As for the justice, I hold decided views that they were most unjust and cruel...To try high ranking military officers on such a charge as 'planning aggressive warfare,' or because malpractices occurred in the area of their command, and to inflict heavy sentences upon individuals for doing what it was their obvious duty to their country to do, to me savours more of vengeance than justice."

Cork & Orrery

Admiral Of The Fleet, The Rt. Hon. 12th Earl Of Cork and Orrery, G.C.B.
Commander-in-Chief, Home Fleet and Portsmouth
In Norway campaign, 1940

"The Nuremberg Charter under which Doenitz was tried created alleged crimes for which there is no precedent or justification in international law or usage. Applied impartially, it would have rendered officers of the Allies' Fighting Services liable to similar penalties, if their countries had been defeated. It made officers responsible for actions committed by their subordinates without their knowledge or approval. It also rendered subordinates liable to severe penalties for obeying orders, though their own law enforced penalties for disobeying them. It is deplorable that civilised Governments should have revenged themselves on Officers, who in the light of history, merely did their duty."

K. G. B. Dewar.

Vice Admiral Kenneth G. B. Dewar, C.B.E.
Commanded H.M.S. *Royal Oak* and *Tiger*

"As to the particular question, whether the unrestricted submarine warfare should be classified as a war-crime, my opinion is that any restrictions on the conduct of a submarine campaign against enemy shipping would certainly impair the success of the campaign. Of course, particular cases of wanton and unnecessary cruelty towards the personnel of the torpedoed ships should be liable to punishment, but such isolated cases do not, as a rule, reflect to the High Command. Consequently for any such cases Admiral Doenitz could not be held responsible, because his job was to conduct the whole campaign, which he did, as any other professional Officer in his position would try to do. The legality of the 'International Military Tribunal' [was impaired] by feelings which were running so high as to interfere with the application of Justice."

Rear Admiral Constantine Alexandris, Royal Hellenic Navy
Commander-in-Chief of Greek Naval Forces, 1943-1945

"Regarding the War Crimes Trials following World War II, where the military leaders were placed on trial for acting in their professional duties, I have always resented them as unfair and resembling the 'carpet-bagger' tactics as practiced against our Confederate heroes of the War between the States in 1861-1865. I agree with Admiral Daniel V. Gallery, in his latest book, *Twenty Million Tons Under The Sea,* as it relates to Admiral Karl Doenitz, wholeheartedly. Please convey to Admiral Doenitz my compliments and best wishes for the future as well as my personal regrets for the injustices handed him by the so-called 'International Military Tribunal.' "

Rear Admiral William W. Studdert, U.S.N.R.
Officer in Command, Construction Regiments, Pacific, World War II

"...Like other professional officers, I was gravely concerned at the precedent established at Nuremberg and in Tokyo. By our own active participation in those post war trials, we have assisted in establishing a precedent which might be used to try, condemn and execute military leaders of the United States in the event that this country was defeated in some future conflict. Every professional officer of the Armed Forces of every country of the world is required by his regular and official duty to plan for possible future wars with every potential enemy. If this can later be declared an international crime, then every professional officer is all his life in jeopardy. Grand Admiral Doenitz of the German Navy was a highly competent professional officer. While he was our enemy in war time, those of us who were professional officers still admired his professional competence. Our own Navy in fact adopted many of the tactics and methods of submarine warfare originated and directed by Admiral Doenitz. As victors our submariners were 'heroes.' By the Nuremberg doctrine, in defeat they would have been criminals."

Rear Admiral Leslie E. Gehres, U.S.N.
Commander, Fleet Air Wing 4, World War II

"Grand Admiral Doenitz did only what any naval officer in any Navy similarly assigned would have done; his duty...Admiral Doenitz carried out his orders. If that's a crime, then we are all guilty. But the real guilty ones are the British Admiralty, the French Department of the Marine, and the Navy Departments of all countries, including our own. They are the guilty ones, not the officers who obeyed their orders. Admiral Gallery's vigorous and contemptuous characterization of the 'so-called' War Crimes Trials is much too mild, too courteous. Who were the trial members? Were they competent to handle such important and such far-reaching questions? Shall we call them 'spades' or just damned old shovels? There are, unfortunately, many damned old shovels in this world."

Commodore Julius F. Hellweg, U.S.N.
Commander, Destroyer Division 4
Commanding Officer, U.S.S. *Oklahoma*

"On the subject of the Nuremberg Trials...I remember coming to the conclusion that as a professional soldier I was glad to be on the winning side. The Nuremberg Trials seemed to be further evidence of the upsurge of internationalism in which the group of victorious nations took upon themselves the task of punishing the losers for not having beaten them! It does not seem fair to me!"

General Sir Andrew Thorne, K.C.B., C.M.G., D.S.O.
Commander-in-Chief, Allied Land Forces, Norway, 1945

"The war crimes trials of military personnel for acts in line of duty set a highly undesirable and dangerous precedent which may plague us some day. Unrestricted submarine warfare, or any other measure which holds promise of success, will always be resorted to in an all-out war whenever there is a question of survival. Any other course would be unrealistic...Admiral Doenitz was unjustly tried and punished."

Rear Admiral Felix X. Gygax, U.S.N.
Commander, Cruiser Division 3, World War II

"I am glad to tell you that the war crimes trials of career officers are one of many items upon which Admiral Gallery and I see eye to eye. They smell. I have always considered them as legalistic hocus-pocus to give semblance of respectability to barbarous vengeance inflicted upon opponents who have merely done their duty on the losing side of a war. A primitive idea supposed to be in disrepute for some centuries. If accepted as a precedent, such trials can only discourage any sort of negotiated peace in future wars. They encourage the unprofitable idea that peace is possible only after at least one side is totally destroyed."

Rear Admiral George van Deurs, U.S.N.
Commanding Officer, U.S.S. *Philippine Sea,* World War II

"It goes without saying that the convening authorities of the War Crimes Tribunals had no jurisdiction over the places, persons, or alleged crimes involved in the War Crimes Trials at the times those crimes were alleged to have been committed. Those 'War Crimes Tribunals' had the same legal status as a Kangaroo Court and conducted those trials with the same regard for justice as could be expected of a Kangaroo Court. As regards the brutality aspect, just how a campaign of 'mass slaughter,' which legalized war is, can be conducted without someone getting killed and others getting hurt is not apparent...The violations of so-called 'humane warfare' by two opposing forces come close to balancing on the 'brutality' scoreboard. Naturally, people behind the lines only get one side of the atrocity picture and they do all the publicizing. From the armed services point of view, if the War Crimes Trials are to become a precedent to be followed in the future we had as well eliminate all national armed services. If a service man cannot carry out the policies and orders of his own government and the senior officers placed over him without running the risk of being tried by an illegally constituted tribunal and hanged by a foreign government, he is not likely to risk his neck very far in support of his own government. The alternative would have to be International Armed Services and the elimination of all aspects of Nationalism, which appears to be exactly what the originators of the War Crimes Trials doctrine were striving for. Had the originators of the War Crimes Trials doctrine been in any degree motivated by justice and the desire to punish the perpetrators of extreme atrocities in time of war they would have at least made some attempt to bring to trial hundreds of Russian officials for perpetrating the most heinous atrocities ever inflicted upon civilized peoples against the Poles and Germans and no doubt against all other peoples who have at any time been under Russian control. The 'War Crimes Trials' can only be justified by Marxist, Leninist, Stalinist and New Dealist doctrines."

Henry C. Flanagan

Rear Admiral Henry C. Flanagan, U.S.N.
Commander, Transport Divisions, Pacific, World War II

"I must say that I thought at the time and still think that the Nuremberg Trials were largely for propaganda purposes and were unwise."

W Gibsone

Major General William W. P. Gibsone, C.M.G., D.S.O., O.B.E.
General Officer, Royal Canadian Army

"At the time of the Nuremberg Trials, I was in command of our Naval Base at Pearl Harbor. Opinion in responsible civilian circles severely condemned the Nuremberg Trials for setting a terrible precedent confronting our own career officers. In the wardrooms and officers' messes of the Navy, the trials cast a deep shadow of gloom. In a service where the law requires explicit obedience to orders from higher authority and when our oath requires that we defend the Constitution against all enemies 'foreign and domestic' it seemed that the government was going too far, particularly when they brought officers of the enemy armed services to trial for what must to them have appeared only doing their duty. Many of us felt that the actions taken were autocratic and had no place in a democracy."

E. W. Hanson

Vice Admiral Edward W. Hanson, U.S.N.
Commander, Battleship Division 9, World War II

"The following represent in summary my views on the treatment accorded Grand Admiral Doenitz of the German Navy and the other strictly military 'offenders' by the International Military Tribunal at Nuremberg. In general, I consider the treatment of military offenders as highly regrettable and attributable to mass hysteria. It was contrary to fundamentals of legal procedure and fairness cherished by the peoples living under Anglo-American traditions. It established the precedent that the vanquished nation is ipso facto the aggressor and, as a concomitance, that specific acts of officers of the victorious nation are blameless. In essence, the Nuremberg Doctrine is that defeat is the great crime of war."

Geo. W. Bauernschmidt

Rear Admiral George W. Bauernschmidt, S.C., U.S.N.
Officer in Command, Naval Supply Depots, Algeria and Marianas Islands, World War II

"It seems to me to be most appropriate that at this time, upon the occasion of the release of Grand Admiral Karl Doenitz from confinement in an 'international' prison for ten years, as a result of his conviction by a War Crimes Trial Court, to make some expression regarding the subject of 'War Crimes'. the trials and the aftermath of same.

"After active service in the U.S. Army for four years during World War II, over 3 years of which was in the European Theatre, which included combat duty and landing on the Normandie (Utah) Beach on D-Day, I was released from active duty in December 1945 and having been elected to the judgeship of the Pennsylvania State Court for the 32nd Judicial District for the term of 10 years (while still in military service in Europe), assumed this office in January 1946. I was re-elected for a second time commencing January 1956.

"During the Summer of 1948, as a Colonel in the Officers' Reserve Corps, I was called to active duty by order of the Secretary of the Army and served as a member of the Commission appointed by him to investigate the cases of German officers and soldiers who had been tried by American Military Courts at Dachau, Germany, in 1946, where the death sentences had been imposed and which sentences had been approved by the Reviewing Authority (General Lucius Clay).

"Examination of the records of trials in over 1,000 cases, interviews with a goodly number of persons, and careful consideration by the three members of our Commission, enabled me to secure a first-hand knowledge of this far-reaching 'experiment' of War Crimes Trials. As a result of this invaluable experience, I am convinced that, in principle, the trial, after the conclusion of a war, of nationals of the defeated nation is unsound...In fact, the broad generalizations of the nature of offenses, the acceptance of ex post facto doctrine, and particularly the rule regarding the legality and propriety of superior orders are contrary to civilized ideals and principles of legal justice. It may be that such trials would be warranted in cases of recognized criminal offenses by individuals, e.g. murder, brutal torture and abuses, etc. However, punishment in such cases could be imposed by the defeated nation itself, even to the extent of making provision therefor in the treaty of peace between the belligerent nations.

"My conclusion is that the entire program of War Crimes Trials, either by International Courts, the members of which comprise those of the victorious nations, or by Military Courts of a single victor nation (as was the case in all of the trials at Dachau which our Commission investigated) is basically without legal or moral authority...The Malmedy Massacre Case is one of those which our Commission investigated. Notwithstanding the terrific amount of misinformation which has been circulated about this horrible tragedy, the record of its trial of the defendants, including Colonel Peiper, is devoid of any competent evidence which would have been sufficient in a court of law in the United States to sustain a conviction...Colonel Peiper and Admiral Doenitz were obliged to spend years in confinement for doing for their country exactly what every good and loyal officer of the American Army did for his country. The fact remains that the victor nations in World War II, while still at fever heat of hatred for an enemy nation, found patriots of the enemy nation guilty of doing their patriotic duty. This is patently unlawful and immoral.

"One of the most shameful incidents connected with the War Crimes Trials prosecutions has to do with the investigations and the preparation of the cases for trial. The records of trials which our Commission examined disclosed that a great majority of the official investigators, employed by the United States Government to secure evidence and to locate defendants, were persons with a preconceived dislike for these enemy aliens, and their conduct was such that they resorted to a number of illegal, unfair and cruel methods and duress to secure confessions of guilt and to secure accusations by defendants against other defendants. In fact, in the Malmedy case, the only evidence before the court, upon which the convictions and sentences were based, consisted of the statements and testimony of the defendants themselves. The testimony of one defendant against another was secured by subterfuge, false promises of immunity, and by mock trials and threats.

"This country owes to Grand Admiral Doenitz and to many other men at the least a humble apology for what we have caused them to suffer. Let us hope that we have learned from these tragic mistakes a lesson we shall never forget, and that never again shall we repeat such conduct...Let us hope that Admiral Doenitz and other enemy patriots will be aware of the fact that there are great numbers of loyal Americans who are ashamed of the behavior of those in our government who were responsible for what was done."

Honorable Edward Leroy Van Roden, President Judge
Pennsylvania State Court, 32nd Judicial District
Colonel, Officers Reserve Corps, U.S. Army
Member, Secretary of the Army's Commission to Investigate the Malmedy Case, 1948

"I do not condone the 'war crimes trials' held at Nuremberg after World War II...Certainly Admiral Doenitz was an effective naval officer. That his conviction of 'war crimes' was illegal is conceded. It seems that combatants make their own rules of warfare insofar as they are able to force them upon their enemies."

Rear Admiral Herbert J. Ray, U.S.N.
Commanding Officer, U.S.S. *Maryland,* World War II
Commander, San Francisco Group, 19th Fleet

"As I stated publicly at the time of the Nuremberg 'war crimes trials,' I condemned these trials as ex post facto, absolutely without any precedent or sanction under international law and therefore crimes against the alleged criminals. The trials were born of a desire for vengeance on the part of the military victors. In the event of another World War, which God forbid, we could find ourselves on the losing side of the fence with our own military leaders being branded as criminals, arrested and tried for defending their own country. I am very glad to join other American citizens in condemning such procedures as those established. Admiral Doenitz was one of the unfortunate victims of the Nuremberg Trials."

Hon. Hugh G. Grant
American diplomat
Dept. of State (Div. of Western European Affairs)
U.S. Minister to Albania and Thailand

"Soldiers do not 'make' and normally do not cause wars between well established governments. Normally only duly authorized governments make war. Soldiers—particularly professional soldiers—are merely military agents of their governments (sworn to protect and support such governments). Therefore, if their military actions are within the bounds of either military international law or accepted practice they should not be held liable for such acts. Further, if their actions contribute definitely to military success of their country they should not be held liable as international criminals, provided they have acted within the policies of their government..."

Lieutenant General Le Roy Lutes, U.S.A.
Commanding General, Army Service Forces, 1946
Commander, U.S. 4th Army, 1949

“My firm belief is that, if we of the U.S. of America could have used the hind-sight we have today, the trials would never have been held. Win, lose, or draw, professional men of all services must be protected from mass hysteria and ruthless, unlawful tactics of those in power, when they have simply performed their duty to the best of their ability in fighting for their country. In war, in many instances, it is impossible for the fighting man to take the time to differentiate between the combatant and the non-combatant; some of the latter will suffer, whether it be in unrestricted submarine warfare or in the release of nuclear weapons...For the ‘war crimes trials’ in general, and for Admiral Doenitz’ trial in particular (in the latter case the question of unrestricted warfare was a prominent part of the agenda), it is my personal opinion that, from a lasting viewpoint of justice and the betterment of humanity in its treatment—one human to another—it would have been better if the ‘war crimes trials’ of World War II had *not* been held.”

Major General Leland S. Hobbs, U.S.A.
Commanding General, 30th Infantry Division, World War II
Commanding General, 9th Corps, Japan, 1947-1949

“It is usually accepted that when diplomacy fails in extreme cases, war begins. Do we accept the principle that it is not aggression until the professional military man fires a shot? How far can one nation push another before it is driven to the force of arms? If both sides were not aggressive—there could be no war—from this then, we can say that during the non-military stages, both are aggressors, each backing a principle. If each side then resorts to war both are still aggressors. It seems to me to be a sad fact that the side that *loses* is the only one that will formally be charged with aggression. In other words, there is no comfort in being second best...Grand Admiral Karl Doenitz...planned for a war which would need to be fought if other pressures failed...I do not hold that his acts in directing the naval forces under his command were other than honorable, and I do feel that his subordinates in general fought honorably as professionals. Are only those on the losing side guilty of war crimes?”

Vice Admiral Charles B. Momsen, U.S.N.
Commander, Submarine Squadrons 2 and 4, World War II
Commander, Submarine Force Pacific, 1951-1953
Inventor, Momsen submarine escape lung

"I think those [Nuremberg] trials were the greatest mistake our government could have made and predict that the precedent set will haunt this country for hundreds of years...I believe that wars are prolonged by observing rules of chivalry and that war should be put down on the weakest point of the enemy. Wars are caused by the politicians and civilians behind the front line, and if you can break their will to fight you can stop the war. The soldiers at the front do not cause wars and often do not know what it is all about. The will of the civilians in the cities is the most vulnerable objective and the next war is going to be waged against them, in spite of our howls about killing women or children or destroying civilization."

Major General Howard C. Davidson, U.S.A.F.
Commander, 10th Air Force, India, World War II

"The infamous 'war crimes trials' will undoubtedly cause future inhabitants of this cockeyed planet to blush with embarrassment. One dislikes to acknowledge any kind of connection, even a human one, with the self-promoted persecutors of men who were simply doing their duty as they saw it. Any attempt to make a man guilty of a crime, which act was not a crime at the time of its commission, is the acme of tyranny. It is, in fact, a perversion of law and justice and ranks high with all other acts of barbarism. Let's call it what is is—naked revenge."

Robert LeFevre
American educator and author
President, The Freedom School

"I do not know if there rested any legal basis for the war crimes trials of men who fought honorably and clearly for their country. It seemed to me at the time of the trials—and does now—that to try any military man for carrying out the legal orders of his government, which he had sworn to do in the prosecution of a war, is manifestly an injustice."

Admiral Harold R. Stark, U.S.N.
Chief of Naval Operations, 1939-42
Commander, U.S. Naval Forces in Europe, 1942-45

"To punish a career officer for zealously carrying out his orders, his duties and responsibilities, is a colossal error in judgement, a grave injustice to the individual concerned, and if left unrequited, used as a precedent for similar cases in the future can well undermine the military service of this or any nation for that matter. Further such misdirected logic or ignorance can well be extended into other fields or professions such as religion, engineering, and even education, resulting in untold chaos which was probably the hidden intention of the 'Trials.' In the last analysis the career officer is the servant of the people of the nation he has sworn to serve faithfully and well. The authority he exercises stems from his fellow citizens. They created him and the position he occupies. If he is to be punished it should be by his own nation..."

Rear Admiral Gordon Rowe, U.S.N.
Commander, Naval Operating Base, Midway Island

"I attended the Nuremberg Trials for several days as a guest of one of the legal profession...One cannot help getting the impression that the law was fabricated...to meet particular circumstances, which surely must be wrong. I feel that the trial of people like Doenitz and Jodl...essentially service men, has created a precedent which might well be found useful in the future by a ruthless and dishonest government...I think, too, that it is very doubtful whether their [Doenitz and Jodl] trial was 'within the law.' "

General Sir Henry Charles Loyd, K.C.B., C.B., K.C.V.O., D.S.O., M.C.
Commander-in-Chief, Southern Command 1942-1943
General Officer Commanding, London District, 1944-1947

"The trials were not based on justice, precedent or international law. They have set a vicious precedent, which, if followed in the event of future war, will give the military commander a choice of a trial for refusing to do his duty or trial as a war criminal if he is on the losing side. The answer will naturally be trial as a war criminal for he will not refuse duty. I am sure that among the military the opinion concerning 'War Crimes Trials' is practically unanimous."

Admiral Laurance T. DuBose, U.S.N.
Commander, Cruiser Division 13, World War II
Chief of Naval Personnel

"I have to say that, in spite of many arguments to the contrary, I do not approve, in principle, of war crimes trials of professional military men."

Hon. Jefferson Caffery, Ph.D., LL.D.
U.S. Ambassador to El Salvador, Colombia, Cuba, Brazil, France, and Egypt
U.S. Ass't. Secretary of State

"I do not believe that a Commander should be considered guilty of a war crime when he is only carrying out orders issued to him by higher commanders or by his Government, such as in the case of unrestricted submarine warfare by the German Navy. I was asked if I would sit on the Court which was assembled to try Field Marshal von Manstein about 1948, but refused because I felt that the whole principle of these war crimes trials was wrong. Another instance which came to my notice was that of General Itagahi, who was commanding the Japanese forces in Malaya when we reoccupied that country. I was General Officer, Commander-in-Chief, Malaya Command, 1945-46. General Itagahi, by his authority, kept under the strictest discipline some 100,000 Japanese troops, although unguarded by us. Every order issued by me was carried out to the letter, almost enthusiastically, and during my time in command I did not receive a single complaint from the Malayan civil population of misbehavior by any Japanese troops. Itagahi was hanged, not, I understand, for any particular crime on his part, but because as Minister of Defense he was held criminally responsible for starting the war against China. If responsibility was to be placed on any one man's head, then surely it should have been the Emperor's, not his Defense Minister's. That, of course, was not politically expedient for Allied policy. In fact, it seems to me that the basis of the majority of the war crimes trials was not founded on true democratic justice, but on a revengeful desire to punish a number of military commanders for all the sin and misery and suffering, inseparable from war."

General Sir Frank W. Messervy, K.C.S.I., K.B.E., C.B., D.S.O.
Commander-in-Chief, Malaya Command, 1945-1946
Commander-in-Chief, Pakistan Army, 1947

"I suppose all military officers are opposed to trying military opponents. Such procedure has never been given international recognition; in the past, conquerors sometimes executed their opponents, but I never heard of any attempt to legalize it. Probably the best example of procedure in such cases was given by my own state, Texas, when Santa Anna was captured. I suppose all Texans wanted to shoot him and certainly he expected to be executed, but General Houston was firm and he was sent home. Probably the trial of Doenitz was the most terrible thing we did, but I am sure we yielded to pressure from Russia."

Admiral Samuel M. Robinson, Jr., U.S.N.
Chief, Bureau of Engineering, and Coordinator of Shipbuilding
Chief, Office of Procurement and Material, 1942-1945

"...the Nuremberg Trial, in this instance, was an ugly miscarriage of justice...only hate and war hysteria could have permitted such a weird concept of war crime. It has always been my contention that if Admiral Doenitz was guilty of any crime in connection with submarine operations, then there would be no limit to the number of officers equally guilty of crime, perpetrated by the 'Head of State.' "

Rear Admiral Arthur T. Moen, U.S.N.
Amphibious Forces, U.S.S. *Geo. Clymer*
(No. Africa and Guadalcanal, 1942-1943)
Commander, Amphibious Division 60 (1945)

"In my opinion, the sentence passed on Admiral Doenitz was unjust, and his trial should never have been held. This is because he never committed any atrocities. I do not regard "unrestricted warfare' at sea, i.e. the sinking of merchant ships, etc., as illegal. We expected our food supplies from overseas to be intercepted, and I certainly never regarded attacks by enemy submarines and other ships on our merchant ships as contrary to the accepted rules of war. I have done a good deal of Intelligence work during my 41 years service, and had 5 months at the Paris Peace Conference in 1919, as a Member of the British Military Delegation. As far as I can remember, there was then no suggestion that 'unrestricted' attacks on our food convoys, etc. were in any way illegal. They were an unpleasant feature of the war, but one that had to be faced...I certainly felt more strongly about the injustice of Admiral Doenitz's sentence than about any other one, for I had never heard of any illegal or barbarous act committed under his orders. I feel strongly that sailors, soldiers and airmen, whose only 'crime' is the effective professional direction of the forces under their command, should not be liable to such trials."

Major General Sir William L.O. Twiss, K.C.I.E., C.B., C.B.E., M.C., F.R.G.S.
General Officer Commanding, British Army in Burma

"At the time of the trials, I could not understand that such irregularities, unconstitutional acts and unjustified trials could possibly take place, and the idea of a civilian court set up to try Naval, Military on Air Force Commandants was unpardonable. To try men who were engaged in combat with an enemy of their country and who were only doing their duty...seemed the grossest travesty of justice. The even-handed justice which had always appeared to be a shining torch in our eyes in my country appeared sadly diminished by this travesty of fair play to one, like I, who had been brought up all my life in military tradition and steeped in the ideals of duty, patriotism and fairness...I have no doubt the officers commanding the three services would have considered that to bring to trial Admiral Doenitz and others of his standing was a miscarriage of justice and contrary to all conceptions of actions in open warfare...I do not imagine for one moment that our Commandants would have acted differently from Admiral Doenitz had they been faced with the problems he had to encounter. Such acts as the Nuremberg Trials of gallant opponents do not augur well for peace in the future. They are merely boding more evil, and more severity for the losing victims after a war, and lower the prestige of the victors. I do sincerely hope that Admiral Doenitz will understand that many of us, and certainly the members of the Forces, deplore the severe actions taken in the Trials in his case, and hope he will have contentment and peace for many, many years to come."

Evelyn Margaret Chetwynd

Lady Evelyn Margaret Chetwynd

"In general, I disapprove of the principle behind the war guilt trials...Once the high command had decided to carry out unrestricted submarine warfare, Doenitz did no more than his duty...He should have been protected by the decision of his seniors."

P. B. Joubert de la Ferté

Air Chief Marshal Sir Philip Joubert De La Ferte, K.C.B., C.M.G., D.S.O.
Commander-in-Chief, Coastal Command, 1941-1943
Director of Public Relations, Air Ministry, 1946-1947

"As it has been my belief that the after-war emotional hysteria was responsible for the trial and imprisonment of the German high-ranking military and naval officers, and that we should reflect with shame upon our efforts for revenge upon men doing what we would do for our own country, I am glad to have my name included in any effort to atone for the injustice done to Admiral Doenitz and to any others who were likewise unfairly treated because they loved their country."

Admiral Frederick J. Horne, U.S.N.
Commander Aircraft, Battle Force,
Vice Chief of Naval Operations, World War II

"...I have often thought of and discussed with others the general question of the Nuremberg Trials and the military personnel involved...I am entirely opposed to trying by Court Martial military leaders after a war simply for carrying out the orders of those who determine the political decisions of the State...I have felt that Admiral Doenitz was *not* subject to trial...I do not hold the Admiral guilty for ordering attacks with no warning on merchant vessels. That is a submarine's only excuse for existing—to destroy by stealth...Working on war plans or preparing for a move against an enemy in order to carry out the political decisions of the Head of State, is certainly no crime; that is the recognized duty of a military leader...I do not think that he [Doenitz] should have been tried...All nations that had submarines resorted to similar tactics during both World Wars, and I venture to say that during the last war U.S. submarines sank far more Japanese shipping, with resulting loss of life, than we lost to the Germans."

Rear Admiral Hugo W. Osterhaus, U.S.N.
Commander, Submarine Squadron 4, World War II
Commanding Officer, Submarine Base, Pearl Harbor, T.H.

"The trial of German alleged war criminals, citizens of a defeated country, conducted by judges of a victorious enemy country was in itself a gross infringement of the elementary principles of justice and equity. If such a trial was to be held at all, the judges should at least have been chosen among neutrals. The law on which the trials were conducted had been created *ad hoc* by the victorious enemy Powers after the alleged offenses had been committed, and the court had been set up without any legal or constitutional basis. The acts for which the accused were tried had been committed at a time when they were not considered crimes, thus rendering the whole of the proceedings retro-active and thus utterly anti-juridical. The only parallels were the trials of Louis XVI and Marie Antoinette of France and those of the Neapolitan revolutionaries in 1799; but, in both cases, the judges were of the same nation as the accused. Even so, they were considered utterly illegal, even at the time. The fact that one of the Nuremberg judges was a Russian, i.e. an official representing a government guilty of an infinite number of crimes far worse than any of those attributed to the accused German, deprived the court of any vestige of legality or equity. The manner in which evidence for the prosecution was collected was open to the severest criticism—bribes and offers of rewards, threats, pressure of all kinds. Any scrap of evidence, if unfavorable to the accused, was accepted, regardless of the character of the witnesses. At one moment, even the Katyn massacre, notoriously the work of the Russians, was brought up against the Germans, although afterwards dropped. The prisoners were accused of acts committed in obedience to the orders of their own legitimate superiors. The charge that the accused had prepared plans for war against this or that possible country cannot be upheld, inasmuch as military, naval or air leaders had necessarily to prepare plans in peace time for any possible war against any possible enemy. Had they not done so, they would have failed in their duty towards their own country and its legitimate government."

Hon. Luigi Villari, Grand Officer of the Crown of Italy
Italian diplomatic official
Member, Secretariat of the League of Nations
Member, Italian Delegation, London Naval Conference

"I have always been *unable* to understand why our government ever acquiesced in authority for the so-called 'International Military Tribunal'...It had no authorization or precedent in international law, which has no punitive provisions."

Admiral Charles P. Snyder, U.S.N.
Commander, Battleships, Pacific Fleet, 1939
Inspector General of the Navy, 1942-1946

"I am afraid that anything I can add to the statements of such American mariners as Admiral Nimitz and Vice Admiral Lockwood would be superfluous and anticlimactic. I am in full agreement with the opinions expressed by Admiral Gallery. Admiral Doenitz was an honorable Naval officer. He was convicted of doing his duty, a performance of which any American could have been proud. I wish him well."

Admiral John M. Will, U.S.N.
Commander, Amphibious Group, Western Pacific, 1953-1954
Commander, Military Sea Transportation Service

“It is indeed regrettable that a precedent is apparently being established under which patriotic Senior Commanders of the Army, Navy and Air Force would be condemned, in case of defeat, to criminal trial and imprisonment or shameful execution for performance of duty they have pledged themselves and been trained to perform...In time of war, it is the duty of every patriotic citizen, as well as of members of the armed services, of every country to do everything possible within the limits of his ability, to seek victory for his country. In the case of submarine operations, if the risks of successful attack are endangered by a requirement that the submarine announce its intentions and permit prior evacuation of the target vessels, a commander would be derelict in his duty in endangering the success of his mission and the possible loss of his submarine and crew, by taking such ‘humanitarian’ action. If such so-called ‘unrestricted submarine warfare’ would better attain success, it is incumbent on that commander to so operate. Similarly, a Senior Commander should not be condemned for violations by certain of his subordinates or subordinate units of the accepted military code, where such deviations occurred without his cognizance, approval, or direction. I join...in the views of the many senior Allied commanders and government leaders in opposition to the general war crimes trials...as typified by the case of Grand Admiral Karl Doenitz of the German Navy. I further regret the severity of the punishment inflicted on many of such leaders who were performing their patriotic duties as they saw them but committed the unpardonable and reprehensible crime of having lost.”

Hugh J. Casey

Major General Hugh J. Casey, U.S.A.
Commanding General, Army Service Command, 1944-1945
Chief Engineer, Far Eastern Command, 1946-1949

“I am glad to join those who believe, as I do, that the ‘war crimes trials’ were a disgrace to our American tradition, and equally as bad, they created a precedent which can only mean liquidation of the entire brains of the United States should the Communists prevail in this country. The conviction of Admiral Doenitz was without the slightest justification in my opinion.”

Devin Garrity

Devin A. Garrity
President, Devin-Adair Company, Publishers

"...The Tribunal which was instituted for the Nuremberg Trials had no precedent and presumably created its own...I naturally dislike the idea that a senior officer carrying out his country's policy in wartime should be liable, if unsuccessful, to judgement and punishment by his enemies."

Admiral Sir Herbert A. Packer, K.C.B., C.B.E.
Lord Commissioner of the Admiralty, 1948-1950
Commander-in-Chief, South Atlantic Station, 1950-1952

"The circumstances whereby he [Admiral Doenitz] was confined must be viewed with shame and regret. I say this with utmost emphasis as an American citizen and can only add that I hope this letter will serve as a means of illustrating the fact that many people of the United States are possessed with a sense of honor, integrity, and principle."

George B. Fowler
Business executive
Treasurer, Valley Paper Company

"The decision to try in court the military commanders of the defeated nations of World War II has created a precedent in international law which will undoubtedly result in similar trials for military commanders of all defeated nations in future wars. Military commanders in war are in fact instruments of national policy which they did not create, and, therefore, they cannot be held responsible for the policy which they implement. The anti-submarine warfare campaigns of all nations in World War II, I am sure, will be considered by future generations in the light of future wars which we now envisage, relatively humane and moderate in nature. By and large, I believe that the average citizen realizes that the war crimes courts have served no useful purpose to this generation or generations to come, and that their actions should be reviewed in the light of reason and not emotion."

Vice Admiral Alvin D. Chandler, U.S.N.
Commander, Destroyer Division 41, World War II
President of The College of William and Mary

"My service during World War II was in command of an armored division throughout the European campaign, from Normandy to Saxony...My division lost quite a number of officers and men captured between July 1944 and April 1945. In no instance did I hear of personnel from our division receiving treatment other than proper under the 'Rules of Land Warfare.' As far as the 6th Armored Division was concerned in its 280 days of front line contact, there was no 'atrocity problem'...Frankly, I was aghast, as were many of my contemporaries, when we learned of the proposed 'war crimes' trials and the fact that military commanders were among the accused. The expression was heard among division commanders; 'A general should make certain that he is on the winning side'...It is my understanding that the 'war crimes' tribunals were neither constituted nor guided by internationally recognized legal authority, but that the victors devised ex-post-facto rules to justify their procedures. Possibly this was an aftermath of the 'unconditional surrender' policy which needlessly cost so many lives without adding to the measure of victory (if, in fact, it did not greatly reduce it). I firmly believe that the 'war crimes trials' were ill-conceived, vindictively executed, and served only to lower the dignity and prestige of America. Furthermore, if their purpose was to deter aggressors, they were a dismal failure. I know of no general officer who approved them."

Major General Robert W. Grow, U.S.A.
Commander, 6th Armored Division in Europe, World War II

Admiral John E. Gingrich, U.S.N.
Deputy Chief of Naval Operations, 1953
Director, Security and Intelligence, Atomic Energy Commission
Commander, naval forces, Korean War
Vice President, International Telephone and Telegraph Corp.

"It is quite plain to me that we have not only not advanced in the Humanities, but have today both because of our own, and because of enemy conduct, retrogressed in some respects to the level of the cave man. In World War II, certainly both sides violated the Rules of the Hague Convention which we had hoped were international laws. In the Korean war, the enemy paid little attention to the rules of war. Because of these unfortunate precedents, it is my opinion that in any future war the rules for treatment of the defeated will be about as humane as the culture of the victor, and no more so. By the 'war crimes trials' in which the victor judged the defeated, we set a precedent which we did not apply to our commanders simply because we were the victors. Our own submarine fleet was certainly designed to sink enemy tonnage, with no means of rescuing personnel. Although the Germans employed the submarine unrestrictedly in World War II before we did, that does not change the fact that we also committed the same acts later, for which Admiral Doenitz was tried and convicted. I have always looked on the 'war crimes trials' as an unlawful revengeful act rather than a court of justice."

"The International Tribunal was not a military tribunal at all, in any sense of the term, based as it was, on 'ex post facto' concepts, directly in violation of Anglo-American Constitutional principles. International law has no punitive provisions, resting entirely on comity. I have read...with great interest Rear Admiral Gallery's opinion of the trial of Admiral Doenitz as 'barefaced hypocrisy' and an 'insult to our submariners'...This being so, I think it is right."

Rear Admiral Edvard Christian Danielsen, Royal Norwegian Navy

"I consider the trial of the German officials after World War II was outrageous and cannot be condoned."

Major General James Kelly Parsons, U.S.A.
Commanding General, 3rd Corps
Commanding General, 2nd Division

"I graduated from the first Submarine Class at New London, Connecticut in 1916—and had submarine duty off and on, through the years, until almost the beginning of World War II. It also happens that I was briefly involved in anti-submarine business in World War I. In World War II, one of my principal jobs was as Chief of Staff of the 10th Fleet (our anti-submarine organization in the Atlantic). Aside from Admiral King (Commander-in-Chief), I was probably one of the chief opponents of Admiral Doenitz. He, in my view, used all of the tricks in his bag...I agree completely with Rear Admiral Gallery's expressed opinions. Doenitz did a proper military job. Had he not been bothered by Goering's lack of cooperation, we would have had a much tougher time...I shall probably never have the pleasure of meeting Doenitz but I should really be most pleased to have that opportunity to discuss 'old times.' "

Admiral Francis S. Low, U.S.N.
Chief of Staff, 10th Fleet, Atlantic, World War II
Commander, Service Force Pacific Fleet
Deputy Chief of Naval Operations

"I agree with Admiral Gallery that these 'war crimes trials' were a libel on the naval and military professions in general, and the trial and condemnation of Admiral Doenitz was an insult to both British and American Submariners, and that of Admiral Raeder to those great officers who commanded the American and British Navies. All were loyal and patriotic seamen whose common 'crime,' presumably, was that they gave effect to the war policies of the Civil Power which, as we know from experience, is apt to be more bellicose and bloodthirsty than are its servants—the fighting men...With regard to 'unrestricted submarine warfare,' I wrote in 1931: 'Considering our own submarines only, it is clear that they will never be used in the piratical manner which Germany herself now deplores. It is true, however, that unless so employed they are singularly inefficient for interference with Trade.' But the arming of merchant ships owing to the limitations of submarines and their vulnerability to gunfire on the surface, turned armed merchant ships into warships, thus compelling submarines to sink at sight unless their value was to be reduced to the vanishing point. In the second world war this was quickly recognized, with the result that the sinking of merchant ships without warning became established as an accepted practise by Allied submarines, as emphasized by Admiral Nimitz when honorably testifying in defense of Admiral Doenitz. Because merchant ships form the most vital, and vulnerable, arm of the Defense Forces of non self-supporting island Powers, such as Britain and Japan, we must accept the fact that they will inevitably be the chief, and quite legitimate, target of attack in the event of another major war..."

Captain Bernard Acworth, Royal Navy, D.S.O.
Served for 18 years in submarines and commanded anti-submarine flotilla
Author on naval subjects

"It was my opinion at the time of the Nuremberg Trials, and still is, that the officers concerned were not treated in a way corresponding to the principles of justice and democracy."

Vice Admiral Thore Horve, Royal Norwegian Navy, C.B.E., D.S.C.
Commander-in-chief, Norwegian Navy, 1946-1949
Chairman, Norwegian Delegation to N.A.T.O.
Commander, Imperial Ethiopian Coast Guard, 1955

"I agree with the opinion expressed in the editorial from the *Chicago Tribune.* My father was a Justice of the Supreme Court of the State of New York. I remember thinking at the time of the trials how outraged he would have felt by the *ex post facto* nature of the rules under which the convictions were decided upon. I should like to join in apologizing to Admiral Doenitz."

Virginia C. Gildersleeve, Ph.D.
American educator
Dean Emeritus of Barnard College

"I was not consulted when the decisions were being made to hold the 'war crimes trials' but had I been so consulted, I would have been energetically opposed to it."

Major General Harry J. Malony, U.S.A.
Commanding General, 94th Infantry Division, 1942-1945
Presidential Minister to Greece, 1946
Consultant to Dept. of Defense, 1950-1951

"It seems to me that the whole concept of the 'War Crimes Trials' stemmed from a rather widespread, but completely naive idea of the role of military personnel in the discharge of their responsibilities to the governments they serve. Many otherwise intelligent individuals seemed to think that wars could be fought spontaneously after the declaration of hostilities and that any prior planning, especially war plans against a specific Power were immoral...I served in the Holland type U. S. submarines for nearly five years, 1923-28, and never entertained any doubt that the Rules of International Law applying to submarines were idealistic and unrealistic. We kicked this subject around a great deal in the Naval War College where I was a student 1933-34, always with the conclusion that submarines of all combatants would be used in the next war just as they were indeed used in World War II. Mr. Justice Jackson lectured at the National War College, where I was a student 1946-47, after his participation in the Nuremberg Trials. I doubt that he would have liked to repeat the experience, for the student body of top-flight Army, Navy and Air Force Officers made no attempt to hide their hostility to his thesis. During the question period the whole concept of the legality of the trials was condemned and one final observation made by a student was to the general effect that the 'precedent established by the trials had but one value; that of placing a higher premium than ever on being on the winning side.' "

Hugh H Goodwin

Vice Admiral Hugh H. Goodwin, U.S.N.
Commander, Carrier Division Two, 1953-1954
Commander, Naval Forces Philippines, 1954-1956
Commander, Naval Forces, Continental Air Defense Command, 1956-1958

[To Grand Admiral Doenitz]

"The writer, son of Rear Admiral Louis Kempff, U.S. Navy, Class of 1861, U. S. Naval Academy, considers it a privilege to express his views in relation to the Nuremberg War Crimes Trials. The fact that the trials(?) were based on 'ex post facto concepts' made the court(?) completely wrong, and you, distinguished Grand Admiral, completely right. You were true to your sworn oath. Nuremberg failed in its duty—utterly!"

Clarence S. Kempff.
Vice Admiral, U.S. Navy, Retd;

Vice Admiral Clarence Selby Kempff, U.S.N.
Commander, Battleships, Pacific Fleet
Commandant, Mare Island Naval Shipyard

"I think that the conviction of Admiral Doenitz by the Nuremberg Tribunal was a mistake and an injustice. I would be glad to have Admiral Doenitz know this. He fought the war with credit and distinction."

Vice Admiral Fitzhugh Lee, U.S.N.
Commander, Naval Air Technical Training Center, Memphis
Deputy Commander, U.S. Atlantic Fleet, 1960
Commandant, National War College

"I have never spoken to any military man of experience about the trials of German leaders, both military and civilian, who did not agree that those trials were a vicious attack on the mental attitudes of men whose knowledge and ability are essential to any nation whose existence is threatened in time of war. Admiral Doenitz was merely doing what he knew was his duty, as were we all."

Major General G. Ralph Meyer, U.S.A.
Commanding General, Anti-Aircraft and Harbor Defenses, Canal Zone
Commander, Anti-Aircraft, U.S. Army

"...In the case of Admiral Doenitz, I feel strongly that his conviction was wrong. I believe that he acted as a Naval Officer and Patriot."

Vice Admiral Edward O. McDonnell, U.S.N.R.
Commanded aircraft carriers in World War II
Holder, Congressional Medal of Honor
Partner, Hornblower & Weeks

"Being neither an officer nor a lawyer, I have no title to pronounce on the conduct of the court. But I am quite clear that any trial of defeated foes by their victors is a mistake and a precedent which should not be followed among what are commonly described as civilised nations."

Dr. George Peabody Gooch, C.H.
British historian and author
Fellow of Trinity College, Cambridge
President of the Historical Association

"I have felt strongly that professional soldiers should not be tried subsequent to the loss of a war for acts committed during combat which were in strict accordance with directives issued by political superiors...some years ago, I expressed myself in no uncertain terms to Justice Robert Jackson relative to the trial of Generals and Admirals for doing their duty in time of war. There is no doubt in my mind that certain of the German trials constituted political reprisal."

Major General Kenyon A. Joyce, U.S.A.
Commanded 9th Army Corps, World War II
President, Allied Military Control Commission for Italy, 1943-1944

"I am indeed glad to associate myself with the list of distinguished military and naval leaders who have registered their disapproval of the proceedings of the International Military Tribunal at Nuremberg, particularly with respect to the war crimes trial of Grand Admiral Karl Doenitz. I have always felt that the war crimes trials at Nuremberg were inspired by vengeance, were conducted without regard to international law and resulted in findings that were a blot on Anglo-American records of justice."

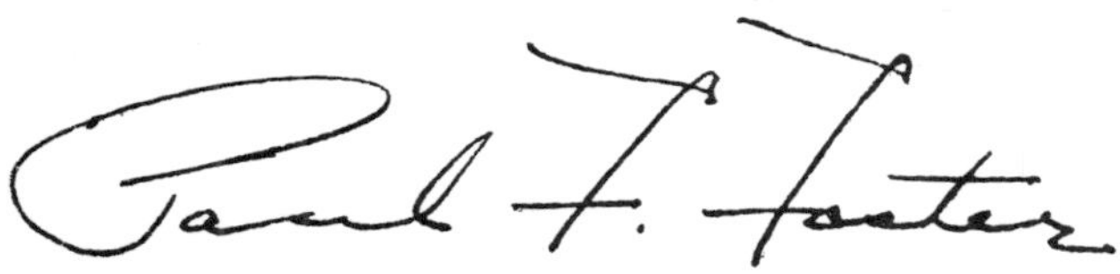

Vice Admiral Paul F. Foster, U.S.N.R.
General Manager, United States Atomic Energy Commission
U.S. Representative, International Atomic Energy Agency
Holder, Congressional Medal of Honor

"I agree with Rear Admiral Daniel V. Gallery, U.S. Navy, and Major General J.F.C. Fuller. General Fuller and I are very old friends and we have discussed this on several occasions, and there is nothing I could add that has not been said already. My view is that a law must apply to all. Had this been applied at the time of these trials, there would have been a number of ranking officers among the victors who stood trial. I hope you succeed in destroying the dangerous precedent created."

F. F. Worthington

Major General Frederick F. Worthington, C.B., M.C., M.M., C.D.
General Officer Commanding, Armoured Division, 1942
Canadian Pacific Command, 1945; Western Command, 1946
Civil Defense Co-ordinator for Canada since 1948

"As a professional soldier, I believe that Grand Admiral Karl Doenitz loyally and valiantly fulfilled his duties by taking all the means in his power to insure his country's victory in the Second World War, courageously coming to grips with the hard responsibilities of command. I believe sincerely that no professional soldier could ever consider Grand Admiral Karl Doenitz as a war criminal. I think that the illegal and unjust sentence which condemned him to ten years of imprisonment ought to be considered as a simple abuse of power on the part of the impassioned conquerors."

E. Calvo
General de Ejercito

General of the Army of Chile, Enrique Calvo Gallegos
Commander-in-Chief, 5th Division, Chilean Army
Chief of General Staff, 1944

"Any military leader who does not do his utmost for the nation for which he serves is certainly guilty of disloyalty. Unswerving obedience, loyalty, perseverance and diligence have always been required of all military leaders. General Robert E. Lee was a regular officer of the Army of the United States prior to the Civil War. The fact that he resigned his commission and became the leading General of the Confederacy was never used as a reason for subsequent court-martial and punishment. Lee has always been honored and respected for his position. He believed in the cause of his native land, and did his utmost to bring that cause to a triumphant conclusion. I feel the same attitude should be taken toward German officers who did their utmost for their country..."

Vice Admiral Charles P. Mason, U.S.N.
Commanded U.S.S. *Hornet* at Battles of Midway and Santa Cruz
Commander, Naval Air Stations, Hawaii
Mayor of Pensacola, Florida

"...Military personnel who carry on war operations in a normal manner should not be charged and tried because their country started a war and lost it. The rules for conducting war change with the development of weapons, and what may have been considered uncivilized and barbarous in one age, may later be considered normal. Unrestricted submarine warfare is a case in point, as is the bombing of civilian areas with widespread destruction of civilians and their buildings and homes, and only incidental damage to military targets. During World War II, I always considered shipping as a military target. For air attacks, I tried to destroy military targets, such as ships, airfields, aircraft, naval facilities, factories, etc., and to keep the damage to purely civilian areas as small as possible."

Admiral Raymond A. Spruance, U.S.N.
Commander, Central Pacific Force in Saipan, Tinian and Guam Operations
Commander, 5th Fleet, Central Pacific Operations, 1943-1945
Commander-in-chief, Pacific Fleet, 1945-1946
President, Naval War College, 1946-1948
U.S. Ambassador to the Philippines, 1952-1955

"I wish to advise that I feel very strongly in respect to the Nuremberg Trials. In my opinion, this whole procedure was a result of mass hysteria and conducted in spirit of mob violence. Acceptance of the concept of the Nuremberg Trials would require every man in uniform to violate his oath to protect his own country, and would place a penalty on his 'will to win.' I sincerely hope that there will never be a recurrence of the Nuremberg Trials, but if that should be the case, that the United States refuses to be a party to it. I hope the above makes my position clear, and you are at liberty to quote me at any time or place you may have occasion to do so."

Major General Thomas O. Hardin, U.S.A.F.R.
Commanded Air Transport Sectors, Africa and Pacific, World War II
Director of Technical Inspection, 1950-1952
Executive, Pan American World Airways

"In reply to your letter with reference to conviction and sentence to punishment of Grand Admiral Karl Doenitz of Germany as a war criminal, I will say that such conviction and punishment were based on very doubtful logic..."

Major General Grandison Gardner, U.S.A.F.
Commanded Air Proving Ground Command, World War II
Member, U.S. Strategic Bombing Survey

"In my opinion, there were no legal grounds for the Admiral Doenitz trial. He was carrying out the orders of his superiors. Every military man, including our own, is placed in jeopardy in war if he follows the same course, and undoubtedly some of our commanders did."

Brigadier General Frank P. Lahm, U.S.A.F.
First airship and balloon pilot in U.S. Army
Set two endurance records with Orville Wright
Commanded Air Service, 2nd Army, A.E.F.
Won Bennett cup, international balloon race, 1906
Chief of Aviation, 1st Army, 1940-1941

"As a military man, I think it was a sad day for my profession when the 'do-gooders' got control at the Nuremberg Trials. We have now set a precedent—no military commander can ever afford to lose—he will automatically be guilty of 'war crimes' and will probably lose his head."

Vice Admiral Herbert S. Duckworth, U.S.N.
National War College, 1946
Staff, Air War College
Aviation Planning Office of the C.N.O.

"To prosecute the war with aggressive resolution is an accepted necessity and during this period public feeling runs hot and hateful. Oft times more hateful than the military personnel actually engaged. To prosecute the peace is a different matter. History has been repetitious where the conquerors and the vanquished have in a very short time become bedfellows. In order to transpose in an orderly manner from the one to the other, I believe it requires a cooling of the hatred that has been built up especially among the non-military. The so-called war criminals should be retained in custody commensurate with their position in their respective country for sufficient time to allow the feelings of the conquerors to subside. If this was done in the case of Admiral Karl Doenitz, the facts would have time to filter through to the public and the demand for retribution would have diminished to the degree where he would never have been sentenced to prison for ten years."

Major General James H. Davies, U.S.A.F.
Commanding General, Alaskan Air Command
Commanding General, 5th Bomber Command
Commanding General, 313th Bomber Wing

"...with respect to the Nuremberg 'war crimes trials,' I think there was absolutely no justification for such trials, and in particular that of Grand Admiral Karl Doenitz, Commander-in-Chief of the German Navy. I am terribly afraid that the Allies have established a precedent which will operate against all the military commanders in future wars. I suppose Castro could justify his executions on the same basis."

Rear Admiral Norborne L. Rawlings, U.S.N.
Director, Newport News Shipbuilding and Dry Dock Company
Commanded Naval Dry Docks, San Francisco, World War II

"I am in thorough agreement with the opinions expressed by many of our most distinguished Flag Officers—that the prosecution of any form of war, submarine or surface or air, to the best of their ability, is their duty and a matter of professional pride to any officer worthy of the name. Admiral Doenitz has every reason to be proud of the achievements of the officers and men of the Submarine Navy under his command, and of the material excellence of their ships—turned out in unprecedented numbers under stress of war. Also, I share in the belief that the legal basis for the trials was flimsy in the extreme, ex post facto in character, and without precedent in International Law. As stated in my review of Admiral Ruge's *Der Seekreig,* any professional naval officer 'cannot but be lost in admiration of the accomplishments of the German Navy.' Admiral Doenitz has my sincere respect for his professional attainments, and my best wishes for his future happiness."

Vice Admiral Walden L. Ainsworth, U.S.N.
Commander Destroyers-Cruisers, Pacific Fleet, World War II
(Kula Gulf and Solomons campaigns)

"I do not like war crimes trials against soldiers who have only done their duty. Grand Admiral Karl Doenitz is, in my opinion, innocent. I agree with Rear Admiral D.V. Gallery."

Major General, The Baron Göran Gyllenstierna, Royal Swedish Army
Inspector of Swedish Cavalry

"I can fully accept the views of Admiral Gallery."

Vice Admiral Claes Lindsstrom, Royal Swedish Navy
Chief of Submarines, 1930
Commanding Admiral, East Coast, 1937-1942

"I will say that I consider the 'war crimes trials' to have been unwise, without support of law, and precedent-setting. If, in a future war, the United States is defeated, the Robert E. Lee or Douglas MacArthur of that day will probably be tried and hanged for doing his duty and carrying out legal orders of his government. I will state further that I do not approve of court-made laws, either now or in the past. Courts are created to judge under existing laws, not to make new laws...Admiral Doenitz was a member of a group illegally tried because of hysteria and a desire to punish somebody."

Major General Charles T. Harris, Jr., U.S.A.
Ass't. Chief of Ordnance, War Dept., 1938-1942
Commanding General, Aberdeen Proving Ground, 1942-1946

"An officer, career or otherwise, regardless of grade, must carry out the orders of his superiors. In the case of senior commanders, this superior is the head of state. A. career officer is obligated to obey these orders; if he fails to do so, or refuses, he is guilty of insubordination. Should he be punished for obeying the orders of his superiors by the courts of the victors? My reply is: Emphatically No... 'Unrestricted submarine warfare' is humane in contrast with the bombing by aircraft of populated areas. If bombing is justifiable, then 'unrestricted submarine warfare' is equally, if not more justifiable, as a legitimate means of defeating an enemy."

Major General John B. Anderson, U.S.A.
Commanding General, 16th Corps, World War II

"I agree with you and your efforts, and you may quote me as concurring in the sentiments expressed in the editorial published in *Chicago Daily Tribune* under date of October 6, 1956."

Vice Admiral Wilder D. Baker, U.S.N.
Commander, Cruiser Division 14, World War II
Chief of Staff, 2nd Fast Carrier Force, Pacific Fleet

"On the War Crimes Trials in general and the Doenitz case in particular, I have always thought that these trials were a mistake and that military commanders on the losing side should not be tried for war crimes by International Military Tribunals set up by the victors..."

Major General William F. Tompkins, U.S.A.
Director, Special Planning Division, War Dept., 1943-1945

"The trials of career Military and Naval Officers, such as Grand Admiral Karl Doenitz...are unjustified, in my opinion, on the basis of any effective or vigorous direction of war as required both by their commissions and orders from their Governments. Personally, I have great professional respect for Admiral Doenitz...I believe that War Crimes Trials of professional Military and Naval Officers have set a dangerous precedent."

Sincerely,

Vice Admiral Earle W. Mills, U.S.N
Chief, Bureau of Ships, Navy Dept.
President, Foster Wheeler Corporation

"I feel that the sentencing of Grand Admiral Doenitz is—as Admiral Gallery says—a simple hypocrisy. Submarine warfare, since it is warfare, is no more criminal than any other form of destruction of the enemy which is, after all, the goal of war. Furthermore I think that everything which has been styled as 'war crime' is in fact a scandalous hypocrisy. Let us suppose that tomorrow an atomic war breaks out. How could this massive destruction of innocents not be considered the very embodiment of an atrocious war crime? If there must be international laws which govern war, it is imperative that this law be promulgated by consent and by general agreement, and in this case—but only in this case—those who have broken the rules of this international law could be considered responsible. Until that time, any legislation devised *post facto* and applied by tribunals whose bias is obvious, cannot be considered as morally valid."

Honorable Pierre Etienne Flandin
French jurist and statesman
Advocate at the Court of Appeals
General Counsellor, Department of l'Yonne, 1955
Prime Minister of France, 1934-1935
Minister of State, 1935-1936
Minister for Foreign Affairs, 1936

"I am glad to go on record as disapproving completely the whole concept of the Nuremberg Trials, for two reasons. The trials had no basis in past legal history. They established a very dangerous precedent in international law which may affect American fighting forces in future wars. Our country has always held in highest esteem the idea of government under law. But by 'law' we mean principles established by duly constituted law-making bodies, in accordance with the existing body of law, and effective only against crimes committed after the prohibition was formally established in law. In other words, we are vigorously opposed, as a nation, to executive-made law, judge-made law, ex-post facto laws, and anything else which lowers the respect for government under laws made with the consent of the governed."

Hon. William E. Jenner
American lawyer and legislator
U.S. Senator from Indiana, 1934-1942, 1944-1959

"I am of the opinion that the Nuremberg Trials constituted a very dangerous precedent. Under such a precedent, the President of the United States...could be arraigned and found guilty for authorizing the use of the Atomic Bomb at Hiroshima...This could also include all Cabinet officers, the Joint Chiefs of Staff and immediate subordinates engaged in carrying out their orders. The trial of Admiral Doenitz was the most flagrant of the injustices indulged in at the 'International Military Tribunal.' If we were by chance defeated in a war, all our leaders, both political and military, could be brought before a Tribunal where injustice and vindictiveness would prevail. Any justification of the Nuremberg Trials is simply playing into the hands of pacifists and traitors who would make this country defenseless by barring the use of aerial and atomic war and submarine warfare."

Major General Richard Curtis Moore, U.S.A.
Commanded Panama Canal Dept. and 18th Infantry, 1938-1939
Deputy Chief of Staff, U.S. Army, 1940-1942
Member, Joint Production Survey, Joint Chiefs of Staff, 1943-1945

"I was of the opinion that the victorious nation was indulging in hypocrisy in bringing the reputable German military leaders to trial for war crimes. I had the impression at the time, and still retain the impression, that a precedent was set for the future wherein the nation which lost the war would witness all their military and political leaders being executed, regardless of the cause of the war. Personally I have had the deepest sympathy for Admiral Doenitz since...he was carrying out his military duties in a war which was initiated by political leaders. I cannot see how any career military man could have taken any other line of action. With reference to the charges of Admiral Doenitz indulging in unrestricted submarine warfare, I cannot see that this is any different in degree than the indiscriminate aerial bombing of cities without too much regard as to whether they contained any worthwhile military targets. Admiral Doenitz has my deepest sympathy because of the manner in which he was treated as a result of his wartime military activities."

Admiral E. T. Wooldridge, U.S.N.
Commandant, The National War College
Commander, Second Fleet, U.S. Atlantic Fleet
Commander, Battleships-Cruisers, U.S. Atlantic Fleet
Commander, N.A.T.O. Striking Fleet

"The Nuremberg sentence of Grand Admiral Doenitz for his activity in performing his duty as commander of the German Navy appears to me as a disgrace for the tribunal, for the victors and for humanity. It was a shameful manifestation of the 'Vae Victis' mentality."

Lieutenant General Erik Testrup, Royal Swedish Army
Military Governor of Stockholm, 1937-1954
Director of His Majesty's Military Hospital since 1947

"I did not and never have agreed with the principle of trial of professional soldiers for carrying out the orders of their political superiors."

Major General Frederick L. Anderson, U.S.A.F.
Commanding General, 8th Bomber Command, 1943
Deputy Commander, U.S. Strategic Air Forces in Europe, 1944
Deputy U.S. Special Representative in Europe, rank of ambassador, 1952

"I concur in the views...relative to the 'trial' and 'conviction' of the so-called 'war criminals,' and in particular to that travesty of justice which imprisoned Grand Admiral Karl Doenitz for ten years. It should be humiliating to every thinking citizen of the United States to realize that we use one code of behavior for ourselves, but apply quite another to our enemies."

Rear Admiral Mays Livingston Lewis, U.S.N.
Commanding officer, U.S. Naval Station, Mers-El-Keber, North Africa, 1943
Commander, Northern Group, 16th Fleet, 1945

"I agree heartily with the ideas expressed by Admiral Gallery when he calls the 'War Crimes Trials' a 'libel on the Military Profession'. Also, to brand as criminals Admiral Doenitz and others whose only crime was that of carrying out their military duties, is as repugnant to me as it must be to all clear thinking men today. It is my sincere hope that bringing this hypocrisy before the world in its true light may help prevent its becoming a precedent and thus a dagger held at the throat of military leaders the world over."

Vice Admiral Delbert S. Cornwell, U.S.N.
Commanded U.S.S. *Suwanee* and *Philippine Sea*
Commander, Carrier Divisions 15 and 4, 1951-1954
Commander, Fleet Air, Jacksonville, Florida, 1955

"Concerning the 'International Military Tribunal' constituted by the victors to submit to judgement as 'War Criminals' the highest Military and Naval Chiefs who, fulfilling their duty, developed a plan of operations ordered by the Government which they served—permit me to give you my personal estimation; it is this: 1. The constitution of this Tribunal constitutes a disgrace for the nations which instigated it and soils the brilliance of the splendid victory obtained by them. 2. It sets a terrible precedent which a future war may unfortunately have to overcome. The injustice of the verdict which condemned Grand Admiral Karl Doenitz also affected Admiral Raeder whom I had the honor of knowing personally in 1928 at Kiel when he was in command of that naval base, and in circumstances in which the undersigned was commanding a warship of Chile which made a port-of-call in that port. The opportunities which I had to deal with him, as much in his home as in the ship of my command, left me with the impression that Admiral Raeder possessed all the qualities of a superior man and as such was he esteemed by his subordinates among whom he enjoyed great prestige. He had been Chief of Staff of the Battle Cruiser Squadron which was commanded by Admiral Hipper in the First World War, in whose encounter with the similar squadron commanded by Admiral Beatty at the beginning of the great Battle of Jutland, inflicted heavy losses by sinking two of Beatty's battle cruisers. I cannot conceive that chiefs of the stature of Doenitz and Raeder could have been condemned and judged as 'War Criminals.' "

Vice Admiral Julio Allard Pinto, Navy of The Republic of Chile
Chief of submarine flotilla, 1929
Commander-in-chief, Chilean Navy, 1938
Minister of the Interior, Cabinet of President Juan Antonio Rios, 1943

"I, in company with many others, abhorred the so-called 'War Crimes Trials' of the professional military officer. This was based on the fact that the professional fighting man is not a free agent. Admiral Doenitz was a professional Naval Officer, doing that which political superiors deemed essential. And our own General Grant wrote the precept for total war in the 1860's. I admire General U.S. Grant, so I guess I'll have to class 'unrestricted submarine warfare' as total war."

Rear Admiral Glenn E. Trester, U.S. Coast Guard

"I have always believed that to condemn a soldier for having obeyed the orders of his superior is the gravest of errors and renders impossible any real discipline in an army. As far as the trials of German military men are concerned, I have always considered it particularly erroneous to have them judged and sentenced after having signed the armistice with them. As for the role of Admiral Doenitz...I have enough confidence in General Weygand and M. Pierre-Etienne Flandin to believe that their opinion is correct."

Hon. Jacques Isorni
French jurist and statesman
Defense counsel for Marshal Petain
Deputy of Paris in the National Assembly

"Under modern conditions, no officer should be tried for conducting unrestricted submarine warfare. Submarines can conduct no other type of warfare and live. The missile has now been added to submarine armament. Even if aimed at purely military shore targets, casualties will be great in highly populated areas among civilians. This shore danger and unrestricted submarine warfare at sea must be recognized as legitimate."

Major General Guy V. Henry, U.S.A.
Italian and European theatres, World War II
Head, Inter-Allied Personnel Board
Chairman, U.S.-Canada Defense Board

"With reference to your letter concerning Admiral Gallery's book, *Twenty Million Tons Under the Sea,* I have read the enclosures with great interest and am in full accord with the sentiments expressed concerning the 'War Crimes Trials,' that they were *ex post facto* in nature, that there was no provision in international law for such proceedings, and that they have established a dangerous precedent for the future."

Major General Charles V. Bromley, U.S.A.
12th Armored Division, France and Germany, 1944-1945
Civil Administrator, the Ryukyu Islands
Commanding General, The Armored Center

"We learned much to our dismay the full meaning of the war guilt clause in the Versailles Treaty only too late, and as we uncover some of the antecedents of World War II, we are once again in the position of wondering who actually was guilty of aggression. I personally believe that the time has come for a courageous re-examination of all 'war crimes' trials in which the United States participated at the end of World War II and for an official disassociation of this country from those aspects where there was no basis in a pre-existing treaty, statute or agreement. The 'war crimes' trials of the military in particular have placed an unfair burden upon the military of any nation, and the full implications of what this can mean have been available for all to see in 1959 in the trials in Cuba and Iraq. It is a source of embarrassment to me, and I believe that it should be a source of shame to all Americans to see such proceedings carried on within a framework to which this country has lent its blessing. Let us all hope that the day is not far away when the United States will have the leadership and intellectual courage to redefine its position on this matter. There are too many of our allies who are already condemned as war criminals by the Communists for us to allow this strange code of injustice to remain on our books."

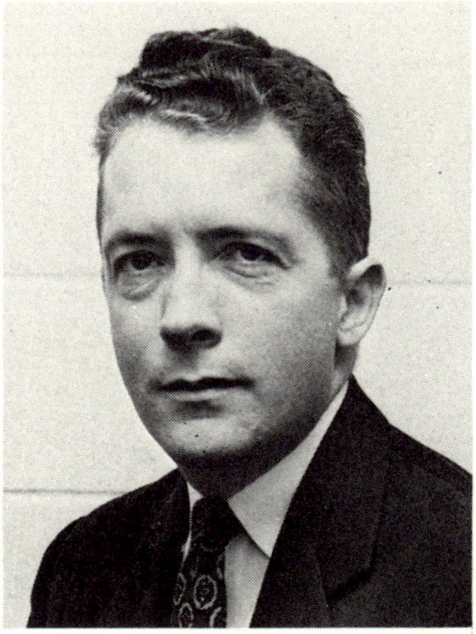

Richard L. Walker

Professor Richard L. Walker, Ph.D.
Chairman of the Department of International Studies of the University of South Carolina

"There is no doubt that the sentence delivered in the judgement of Admiral Doenitz pronounced by the Special Tribunal of Nuremberg was an unjust act, possibly due to the disorientation existing in the world at the end of a bloody war which unleashed passions and in which chivalry was forgotten. Any naval officer in the world, in a situation similar to that of Admiral Doenitz, would have to behave as he did, in defense of his country, all the more so because, since the first World War, the application of the norms established in international treaties were inapplicable and impossible to observe. In practical terms, on all the seas, there were no non-combatant merchant ships and practically all were potential warships in the service of the enemy."

Carlos Rotalde

Vice Admiral Carlos A. Rotalde, Peruvian Navy

"I entirely agree with your point of view that the Admiral's [Doenitz] crime was the effective professional direction of the wartime navy of his country, a 'criminal standard' under which any career military or naval officer could be convicted. What my friend Rear Admiral Gallery, U.S. Navy, states in his latest book is the real truth: "a barefaced hypocrisy," or is it necessary to remember the indiscriminate bombing of German towns, the operations of the U.S. submarines in the Pacific and the atomic bombs over Hiroshima and Nagasaki? What of all the huge expenses invested to exploit atomic power and ballistic missiles? Is it possible to dedicate these weapons to hit only military objectives?...You are doing a fine work for the benefit of the historical reappraisal of the dangerous precedent set at Nuremberg."

Vice Admiral Roque A. Saldias, Peruvian Navy
Minister for Navy and Air Force, Peru, 1937-1939
Prime Minister and Minister for Navy, 1947
Minister for the Navy, 1948
President, Council of Ministers and Minister of Marine, 1954

"My opinion of the 'War Crimes Trials' in their entirety is that they were a throwback to the days of barbarism, a proof of man's inhumanity to man, a complete lack of a decent respect for the welfare of our fellow-man, and a violation of all elements of justice and decency. Any understanding and righteous human, according to my creed, is happy that Admiral Doenitz has lived to see an intelligent world regret those terrible errors. Others, less important but equally honorable unfortunates, such as General Homma of Japan, paid for their defeat by being executed. I am delighted to have the opportunity to express my thoughts on this matter and hope that some form of restitution may be made to many others."

Major General Clements McMullen, U.S.A.F.
Commanding General, Far East Air Service Command, World War II
Chief of Staff, Pacific Air Command, 1946

“I am grateful for the opportunity of being one of many World War II veterans to pay homage to a truly great naval officer. During 1944, I commanded the Northeast Greenland Task Unit of the U.S. Atlantic Fleet. I believe that one of the most remarkable and heroic feats in submarine history was the navigation of a German submarine under approximately 100 miles of pack ice, to surface in the shore lead and attack one of my ships, the *Northland.* I had completely discarded such a possibility in my estimate of the situation. We think of the trans-polar sub-ice navigation by the *Nautilus* and *Skate* as outstanding. Yet, in 1944, before the advent of the inertial system of navigation, atomic propulsion and other modern implements to endurance; this intrepid German Commander (supporting *Operation Edelweiss*) contended with the swift East Greenland current bearing icebergs as well as a moving carpet of sea ice across unsounded depths. I am sure Admiral Doenitz has received many compliments upon his professional achievements to which I humbly add my congratulations. Perhaps more to the point was my conversation at dinner in the cabin of the *Eastwind* (1944) with Ober Leutnant Karl Schmidt (German Naval Artillery) who agreed that only an outstanding leader would inspire submariners to deeds of daring. I mentioned at the time: ‘I wish we had Admiral Doenitz on our side.’ I think our policy of trying German leaders for ‘war crimes’ was stupid. We could have learned a lot from these men who kept Germany fighting almost six years when she was supposed to be bankrupt.”

Charles W Thomas

Rear Admiral Charles W. Thomas, U. S. Coast Guard, M.S., A.M.
Commanded icebreakers *Northwind* and *Eastwind*
Commander, Greenland Patrol, U.S. Atlantic Fleet
Commander, Task Group 43.6, U.S. Atlantic Fleet (Antarctic)
Administrator, Univ. of Washington scientific investigation of polar phenomena

“I am opposed to so-called ‘war crimes trials’ against career military officers for carrying out orders or duties in connection with their military position.”

T. F. Donohue

Rear Admiral Timothy F. Donohue, U.S.N.
Task Group Commander at Okinawa (Minesweeping)
Ass’t. Executive Secretary to Secretary of Defense
Intelligence Officer, 3rd Naval District

"Hypocrisy is always present in emotional situations, and that, of course, is what happened after the war. A person in the military Service takes an oath to do all he can to defend the government that he serves. The Germans were doing just that, in most cases at least. Unless some act of an individual is personal in its nature and cruel beyond the requirements of war, he should not be held guilty of carrying out the policies of his country. I am thinking of Wirt of Andersonville, in which case his deeds went far beyond those required to carry out his job. In the Doenitz case, the trial was nothing in the world but the hypocrisy of righteousness which we victors could indulge in because we won. There was no authority to review the decisions which would have dared question the acts of the trial court. Wrong as it was, it may serve a very valuable purpose in preventing another such travesty on justice in the future. I believe that the world has come to see the injustice of those accusations."

Admiral Harold M. Martin, U.S.N.
Commander, Carrier Division 23 and Task Force 49, Pacific
Commander, Carrier Division 2 and 5, 1947
Commander, 1st Fleet and 7th Fleet, 1951-1956

"You ask for my personal appraisal of the trial and conviction of Admiral Karl Doenitz just after the close of World War II. Should this trial, conviction and punishment pass into history unchallenged by men of good will throughout the world, and especially by career officers of the armed forces of all nations, victory only can save great combatant leaders such as our own MacArthur, Hart, Eisenhower, and Halsey, from being judged and punished as 'War Criminals.'"

(Photo by U.S. Army Signal Corps)

Major General Robert M. Danford, U.S.A.
Chief of Field Artillery, 1938-1942
Commandant, U.S. Military Academy, West Point

"To use a familiar expression, 'what is sauce for the gander is sauce for the goose,' is an accepted principle of life equally applicable to individuals as also to nations. When one quarrels with another in private or in public or when one nation fights another on the battlefield or on the high seas or in the air there are and should be certain laws to be observed which in day-to-day life we call 'laws of the game.' If it is true of individuals that 'nothing is fair in love and war,' it is equally true of warring nations. If this is accepted, then after the cessation of hostilities between nations when treaties are signed, when questions of repatriation etc. are discussed and solved, there should be an end of all ill feeling or malice between the victor and the vanquished. That is the eternal law of life.

"Secondly, a soldier must obey his commander and keep to his post. On this hypothesis, Grand Admiral Karl Doenitz's sentence of ten years confinement was not only inhuman but it was an illegal sentence which cannot be supported from any point of view, military or international. It is true, in the words of an eminent jurist that 'international law is the vanishing point of jurisprudence' but that doctrine must be qualified by international morality. Looked at from this angle, the international military tribunal or the 'war crimes trials' lose all significance because when the war terminates, the rancour or bitterness between nations, victorious or vanquished should disappear from their hearts and a new chapter should open up. These sorts of trials—like the trial at Nuremberg—lay down dangerous precedents for all time to come. It was an innovation after the last world war. Sufficient unto the day is the evil thereof. World opinion should be mobilized against such precedents and the U.N.O. should be persuaded to take up this question on broader grounds of humanity, because, in the words of Robert Browning, 'it is one more triumph for devils and sorrow for angels: one wrong more to man, and one more insult to God.' "

Hon. Sudhir C. Mitter, LL.B.
Indian jurist
Senior Advocate, Supreme Court of India

"I have retired from public life but to assist you I am sending an opinion by Mr. S. C. Mitter, Barrister-at-Law, an eminent leader of the Calcutta High Court Bar, a reputed Senior Advocate of the Supreme Court of India, and a respected public man, as I think his view represents that of the majority of well-informed educated opinion here."

Hon. Justice Kamal Chunder
Judge, High Court of Calcutta from 1946

"The real culprits in the 'War Crimes Trials' were not those being tried, but were those doing the trying."

Honorable R. Carter Pittman
American jurist and business executive
President, North Georgia Oil Co.

"As to trials of 'War Criminals,' we have set a precedent which, should we have a war with the Soviets and should the Soviets win (not unlikely since they would strike first), we might expect our President, the Secretary of Defense, and each high commander to be brought to trial as a 'War Criminal.' We would think it barbarous, of course, but after all, *we* started it. As to submarine warfare, it is no more to be condemned than any other form of surprise attack, as for example night bombing, night surprise attack and atomic bombing of cities. Incidentally, *we* initiated that form of warfare also. Warfare has deteriorated to the days of Tamerlane. Who is to blame? I do not know, but I do know that we are not free of our share. The 'War Criminal' idea was our worst error."

Major General Charles E. Kilbourne, U.S.A.
Lieutenant General of the National Guard of Virginia
Director, War Plans, Dept. of the Army, 1932-1935
Commander, Philippines Dept., 1936
Commanding General, 2nd Army
Superintendent, Virginia Military Institute, 1937-1946

"I believe that it is impossible to declare military leaders war criminals, whatever their rank, who have simply defended their country and executed the orders received to assure that defense...I therefore believe with M. Pierre Etienne Flandin that submarine warfare is no more criminal than any other form of destruction of the enemy, which after all is the aim of the war itself. The condemnation of Admiral Doenitz does not seem just to me."

General of the Army Maxime Weygand
Member of the French Academy
Commander-in-Chief of the French Army, 1931-1935, 1940
Minister of National Defense, 1940

"Even at the time of the trial and conviction of Grand Admiral Doenitz, I had remarked that he was being denied the benefit of equal laws and of equality before the law by prosecuting him for an act which had been indulged in by British and American admirals also. To apply the principles of private morality to soldiers and sailors engaged in a war between nations was totally unjust, as it amounted to applying *ex post facto* concepts and against one side alone. Many a soldier, sailor and airman can be convicted of murder and sentenced to death for killing his opposite numbers in the enemy army, a thing which no jurist can approve of under existing international law. If this mad principle had been applied to both sides impartially, no such trial and conviction would have been possible. I attribute Doenitz's trial, conviction and sentence to be due to the passions engendered by the War with its demoralising effect on even judges and other normally good men. It was *a war crime,* though committed by an International Tribunal. No other defence or explanation is possible except that it was a vindictive act perpetrated in anger, an act which would not be justified even by the Hammurabi Code."

Hon. Justice Ayilam Subrahmanyayyar Panchapakesa Ayyar
District and Sessions Judge at various circuits in India from 1932-1948
Puisne Judge, High Court of Judicature, Madras, India, since 1948
Director of Legal Studies, State of Madras
Author of 28 books

"The permanent rules of international law declare that prisoners of war should be treated with the utmost consideration while confined by the winners in any war. This same concept holds true in the Cuban trials, and there seems to me to be a clawing spectre of a will to do violence to anyone who has opposed you in wartime matters...I certainly approve of honoring our enemies when they acted in their wartime duty of opposing our forces."

Rear Admiral Jesse G. Johnson, U.S.N.
Ass't. Task Force Commander, Atlantic, 1943-1944
Captured German Submarine *U-505,* 1944
Commanded U.S.S. *Webster*

"I am glad to join my friends and contemporaries in an expression of my views on the Nuremberg trials for transmission to Grand Admiral Karl Doenitz. Briefly, I consider the greatest crime of World War II to have been the 'war crimes trials'. These were a crime against those who were tried and a higher crime against Western Civilization. The principal General Rules of War in International Law applied the precepts of the Mosaic Ten Commandments to sovereign national states. The Commandments set forth the limitations which men must of necessity impose upon their own conduct if they wish to coexist in security and tranquility. Any penalties incurred through breaching the Rules of War are incurred by man and his civilization. These appear not to have been at issue during the trials. The crime of those at the bar rested in their having lost the war. This loss had been due largely to an outrageous tactic called 'strategic' bombardment, whose objective was to 'shatter civilian morale' by direct attack on civilian populations in deliberate defiance of the principal General Rule of War in International Law. By punishing the vanquished, instead of those responsible for the barbaric tactic, the Nuremberg Trials made absolutely certain the fact that in another war every weapon, however barbaric, will be used without limit or regard for the survival of mankind or civilization. By thus reversing the course of the history of Western Civilization, the Nuremberg Trials actually signed the death warrant of man and civilization. If by making known to Grand Admiral Doenitz the views of thoughtful Americans, we can make some restitution for the crime of the war crime trials, we will at least measure up to the minimum requirements of simple Justice."

Eugene E. Wilson, D.Sc.
Naval aviator, aircraft manufacturer and author
Chief of Staff, Aircraft Squadrons, Battle Fleet, 1927-1928
Chairman, Board of Governors, Aircraft Industries Ass'n. of America
President, United Aircraft Corp.

"I hesitated to express an opinion on the Doenitz case because I was not a combat officer while on active duty, having spent most of my life in designing, building and repairing naval vessels. However, on thinking it over, it seems to me that if the principles on which the trial of the Admiral were based were carried to a logical—or illogical—conclusion, those of us who designed and built submarines would be equally guilty with the Admiral. Furthermore, from my studies at the Naval War College, I fail to recall any justification in international law for the sort of trial the Admiral received. Therefore, my sympathies are with him."

Rear Admiral Alexander H. Van Keuren, U.S.N.
Technical Advisor, London Naval Conference (1930) and General Disarmanent Conference (1932)
Chief, Bureau of Ships, 1942
Director, Naval Research Laboratory, 1942-1945

"Having been a professional soldier all my life, I am sure that I would have carried out during the time of war any order from my legal superior. Especially if the order pertained to combat operations would I have gladly carried it out, even though it would have meant death to me or even if it did not coincide with my own moral and ethical code. All orders, whether they directed bombing operations on open cities in Germany or unrestricted submarine warfare in the Pacific, were invariably carried out to the best of the ability of the subordinate receiving the instructions or orders. I felt at the time of the Nuremberg Trials that many, including Admiral Doenitz, were simply carrying out their orders, and I am sure that had I been in his shoes, I would have done the same. It seems to me that the precedent set by the War Crimes trials of career officers would have the direct opposite effect on any professional corps of officers as was hoped for and anticipated by those setting up the trials. Knowing that if you lost the war you would likely be tried for having carried out your duties, would, in my estimation, make you less likely to adhere to the niceties of war, if there are any such things, and would cause you to try to win at all costs under any circumstances."

Delmar T. Spivey

Major General Delmar T. Spivey, U.S.A.F.
Prisoner of War, 1943-1945 and senior officer of P.O.W. Camp of 9,500 officers
Chief, War Plans Division, U.S.A.F., 1949
Vice Commander, 5th Air Force, and Japan Air Defense Force
Commandant, Air War College, 1954
Superintendent, Culver Military Academy

"If I go out on the street and shoot and kill a man, I am justly tried for murder, as there is a law against murder. If, however, we are in war and I sight an enemy and shoot and kill him deliberately, I am doing my duty. And if I kill enough to make comment, I am decorated. Here lies the fundamental difference. There is no law to punish anyone for killing in war time. In war, we must obey the orders received from our commander. That is what we are trained to do. We would be court-martialled if we disobeyed. Everyone in service in World Wars I and II was responsible to higher authority, and was pledged to carry out all orders he received from that authority. There was never any law that required punishment of acts of war. So, the Nuremberg Trials were illegal—a reflection on discipline. I hold Admiral Doenitz in the highest esteem, and his trial and imprisonment were outrageous."

Rear Admiral John Wainwright, U.S.N.
Commanded Yangtse River Patrol, 1938
Commanded 3rd Battleship Division, 1940

John Wainwright
Rear Admiral

"I have long held firm views on the trials of military persons for what I always regarded as political 'crimes.' In fact, I felt so strongly on the matter that I asked to be excused as the proposed president of a military court-martial which was to try General Homma in Manila. I quite agree that the 'war crimes trials' following World War II set a very unfortunate precedent. Most definitely I did not subscribe to that post-war policy, and of course that includes the Doenitz trial."

Major General Robert S. Beightler, U.S.A.
Commanding General, 37th Infântry Division, 1940-1945
Commanding General, 5th Armored Division, 1948-1949
Director, Ohio Department of Highways
Executive Director and Member, Ohio Turnpike Commission

"Please add my commendations to those which you have already received for the excellent work being done to clarify the mystery of the 'International Military Tribunal.' It gives me great pleasure to endorse this movement and you can count on my support. From the first announcement of the 'trials,' I questioned the legality and endeavored to find from someone the basis upon which the body could legally function. To this date, I have as yet to be satisfied. I am convinced that the future morale of military personnel is in jeopardy as a result of these 'Trials'. This opinion is based upon conversations with both active and retired military personnel of this country and many foreign military friends and diplomats."

Major General Leigh Wade, U.S.A.F.
Commander, Air Base, San Antonio, Cuba, 1941-1946
Air Attache, U.S. Embassies at Athens and Rio de Janeiro, 1949-1953
Commander, Air Force Section, Joint Brazil-U.S. Military Commission, 1953-1955

"There appeals to me the awful furor that would have been raised had the tables been reversed and our enemies, by chance, had been victorious and, with or without trial, had imprisoned or hanged our commander in Europe for the alleged death of many innocents. Suppose they, under the same conditions, meted out like treatment to Mr. Churchill. Or in the Pacific, had the Japanese won, would General MacArthur and Admiral Nimitz been swung from a hanger's scaffold and Mr. Truman guillotined? God forbid. The very thought of such is terrifying, in the case of patriots who offered their lives for their country and, in so doing, brought about the death of non-combatants among the enemy. If there be such a thing as civilized warfare, the Allies were, in my opinion, guilty in some instances of betraying civilization. But to single out a few individual officers for punishment is not fair, just or sensible. An officer of any Government in time of war who does not use every means at his disposal to defeat his opponent on the field of battle, land, sea or air, is derelect in his duty. By the same token, any person who offers his life in the service of his country, in high position, with the knowledge that he may fill a convicted criminal's grave for doing his level best is, shall we say, exceptionally devoted, extraordinarily brave or just plain foolhardy. Why should any high officer be punished by a strong conqueror for something which in the winner's ranks would bring praise, decoration and promotion?"

Major General Frederick Gilbreath, U.S.A.
Commanding General, San Francisco Port of Embarkation, 1941-1944
Commanding General, South Pacific Base Command, 1944-1945
Commanding General, Army Service Command, 1945

"I have always felt that the Nuremberg trials were ill conceived and were not in any way based upon sound law, either international or domestic. I had the pleasure of listening to that great statesman, Senator Robert A. Taft, debate the Nuremberg trials with. . . Senator Fulbright, and it made a great impression upon me. It is inconceivable that anyone who believes in fundamental principles of fair play by the rule of law can justify the so-called War Crimes Trials at Nuremberg."

Loyd Wright, American attorney
Chairman, International Bar Association
Chairman, Commission on Government Security

"No one who has been in the naval service and understood what is meant by 'devotion to duty' can fail to have anything but sympathy for Grand Admiral Karl Doenitz. I shall always have doubts about the whole 'War Crimes Trials,' both in Germany and in Japan. I am unable to understand how one can try an officer for obeying orders or for doing his duty. It makes no difference what flag he fights under. To me, the War Crimes Trials of Nuremberg and elsewhere are one illustration of the greatest danger of our times: mass pressure based largely on little information and perilously close to mass hysteria. This mass pressure is in large measure based upon a sentimental, unrealistic, and dangerous interpretation of equality among men. I do not deny the excellence of the Roman and U.S. dream-ideal of 'equality before the law' and 'equality of opportunity' to serve and to demonstrate excellence. But this faith rests on a firm belief in the importance of 'quality' in human affairs. Plato held up the ideal of 'proportionate equality' as worthy of emulation. To me, this all boils down to cherishing whatever quality and whatever excellence appears in our society, our polity, our economy (including capital and labor), and, above all, in our cultural aspirations. Even the Marxists seem to realize that 'man does not live by bread alone.' "

George B. Fowler

George B. Fowler, Ph.D.
Professor of History, University of Pittsburgh
Member, Institute For Advanced Study, Princeton, 1953-1955

"I believe the 'Nuremberg' convictions set a dangerous precedent for high military commanders of the future...Once a nation is committed to war, the military commanders should proceed under the internationally accepted codes of war. But they must also do their 'utmost,' and thereby hangs a broad interpretation, and war being what it is, must inevitably lead to the adoption of ruthless measures. Admiral Doenitz appears to have inherited the odium, fancied or real, of his high military associates and suffered accordingly."

Rear Admiral Earl G. Rose, U.S. Coast Guard
Commodore, Greenland Patrol, 1943-1945
Commander, Task Force 24, 1945-1946
Chief of Operations, U.S. Coast Guard, 1946-1949

"As far as the Nuremberg Trials are concerned, I never was in sympathy with them—at least I never was in sympathy with placing on trial an officer who presumably was merely carrying out his orders."

Honorable Sinclair Weeks
U.S. Secretary of Commerce, 1953-1958

"You are authorized to use my name as an individual who agrees with Rear Admiral Gallery that these trials were a 'libel on the military profession' and, in certain instances, 'barefaced hypocrisy.' Since the beginning of time, nations at war have directed their efforts toward victory by overcoming the will to resist of their enemies and by depriving those enemies of the means with which to wage war. In furthering victory for the Allied Forces, the United States directed its submarine warfare on an 'unrestricted basis' and utilized its airpower, as did England, against centers of population as well as strictly military targets. If the Allies considered this use of their military forces compatible with attaining the ultimate objective of war, I find it most difficult to understand why certain military officers of the opposing forces should be charged with crimes against humanity and punished either by execution or imprisonment."

Lieutenant General Harold L. George, U.S.A.F.
Ass't. Chief of Staff for War Plans, A.A.F., 1941-1942
Commanding General, Air Transport Command, 1942-1946
Senior Air Force Representative, U.N. Military Staff Committee

"About the Nuremberg International Military Court, I must say that: it represents a setback in juridical order; a distortion of the concepts of our civilization; an unworthy attitude of the moral conscience of Western men. What was done in Nuremberg has the seal of the Orient, that vengeful spirit that practices 'a tooth for a tooth, an eye for an eye,' without remembering that Justice cannot seek vengeance...And were there criminals at Nuremberg? That is, were there on one side men who maintained social harmony (meaning human solidarity in relations among themselves), and on the other side men that deliberately disturbed that harmony? The answer is only one: on both sides, men involved in a struggle of life or death were breaking that harmony. Thus, in that immense conflict, there were no means of distinguishing among death of men on the battlefield, death in the bombings of cities or in concentration camps. All was death, all was ruin, all was massacre, all was annihilation. And there are Hiroshima and Nagasaki, with the thousands of innocents annihilated by the atomic bombs demanding (within the same Nuremberg spirit) that the authorities that ordered their use, and the pilots who carried and dropped them from above, and the scientists who manufactured them, all be included in the roll of war criminals. The truth is that Nuremberg's monstruous example is generating War Courts throughout the world. These courts, forgetting the two thousand years of Christian Civilization, revive the beastly Roman 'vae victis.' And there is Cuba, the recent example. Let us condemn Nuremberg. Let us condemn the trials where men can be tried for errors made as consequence of other errors; for justice presupposes that defense of social order against a disturbing agent of same, and not the revenge of a group of disturbing victors against other disturbing vanquished."

Ignacio Jose Verissimo, Marshal of the Army of Brazil
Commander, 5th and 8th Military Regions
Commander, 3rd Army

"It is quite obvious that the War Crimes Trials of 1946 and following were applying ex post facto law, if they were applying any law at all."

William Ernest Hocking, LL.D., Ph.D.
Alford Professor Emeritus of Harvard University
Chairman, Division of Philosophy and Psychology, Harvard

"In my opinion, the so-called War Crimes Trials, held at Nuremberg and elsewhere, must be considered a travesty of justice and a most unfortunate precedent in international law. No trial of vanquished by victors in the immediate aftermath of a great war which aroused the strongest passions could satisfy the standards of objective, impartial justice. A truly grotesque feature of the Nuremberg indictment was the inclusion of the charge that the Germans had massacred some thousands of Polish war prisoners in the Katyn Forest, whose bodies were discovered in the Spring of 1943. Actually the evidence is so overwhelming that the Soviet political police murdered these prisoners that the charge was left shamefacedly undecided, and nothing more was heard of it. In other cases, the Germans were charged with war crimes for procedures (submarine sinkings without warning) which were practiced by the United States and other Allied Powers. The question of how far a military or naval officer may disobey orders given by superior authority was raised without any satisfactory answer. What seems especially obnoxious about the so-called war crimes trials is that they set a precedent for ending every future war with a massacre of the leaders of the defeated side. No matter what the right or wrong may be as to the origin of the war, the victors now have a precedent for acting as judges in their own cause. There have already been threats in communist countries to try as 'war criminals' those who advocate defensive military measures in non-communist countries. There may be a case in abstract justice for an independent neutral tribunal that would condemn impartially all who have committed atrocities in the conduct of war (although in this age of weapons of mass destruction it would be a little hard to define 'atrocities'). This, however, seems impracticable. There is no case in law, morality or political expediency for setting up so-called courts of victors to pass pre-fabricated sentences on vanquished."

William Henry Chamberlin
Author and journalist
Correspondent of the *Christian Science Monitor* and *Wall Street Journal*

"All I can properly say is that the Allies had the monstrous precedent of the United States' trial and execution (August-November 1865) of Captain Henry Wirz, Army of The Confederate States of America, for alleged war crimes; and that this trial and execution violated both domestic and international law, in my opinion, and placed a stigma upon the honor of the United States."

William M. Robinson, Jr.
American civil engineer and author on the Civil War
Colonel, A.U.S.; built airfield on Guadalcanal, World War II

[To Grand Admiral Doenitz]

"...We have a saying in my country that when one is too close to the forest one cannot distinguish the individual trees. We are still comparatively close to the events of the Second World War and it will be many years yet before those events are reviewed by the calm dispassionate eye of the historian. But, when that day does come, I personally believe that your reputation as a Naval Officer and as a fighting Admiral will stand secure and established."

[To the Editors]

"...As a submarine Admiral whom I knew to be held in the deepest admiration and respect by Officers and Men of the U-Boat Fleet, I held Admiral Doenitz in respect myself, and there is no doubt that he handled his U-Boat Arm with masterly skill and efficiency. In return he was served with great loyalty."

(As Admiral 1951; Courtesy Imperial War Museum)

Yours Sincerely,
George Creasy.
A.F.

Admiral of the Fleet Sir George E. Creasy, G.C.B., C.B.E., D.S.O., M.V.O.
Director, Anti-Submarine Warfare, Naval Staff
Commanded battleship *Duke of York*
Rear Admiral of Submarines
Fifth Sea Lord, Vice-Chief of the Naval Staff
Commander-in-chief, Home Fleet
Allied commander-in-chief, Channel Command, N.A.T.O.

"...If we accept the justifications given for the trial of Doenitz, I as a professional military man, those of my colleagues in this country who have attained to positions related to planning, and military men in every other nation, however peaceful its aims and policies, who have planned for their nation's defense, are guilty with Doenitz of 'conspiring to wage aggressive war.' This is absurd...To try men for faithfully serving their countries as military commanders or staff officers is basically unjust. Obviously only those who serve defeated nations will be punished. Those who performed the same duties for the victors will continue to be acclaimed as heroes and patriots. This double standard is obviously unfair."

Brigadier General E. H. F. Svensson, U.S.A.
Chief, Planning Division, G-3, Dept. of the Army, 1955-1956
Chief, Military Mission to Turkey, 1956-1958

"I feel that the effective direction of the wartime Navy is the direct responsibility of the officer placed in charge of such operations, and it is his duty to perform this function to the best of his ability in the best interest of his country. To be punished or confined in prison for serving his country in such a manner would place all responsible commanders of the nations fighting to achieve victory in a position subject to conviction. I do not believe this action is in conformity with the rules of warfare."

Vice Admiral Richard F. Whitehead, U.S.N.
Commander, Support Aircraft, Pacific Fleet, World War II
Chief, U.S. Naval Mission to Brazil, 1952

"I consider that the condemnation as 'war criminals' of those such as chiefs of the Armed Services who served their country with patriotic decision and sublime heroism, enduring the lamentable consequences which wars carry in their wake, was a sad and reprehensible episode of the Second World War. The unjustified and unfortunate Nuremberg Trials will always afflict the conscience of the victors. May there go out to Grand Admiral Karl Doenitz, Commander-in-Chief of the German Navy, who has been made even more glorious by the martyrdom which he suffered, our fervent admiration."

Hon. Alberto Freundt Rosell, Republic of Peru
Professor of Criminal Law, San Marcos University, 1922-1940
Dean of Faculty and Economics, 1940
Minister of Foreign Affairs, Minister of Justice
Peruvian Ambassador to England, and to Brazil

"In *Victors' Justice* I pointed out nearly 25 years ago some legal, moral, and practical objections to the trials of Germans and Japanese in victor courts that were held after the defeat of Germany and Japan in 1945. Since then I have learned of many more. It is on this account that I venture to say a few words about the trial, conviction, and imprisonment of Grand-Admiral Karl Doenitz.

"Admiral Doenitz was accused of having promoted preparations for aggressive war. As the late Captain Russell Grenfell, of the British Royal Navy, stated in the witness-box at the trial before an American court at Nuremberg of Admiral Schneewind, every allied government employed officers who 'promoted preparations for' war, and neither any such officer nor anybody else could tell during those preparations that the coming war was not going to be 'aggressive.' Largely on this evidence, Admiral Schneewind was acquitted, and the precedent which had been set up earlier by the international military tribunal at Nuremberg in finding Admiral Doenitz guilty was set aside. Admiral Doenitz was pronounced guilty of 'having waged aggressive war.'

"The tribunal did not bother to show that any naval officer anywhere had ever won praise and approval for refusing to fight for his country on the plea that the war in which his country was engaged was 'aggressive' or that for a sailor or soldier to engage in war when ordered had been till that moment, whatever the circumstances, a crime, or that it was even then a crime for anybody except a German.

"Admiral Doenitz...was sentenced to ten years' imprisonment, and with other Germans similarly sentenced by the international military tribunal was sent to Spandau. Germans and Japanese detained by the victors elsewhere had portions of their sentences remitted. For instance, the United States government began putting prisoners of this character on parole in 1950. The Australian government released prisoners who had completed one-third of their term or, if the sentence was for life, after ten years. Admiral Doenitz was made to serve the full ten years to which he had been sentenced. Indeed, he was detained longer still. For whereas the length of sentence ran for all other 'war crimes' detainees from the date they were taken into custody, his was declared to run only from the day he was sentenced. Thus he may be said to have been the victim of a double abuse of justice, once in being tried and pronounced guilty, and a second time in being detained for about a year and a half longer than a convict under similar sentence would have remained in any other prison.

"The case of Grand-Admiral Doenitz shows very well how deplorable it is that the general assembly of the United Nations should have attempted to get the iniquities of the Nuremberg trial repeated at the end of any future war in which a member-state of the United Nations is victorious. In 1951 the general assembly caused to be drawn up (*a*) a code of international offences against the peace and security of mankind, and (*b*) the draft statute of a court of international criminal justice, both modelled on the Nuremberg international military tribunal and its charter. The two documents rest in a pigeon-hole ready to be applied if the opportunity offers."

Montgomery Belgion
English author and journalist
Editor, *N.Y. Herald* (European edition), World War I
Staff, *London Daily Mail, Westminster Gazette*
Secretary, Westwood House School Trust

Montgomery Belgion

"I have no hesitancy in stating that I have always considered that the trials in general, and that of Admiral Doenitz in particular, created a deplorable precedent with implications concerning the conduct of any future war by our leaders, both civilian and military, that are dreadful to contemplate. That unrestricted submarine warfare was recognized as the only practicable type was evident in the conduct of the war by all the navies involved. Certainly our own navy gave every evidence of the unrestricted nature of our submarine operations against the Japanese. We of course had no way of learning what would have been the fate of our leaders had we had the misfortune to be defeated in the war. Perhaps the best lesson to be learned is that we can ill afford to be on the losing side."

Vice Admiral John W. Roper, U.S.N.
Commanded U.S.S. *Wisconsin,* World War II
Chief of Naval Personnel, 1949
Commander, Cruiser-Destroyer Force, Pacific Fleet, 1951

"I am glad to see an attempt to bring some clear thinking upon the Nuremberg trials. It is one thing to prosecute for atrocities and quite another for waging aggressive war. I spent some three months in the winter of 1945-46 in Tokyo studying the war crimes prosecutions there. I resigned because of the illness of my sister, but just about the time I was coming to the conclusion that we were wrong. There was no substantial evidence of atrocities in those cases. We were in effect prosecuting the leaders of the state for waging aggressive war. I remember coming upon the interesting bit of information that at Paris in 1919 when there was a great cry to try and hang the Kaiser, that our delegation, and curiously enough the Japanese, said there was no warrant in international law for such a prosecution. If a state is sovereign, then it follows that its leaders must take the course which seems best for it."

Hon. Amos Walter Wright Woodcock
Counsellor-at-Law and Brigadier General, A.U.S.
U.S. Attorney, District of Maryland
Special Assistant to the Attorney General of the United States
Attorney in Prosecution of Japanese "War Criminals," 1945-1946
President, St. John's College

"My opinion is that an officer who carries out his duty in accordance with directions from his Government can be dealt with as a prisoner of war, but not as a 'criminal prisoner.' "

Major General Birger Ljungberg, Royal Norwegian Army
Minister of Defense, Labor Government, 1939-1942
Representative of Norwegian Defense Dept. in the U.S., 1943

"I have never accepted the concept of 'war criminals,' nor can I do so now. The only crimes which can be defined are ordinary civil crimes; in wars, those who, in fulfillment of their duties, produce victims among civilian populations cannot be defined as criminals. In future wars, this tragedy will be even more accentuated and it will not be just that the conquered be judged for deeds and acts which are inherent in modern warfare, and for the incidents which occur therein common to victors and vanquished alike, and therefore of equal responsibility to both."

Admiral Don Alfonso Arriaga Adam of the Spanish Navy
Commanded torpedo boats, destroyers, and cruisers
Commandant, Naval Base at the Canary Islands
Chief of Staff of the Spanish Navy, 1942-1951

"As between victors and vanquished, it is hard to draw the line between justice and vengeance. If vengeance, over and above that inflicted in the course of hostilities, is merited, a court of justice is not the best instrument to carry out the same. For to the difficulty of securing unbiased judges from among the belligerents, is added that of persuading other peoples than the victors that the proceedings are impartial; and unless neutrals and vanquished are satisfied that the tribunal is impartial, its decisions will carry little more conviction than does a political trial behind the Iron Curtain. Hardly less troublesome is the question of what is a justiceable war crime. Although 'aggression' is presumably under the ban, since the leading governments have renounced war as an instrument of policy, elaborate defense preparations are still considered essential. Where does defense end and aggression begin? It is not necessarily the first shot that creates aggression...To my mind, in point of fact, the aggressor will always be the losing party. War is collective action. To single out individuals for punishment is in general unrealistic and unfair. Those who make the decision to engage in hostilities are subject to the general political atmosphere in the country which they govern. Military, naval and other officials of the government are carrying out orders. If they ceased to do so, anarchy would result...From the foregoing, it will be plain that...I view Grand Admiral Doenitz's condemnation and punishment very much askance."

Hon. John Campbell White, American diplomat
U.S. Minister and Ambassador to Haiti, 1940-1944
U.S. Ambassador to Peru, 1944-1945

"Permit me to join you and the host of career soldiers, sailors and airmen in condemning the tragic hypocrisy engendered at the Nuremberg 'war crimes trials'. Nothing in history has so libeled the military profession or so detracted from its ethic purity. The principle of military thought and action, as a precedent established at the Nuremberg trials, if permitted to perpetuate, would destroy our traditional ideals of patriotism and our sworn adherence to 'duty, honor, country.' The professional soldier has nothing but abhorrence for the violation of our constitutional principles and the travesty on international law flaunted at the Nuremberg trials of career officers —whose only 'crime' was professional competency and patriotic zeal. These trials were, of course, highlighted by the case of Grand Admiral Karl Doenitz. As a professional soldier, I can only hope that Admiral Doenitz may know that American military men feel respect and admiration for his courage, his convictions, his ability, and his dynamic leadership."

E. K. Wright

Major General E. K. Wright, U.S.A.
Chief, Armored Section, 12th Army Group, 1943-1945
Deputy Director, Central Intelligence Agency, 1946-1949
Commanding General, 6th Infantry Division

"It seems rather pathetic to apologize to a man after he has been hanged. For certainly ten years imprisonment was a crime, and its moral effect on the submarine service can never be measured. The acceptance of the submarine as a weapon of war naturally accepted the fact that its success depended upon secrecy of action, without which it was doomed. Those that go to sea in time of war, whether as passengers or crew, do so with the knowledge that their carrier is definitely a legitimate target for the enemy and accept those terms before embarking. How the War Crimes Trials ever got into being, I know not, but if you destroy the 'unrestricted warfare of the submarine,' you might as well plant them in mothballs, not temporarily but forever. I could never condone the Atom Bombs on defenseless cities (Hiroshima). Ships at sea are a wartime target of the enemy and naturally become targets for destruction. 'War is Hell.' "

Rear Admiral Charles R. Train, U.S.N.
Commanded U.S.S. *Henderson* and *Utah*
Naval Aide to President Herbert Hoover
Commander, Cruiser Division 3, and Battleship Division 2, Battle Force

"I considered the Nuremberg Trials unjust for condemning the conquered Admirals as war criminals when, in reality, they did nothing other than defend their country with acknowledged patriotism, and putting all of their professional skill in the service of a struggle in which none of the factions was unduly concerned with respecting International Laws, due to the new methods made necessary by what has been defined as 'Total War.' In my opinion, we have returned to the era whose motto was 'woe to the vanquished,' and we should remember that Rome had to suffer the terrible consequences of what she herself had imposed."

Vice Admiral Carlos Torres Hevia
Navy of the Republic of Chile

"Since the Government of the Soviet Union took part in the proceedings of the International Military Tribunal of Nuremberg, which Government itself is guilty of the most weighty international crimes, recognized as such by civilized humanity, the judgements of this court are null and void. Consequently, the Governments of France, Great Britain and the United States of America have the duty to initiate the revision and annulment of the Nuremberg judgements which were rendered with the collaboration of the Government of the Soviet Union. For this purpose, the Governments mentioned, with the exclusion of the Soviet Union, ought to form an International Court of Cassation *ad hoch* and institute suitable proceedings in it. In any case, the persons who are still serving sentence and those who still have their freedom restricted on the basis of the above judgements of the International Military Tribunal, should be immediately set free."

Hon. Dr. Stasys Lozoraitis
Foreign Minister of the Republic of Lithuania
Head of the Diplomatic Corps of Lithuania

"In my opinion, the war crimes trials were a serious and sad mistake. I regard them as an example of post-war hysteria. They have no relationship with justice as I have been taught to regard justice. Punitive justice should have two objects in view. One, to remove from society a person who has clearly demonstrated that he is unfit to remain in a civilized community and, two, to furnish an example which will deter others from committing similar offenses. Neither of these objects would apply to those who gave their utmost effort in winning the war for their country. I am sure that the judges at those trials would now be among the first to condemn any of their own countrymen for not doing their utmost for their country in a war. Any man in a high position who did not do so should be charged as a traitor. As to acting as a deterrent for the future, I certainly hope that no citizen of the United States would let the results of the Nuremberg trials keep him from doing his utmost in case of war for fear of punishment after the war. The very idea of that makes traitors of us all."

Major General Frank O. Bowman, U.S.A.
Engineering officer, 2nd Corps and 5th Army, World War II
Commanding General, Fort Leonard Wood and 6th Armored Division

"International Law does not contemplate the formation of a tribunal similar to the one at Nuremberg, and there are no precedents in the history of the world of any other similar tribunals. The fact that a treaty was drawn up between Great Britain, the United States, France, and Russia is what served as the basis of the formation of the *sui-generis* 'International Military Tribunal' which was not provided for in international law, nor much less were the rules and procedures followed during the course of the proceedings.

"The campaign of the German Navy which Grand Admiral Doenitz directed, filled me with admiration, because it made manifest the capacity of the Navy of his country, the fruit of rigorous training which the same Grand Admiral knew how to plan. Concerning the 'unrestricted warfare' which the German submarine force waged almost from the beginning of the war, this should be termed a military necessity, bearing in mind the experience of World War I and the progress made in electronic equipment for the detection of submarines, as well as the use of the airplane together with the ships which formed the anti-submarine task forces. If despite this unrestricted warfare (which was also employed by the U.S. Navy in the Pacific) there were months towards the end of the war in which the German submarine losses were greater in number than the number of Allied ships sunk, then, militarily speaking, one could ill ask of the submarine commanders a greater risking of their units in order to wage a more humane war. This is so sure a fact that the U.S. submarine forces acted in exactly the same manner. Their campaign in the Pacific equaled or perhaps surpassed the initial successes of the German submarines in the Atlantic.

"Thus it is not possible to brand as a 'war criminal' a man who had the professional obligation of leading his country on the path of the triumph of its arms. During the Nuremberg trials, Keitel, Jodl and Doenitz stated that they had acted simply as soldiers and not as politicians. Their inclusion as exponents of the policies of Hitler in his 'aggressive war' is solely due to the fact that article eight of the 'Charter of the Tribunal' stated that, 'If an accused asserts that he acted in fulfillment of an order of his government or of his superior, this does not free him from guilt.' In the military order, this article destroys the basic principles of discipline. Since it creates the fear of future liability, subordinates might even go so far as not to respect orders, this carrying with it the consequent chaos in the operations which superiors might have planned."

Rear Admiral Arturo Jimenez Pacheco, Peruvian Navy
Commanded various ships, including a frigate, submarine and cruiser
Chief of Staff, Navy of Peru
Member, Council of State, and Brazilian Border Commission

"Grand Admiral Doenitz was a military man of profession. His duty was to work for his country and for the German Navy. From an officer, it is required that he keep his officers' oath. That has Grand Admiral Doenitz done, and therefore we cannot understand the judgement of the 'International Military Tribunal' at Nuremberg other than as a renewal of the old way of thinking, 'woe to the vanquished,' not worthy of any civilized nation."

Major General L. Melander, Army of Finland
Chief, 2nd Dept., General Staff, 1937-1942
Commander-in-Chief, Finnish Cavalry, 1942-1945

"The Nuremberg War Tribunal was unique in the world's history in that the greatest criminals, being honorably victorious, were sitting at the table of judges, together with the distinguished jurists of the Free World..."

Dr. Kazys Pakstas
Professor of Geography, University of Lithuania
Professor of Soviet Geopolitics, U.S. Army Language School
Professor of Economic Geography, Duquesne University

"With regard to the [trial of Admiral Doenitz], I believe that he was a much maligned officer who, under difficult circumstances, did an outstanding job as his country's naval Commander-in-Chief. Had the Germans won, and had they used the same standards as did we in selecting war criminals for trial—then certainly Admirals King, Nimitz and Lockwood would have been high on their list. Indeed I think the same reasoning applies in the cases of most of the high-ranking officers who were brought to trial..."

Vice Admiral Felix Johnson, U.S.N.
Ass't. Chief of Staff, South Pacific Force, World War II
Commander, Destroyer Force, U.S. Atlantic Fleet, 1948-1949
Director of Naval Intelligence, 1949-1952

[To Grand Admiral Doenitz]

"The conduct of the Nuremberg 'trials' is a disgraceful episode of which real Americans must be ashamed, and the execution and imprisonment of German military leaders and industrialists...is a blot on our national integrity. You, Admiral Doenitz, commanded honorably and well. We regret that your services to your country unjustly led to years of prison as vengeance by those who would ruin our civilization."

Frank H. Cunningham, Litt.D., Ph.D., LL.D., Ed.D.
American educator, author and editor
Vice President, Sequoia University

[To Grand Admiral Doenitz]

"As one who has served in two wars, I must admit that to me the 'war crimes trials' of officers of the Army, Navy and Air Force were very shocking. I, like a good many others, wonder what is meant by 'aggressive war.' As far as I know, the sole purpose of a war from any country's standpoint is to win it. The only difference between a war criminal and a war hero, evidently, is that the latter won. Due to the concepts as established after World War II, the future of military leaders on the losing side is indeed bleak. I don't know whether it is any consolation to you to know that a great many who served in the war feel the same way I do. During WWII I served entirely in the Pacific. If our brand of submarine warfare was anything but 'aggressive,' I am amazed. We had a job to do and we did it. Best of luck."

Major General L. J. Sverdrup, U.S.A.R.
Commanding General, Engineer Construction Command, Southwest Pacific Area, World War II
Commanding General, 102nd Infantry Division, 1946-1957

"As a student of history, politics and military science for more than half a century, I am delighted to express my satisfaction over the release of Grand Admiral Karl Doenitz...In the eagerness of the American People to rearm Germany as a defense of themselves just ten years after the trials of German officers and patriots, I see the worst condemnation of this country to be found in its history."

Hon. Jennings C. Wise
Colonel, 80th Division, A.E.F., World War I
Counsel for the U.S. Mixed Claims Commission, 1921-1923
Ass't. U.S. Attorney General
Author of many books

"Without recounting the generally recognized lack of authorization or precedent in international law, the ex post facto concepts involved, and the violation of Anglo-American constitutional principles, I consider the trial of professional military men for planning and waging war in the service of their country in World War II, as a travesty of justice...I consider Admiral Doenitz to have been the victim of an emotional aberration on the part of the victorious allies that has established a precedent which will return to plague us again and again in future years."

Rear Admiral Clifford E. Van Hook, U.S.N.
Commander, Panama Sea Frontier, 1942-1943
Deputy Commander, 7th Fleet, 1943-1945
Commander, U.S. Naval Forces, Australia-New Guinea, 1945-1946

"In warfare the so-called 'Law' of 'Necessity' frequently supercedes international law and as a result many wrongs may be committed. After World War II the victors could set up what they considered to be the 'Law' of 'Right and Wrong.' Apparently those people who were tried and in many cases punished, were measured by this 'Law.' Such a 'Law' was not a 'Law' in the accepted sense of the word, but it was more of an accepted sense of 'Public Opinion...' "

Rear Admiral Percy W. Foote, U.S.N.
Commander, Destroyer Division 26, 1921
Commanded, U.S.S. *Arkansas,* 1931-1933
Commissioner, Pennsylvania Motor Police, 1937-1939
Inspector of Naval Material, Houston District, 1942

"We deeply regret the fact that any of our United States citizens had any part in those Trials during which Admiral Doenitz, an honorable soldier, carrying out his orders and effectively leading the naval arm of his nation at war, was illegally sentenced to a term in Spandau Prison, West Berlin."

Margaret Hopkins Worrell, LL.B., LL.M.
National President, Ladies of the Grand Army of the Republic
Judge (for 21 years), Probate Court, Dept. of the Interior (Indian Claims)
Organizer, Federal Employees Union, and League of the American Civil Service

"Your interesting endeavour would be of only academic significance if the object were not the criticism of a dangerous precedent, and in particular, to do justice to Grand Admiral Doenitz, classified by a law of circumstance among the war criminals. I suppose that you have set your sights higher and that you seek to find a means of avoiding these errors in the future...I could have limited myself to giving my approbation to the editorial in the *Chicago Daily Tribune*. However I thought that the opinion of a neutral would add nothing to the testimony of high *Allied* personalities who have refused to associate themselves with an action of their own countries, a testimony which does them honor."

Colonel Alfred-Ernest Lederrey, Army of Switzerland
Commander, 3rd Mountain Brigade, 1938-1946
Inspector, 2nd Army Corps, 1938-1953
Professor of military history and author of five books

"I know of no legitimate or good reason why Admiral Doenitz should have been punished for his actions during World War II. He carried on to the end of the Hitler Regime in accordance with the training of the Naval Profession. If a naval officer does otherwise, his oath and training are not worth anything. Admiral Doenitz is not the first, and probably won't be the last, to suffer for supporting his government to the last."

Commodore Thomas E. Van Metre, U.S.N.
Commander, Destroyer Squadrons 7, 11 and 26, 1938-1941
Deputy Naval Inspector General, 1942-1945

"In my opinion, there was no legal principle, and no moral justification, upon which to base the 'War Crimes Trials,' before the 'International Military Tribunal,' in the case of Admiral Doenitz, or any other military or naval officer whose 'crime' was the effective prosecution of his sworn duty to his country. To recognize any such principle of law would be to make a debating society of the military service of any country, including our own, where the officers would have the right to determine whether or not orders received by them were to be obeyed. I feel that the actions of the Allied leaders at the time were dictated by anger and not by statesmanship. They lost sight of some fundamentals. We had been taught from the first day of entrance into the service that orders from our government were binding upon us under all circumstances and without question. Such, also, is the gist of our oath of office as officers. The only safe ground for the military is embodied in the toast, 'my country, may she always be right, but right or wrong, my country.' If the naval treaty, signed by a few of the powers involved, against unrestricted submarine warfare in relation to merchant vessels, were to be construed as affording a basis for some action against individuals conducting unrestricted submarine warfare, the question arises as to why it did not apply to both sides. We conducted such warfare in the Pacific during the war. Certainly, there was no international law upon which to base such trials. There are only a few principles of international law upon which there is wide agreement, and no court, or other agency, for the enforcement of those few principles. Some had hoped that the Court of International Justice at the Hague would someday have prestige enough to partially supply this deficiency, but not so. It seems to me that our position was untenable. It seems to me that the action taken against Admiral Doenitz, and other military officers whose 'crimes' were the prosecution of their duties, was not only without precedent but was a mistake. This precedent, if followed, will result in the trials, by the winners, of all military leaders on the losing side in wars of the future, no matter which side is the aggressor or in the wrong. Each side always calls the other the aggressor, regardless of the facts. Early in the Korean War, when our forces were desperately pressed on the defensive and the North Koreans were at the crest of their offensive, some press dispatches reported that the North Koreans threatened to bring our military officers to trial, when captured, for waging aggressive warfare. It seems to me that the entire episode of the war crimes trials of military officers constitutes an undesirable precedent."

F L Lowe

Vice Admiral F. L. Lowe, U.S.N.
Commanded heavy cruiser, South Pacific, 1942-1943
Member, Logistics Committee, Joint Chiefs of Staff, 1943-1944
Ass't. Judge Advocate General of the Navy, 1944-1945

"Certainly no regular military officer would want to be judged on an ex post facto basis for executing the lawful orders of a superior when they comply with the customs of the times."

Preston V. Mercer
R Adm. U S N (Ret.)

Rear Admiral Preston V. Mercer, U.S.N.
Ass't. Chief of Staff, U.S. Pacific Fleet, World War II
Commander, Destroyer Squadrons 1 and 54
Member, Joint War Plans Committee, Office of the C.N.O.

"War, because of its violence and destruction was not able, nor is it able, nor will it be able, to be tolerable in the normal development of relations between civilized men. But we also know that war is inevitable, just as passions in the world are inevitable. Centuries ago, efforts were made to humanize war, and international agreements which were based on chivalry and generosity towards the vanquished strived to do this. Already in the 19th century, it was possible to confirm that to all the evils of war there was united the advantage of a greater effort during wartime to obtain positive progress in science and industry which had manifestations later in practical peacetime applications. For example, there is no doubt that some campaigns of Napoleon contributed to the deciphering of the secrets of ancient civilizations (as in Egypt), and that motors, steels, aviation and natural energies were placed at the disposal of normal peacetime life after achieving positive advances in the two world wars. That is to say that if war had continued to be a noble contest between chivalrous enemies, it would not have brought only devastation and ruin. But from the moment that the conquered was treated like a slave and all kinds of humiliations and penalties imposed, there disappeared in war that chivalry which was so necessary to humanize it, and we have retrogressed many centuries in the concept of the struggle to defend sacred ideals. What happened at the end of the last World War in the Nuremberg Trials is monstrous, as is the very name of 'war criminal' when such a designation is pronounced by the victors over the vanquished. The only thing achieved by such a system is to indefinitely prolong the hatreds which every war leaves behind it in the inevitable wake of the violent struggle. Modern means of destruction will someday be able to bring an end to humanity if the execrable methods of persecution and vengeance against the vanquished are not abandoned."

Lieutenant General Emilio Esteban-Infantes Martin
Chief of the General Staff of the Army of Spain

"I sympathize with critics of the 'Nuremberg Trials.' "

Carlton J. H. Hayes
American historian and diplomat
U.S. Ambassador to Spain, 1942-1944

“Now that the second World War begins to recede into the past and the clouds of prejudice conjured up by the propaganda to disperse, there must be few persons with any claim to objective thinking who would seriously maintain the legality of the condemnation of Admiral Doenitz and the other ‘German Major War Criminals’ in Nuremberg.

“This is not the place to elaborate the reasons why the process as conducted by the International Military Tribunal must be regarded as lacking in every element of justice. Suffice it to point out that—

1) According to the principles of international law universally recognized up to 1945 and explicitly admitted by the Allied and Associated Powers after the first World War, the Allies had no jurisdiction over the citizens of another sovereign state for acts done in the service of that state.

2) The ‘crimes’ for which the accused were sentenced had for the most part never been declared to be crimes at the time of their committal. The sentences were thus in flagrant violation of the Rule of Law as embodied in the legislation of every civilized country. Incidentally, violation of the Rule of Law by condemnation for acts not previously declared by law to be crimes was one of the offenses with which the defendants in Nuremberg were charged.

3) The Tribunal was composed of citizens of the states which had been engaged in a life-and-death struggle with the state to which the accused belonged. But, in the words of the distinguished jurist and theologian Father Salvatore Lener S.J., ‘he who judges in his own case is not only a *suspect* and therefore a *challengeable* judge; he is simply not a judge. If he sits as judge, the illegality of the process and the nullity of the sentence are absolute and incurable.’

4) The Tribunal condemned the accused for acts ‘contrary to the laws of war’ committed by Germans, while refusing to allow evidence or even mention of precisely similar acts committed by members of the Allied forces,—or by Allied statesmen.

5) The Charter of the Tribunal abolished the rules of evidence which in every civilized country have been introduced for the protection of accused persons against prejudiced and unreliable assertions. The Tribunal consequently admitted to the prejudice of the accused a mass of unsubstantiated malicious rumour in the form of written depositions while refusing to the defendants the elementary right of putting the deponents to the test by cross-examination.

“It would be possible to continue to enumerate instances of the injustice of the proceedings of the tribunal to an almost unlimited extent. I prefer, however, to cite a phrase of Mr. Justice Jackson, the American Chief of Prosecution, as proof that even those responsible for the conduct of the Tribunal were aware of its transgression of the canons of justice:— ‘One of the reasons this was a military tribunal, instead of an ordinary court of law, was in order to avoid the precedent-creating effect of what is done here on our own law.’ [*Trial of the Major War Criminals,* Vol. III, p. 543].

“In other words, not even those to be charged in the future with the gravest crimes were to be deprived of the legal protection which was denied to the statesmen, soldiers and sailors of a defeated Germany. Innumerable injustices were done in the course of the month-long process in Nuremberg; none were more scandalous than those inflicted on Grand Admiral Doenitz, against whom no charge was ever brought forward except that of doing his duty to his country. It must be a matter of satisfaction to any man with a sense of justice to know that he is at last free; it can only be regretted that his release was not accompanied by any expression of regret for the unjustifiability of his imprisonment."

Hon. Charles Bewley, S.C.
Irish jurist and statesman
Member, Inner Bar of Irish Free State, 1926
Irish minister to the Vatican, and Germany
Author of numerous books

"It has been a long time since I expressed my opinion on the illegal and regrettable trials at Nuremberg. In 1948 I translated, from the English, General J.F.C. Fuller's book, *Armament and History*. At that time I wrote a long preface in which I stated the following: 'In this vertical decline of morality, is it permitted to a soldier to point out that only the soldiers, in the last conflict, knew how to respect the laws of war...Even at the hardest moments, the armies in the field behaved correctly toward their adversaries, caring for the wounded, no matter who they were, humanely treating the prisoners...' And this is why one understands General Fuller when he writes, 'I energetically protest against the condemnation, as war criminals, of the conquered generals...In effect, there is no doubt that in ordering the destruction of large enemy cities, which represented an important part of the very basis of European culture and civilization, the Allied political leaders have incurred a dire responsibility before the bar of history.' My opinion has not changed today. Churchill and Roosevelt deserved as much as Hitler, and certainly a great deal more than Doenitz, to pass in judgment before the tribunal of human civilization. The bombings of Cologne, of Dresden and Aix-la-Chapelle were not only military stupidities, they were also evil acts.

"To get back to the case of German military leaders, their trials were a scandal, because if the conquered leaders are automatically brought to trial, where are we going? Who will want to command? And I should like to point out here the difference in attitude at Nuremberg of the American admirals and of the American generals. The American admirals were courageous. They defended their German counterparts and saved their lives. Why didn't the generals of the ground armies do as much? They behaved contemptibly, because I don't think that the German ground armies committed any crimes...But this old story also proves that never since the times of barbarism has the moral level of humanity fallen so low, an ineluctable consequence of the de-christianization of the West, begun in the 18th century, and which will soon make us all slaves of Communist, materialist imperialism."

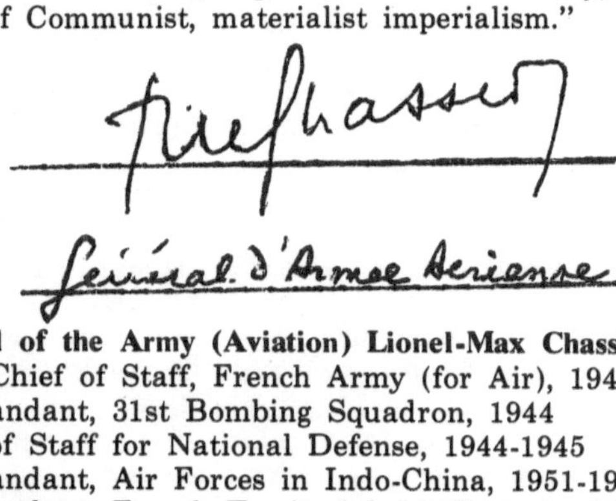

General of the Army (Aviation) Lionel-Max Chassin
Ass't. Chief of Staff, French Army (for Air), 1943
Commandant, 31st Bombing Squadron, 1944
Chief of Staff for National Defense, 1944-1945
Commandant, Air Forces in Indo-China, 1951-1953
Commandant, French Territorial Air Defense, 1953-1956
Coordinator, European Air Defense, 1956-1957
Author, numerous works on military history

"I believe that the expression of my modest opinion on the unjust condemnation of Grand Admiral Doenitz is an act of professional apology to the Grand Admiral, sentiments which, I am sure, every true professional shares...I had to admire the performance of the German soldiers and sailors, patriotic, brave, daring, efficient and self-sacrificing...In both capacities, as a military man and as a political personage, Doenitz acted as a skillful professional, valiant and patriotic, as would have acted—in analogous circumstances—any general or admiral of the Allied Powers, who had moral fibre, that is to say, sentiments of the responsibility of his charge, with honor, abnegation and the spirit of sacrifice, dignity and love of country.

"I consider it an affront that Allied jurisconsults and lawyers of the four large conquering powers concocted the new and unusual laws of war which made possible the sadly infamous Tribunal of Nuremberg...I don't believe that the punishment decreed by them for the Grand Admiral...constitutes a badge of pride and evidences a spirit of justice on the part of those who engaged in it, as well as for the high military chiefs, of the Army as well as the Navy and Air Force, who permitted such persecutory criminal treatment to which Doenitz was subjected during the proceedings, incompatible with the dignity of the high military office of one who had valiantly battled opposite them, not under the pressure of the political power but, above all, imbued with the sentiment of military duty of every commander of troops in the face of the enemy.

"There can be no doubt that from the military point of view the sentence of the Nuremberg Tribunal against Grand Admiral Doenitz carries with it, on the one hand, a confusion in the high commands with respect to the principle of authority in all its vast scale. On the other hand, each ranking commander of troops in the future, this dire precedent having been set, will try to evade his responsibility in order not to be judged as a war criminal in case that the war causes a failure of his campaign, with which will come chaos in the conduct of the overall plans of the war, or will induce these same senior commanders to conduct their operations in a cruel form...in order that a defeat of arms will not lead them to legal proceedings by the victors. In other words, they will not fight for love of country but for the egoistic principle of saving their own lives once peace has been established, for it is now doctrine that a senior officer, once the war is over, may be converted into a hero who is showered with honors and praises by his people, or into a war criminal who will be humiliated and persecuted, condemned to the infamous punishment of the gallows or years in a harsh prison, all according to whether he be victor or vanquished.

"Once hostilities have been entered upon, it is no longer either possible or fitting to deliberate concerning the complex circumstances of every kind which unfortunately involve nations in war and that, in every case, the justice of the cause for which it is being fought is proclaimed before their own people.

"I hope that this brief comment by a general of a Republic, small in size but large in sentiments of democracy and justice, and with a military tradition of which one can well be proud, will be considered as an expression of respect, admiration and affection for Grand Admiral Doenitz for his unjust imprisonment of 10 years as a war criminal, a punishment which, far from constituting an affront to him, is a badge of merit and an escutcheon of pride, not only for him but also for his family and for the institution which he commanded with honor professional capability and self-sacrifice."

General Humberto Benedetti Miranda, Peruvian Army
Commanding General, Infantry Regiment *Maipo,* 1932-1934
Intendant, Province of Valparaiso, 1938
Chief of the General Staff, Army of Peru, 1941

"You have again solicited my views on the legality and propriety of the War Crimes Trials which followed World War II. While I appreciate your invitation to comment I do not think I can add, either a new point of view or new arguments, to that widely discussed and unprecedented procedure. The *ex post facto* concept is of course illegal in our field of jurisprudence. It is my opinion that the procedures followed at Nuremberg and Tokyo were based on that concept. That those trials were international in character does to me appear to legalize a deviation from our national law. For two years I served as Commander, U.S. Naval Forces Germany; I met and became friends of several former senior German naval officers. I cannot now think of any single act of the Allied Powers that created more resentment among those officers than the conviction and imprisonment of former Grand Admiral Doenitz."

Vice Admiral Howard E. Orem, U.S.N.
Director of International Affairs, Office of the C.N.O., 1949-1950
Commander, Amphibious Group 4, U.S. Atlantic Fleet, 1951-1952
Director of Research, Stevens Institute of Technology

"...the trial of Admiral Doenitz has served to bring into relief the question whether the purely professional direction of a fighting service in war by its head can be construed a war crime without some significant evidence that such direction has elements which bring it within the definition of 'crime' as recognized in an International Military Court. Ruthlessness is generally regarded as an essential ingredient in the make up of a soldier who is fighting in the interest of his country...it should not expose its possessor to trial."

Major General Anton Muttukumaru, O.B.E., Army of Ceylon (Sri Lanka)
Advocate, Supreme Court of Ceylon, 1934-1939, 1946-1948
Commander of the Army, 1955-1959
High Commissioner in Pakistan, 1960-1962
Ambassador to Iraq, Iran, Australia, New Zealand, and U.A.R., currently accredited to Yugoslavia, Lebanon, Sudan, Jordan

"The Nuremberg proceeding was a grave error. In effect, whether we like it or not, we are in an age of 'total war,' on land, sea, and in the air. It is therefore inadmissible that military leaders who hold high command in time of war, should afterwards be treated as 'war criminals,' and defined as such before specially set up tribunals, for the sole fact of having carried out in this capacity the general orders resulting from the war policy of their government.

"The trial of Admiral Doenitz was in this respect an error of especial gravity. Unrestricted submarine warfare was practiced in the course of the war not only by Germany but also by the Allies themselves. In any case, it was less savage than the frightful destruction which was carried out by the American Air Force, merely for experimental purposes, on the highly-populated Japanese cities of Hiroshima and Nagasaki with the first atom bombs, at a time when Japan had virtually decided to surrender unconditionally (August 1945)."

Admiral Jean Decoux
Commander-in-Chief, French Naval Forces in Far East (1939-1940)
Governor-General of French Indo-China, and High Commissioner of France in the Pacific (1940-1944)

"...I think that the trials of the War Leaders because they were the Leaders were as great a mistake as a so-called civilized nation could make. I know that I was not alone in this attitude. I believe that General Eichelberger, commander of the Eighth Army, with whom I was fairly closely associated, had substantially the same view. In prosecuting these trials we did no good for ourselves and we set an exceedingly dangerous precedent for the future."

Rear Admiral Paulus P. Powell, U.S.N.
Commanded various task forces in Pacific, World War II
Chief of Staff, 3rd Amphibious Force
White House naval aide to Presidents Hoover and Franklin D. Roosevelt

"I am very glad to have the opportunity to express myself on the case of Grand Admiral Doenitz...There is no basis for holding that those honorable defendants such as Grand Admiral Doenitz were guilty of 'war crimes' or of a violation of the Kellogg-Briand Pact. To say that a professional soldier or sailor who engages in war in accordance with his oath of office and in accordance with the laws of war in general acceptance at the time is guilty of a 'war crime' is not defensible in law, in precedent, or in the concepts of Christian morality...The charge against Admiral Doenitz is without foundation in military, civil or international law. His conduct as a naval officer is above reproach. His direction of the forces under his command was efficient and the operations of his submarines were no more unrestricted than those of our own. The trials of honorable professional military officers at Nuremberg appear, as time lends its perspective to the passions of war, more and more as a gross miscarriage of justice. More and more they appear as the vengeance of the victor upon the surrendered vanquished...I shall take this opportunity to say that I regard [Grand Admiral Doenitz] as one of the ablest naval commanders in history. He served in the highest capacity with honor and distinction. He suffered the injustice and indignity of the Nuremberg Trials with forebearance and dignity. He is an example of the fact that greatness of character is as evident in defeat as in victory."

Vice Admiral Harry Sanders, U.S.N.
Commander, Training Command, Pacific Fleet
Ass't. Chief of Naval Operations (Fleet Operations)
Commander, Mine Forces, Atlantic Fleet
Commander, Cruiser Division 1, Korean War

"I have always judged the Nuremberg trials morally unfair and politically most dangerous. It is to be feared that even that puny attempt at moral discrimination will be found wanting in the next war, where death sentences will rain, on those only, who have not turned coat in time. *Yesterday* said: 'A soldier must obey.' *Tomorrow* will say: 'Obey...whom?' "

Paul Morand
French author and diplomat
French Commissioner on the Danube, 1938
Ambassador to United Kingdom (1940), Romania (1943), and Switzerland (1944)
Author of more than 30 literary works

"...I do not consider the German Admiral Doenitz personally responsible when, for the security of his submarines, he waged 'unrestricted submarine warfare' in order to prevent his own submarines being sunk by enemy warships disguised as commercial ships...It is a leader's fate to suffer...The Athenian people, influenced by demagogues, inflicted the death sentence and executed their admirals who had gained the victory during the battle against the Lacedemonians (Sparta's fleet) at Arginoussais (in 406 B.C.), and this for the reason that they proved unable, owing to the storm, to rescue the life of those shipwrecked during the battle!!!"

General George Kosmas, Royal Hellenic Army
Commanded divisions, groups, and corps during War in Albania, 1940-1941
Chief of Staff of the Greek Army
Member of House of Commons, 1947-1948
Minister of Northern Greece, 1954-1955

"Personally, I believe that the Nuremberg Trials rested on a sheer act of force. The Arabs had no enthusiasm about these trials...Even from a purely international and objective consideration no act deserves the description 'cold blooded murder' more fittingly than the throwing of the two A-bombs on Hiroshima and Nagasaki..."

Omar A. Farrukh, Ph.D.
Lebanese educator and author of many literary works
Member, Arab Academy, Damascus
Professor, Islamic Philosophy and Arabic Literature, Syrian University, Damascus
Member, Islamic Research Association, Bombay

"The truth requires admission that the entire technique of war can have no other target than the mass of civilians. The so-called war crimes of the German U-boats seem, nowadays, simple incidents compared with the colossal slaughter of Hiroshima or the terrifying consequences of a future nuclear war...the civilians of his [Doenitz] own country suffered much by the air raids of the Allied Forces."

General Constantine Ventiris, Royal Hellenic Army
Commander-in-Chief, Greek Army, 1944
Chief of the General Staff, 1947
Chief of Operations (1949), and aide to King Paul

"Grand Admiral Karl Doenitz of the German Navy was illegally tried by the Nuremberg Court. His sentence to ten years confinement was inconceivable! It violates all modern concepts of justice. Both the trial and sentence were without precedent. They violated the rules of war that are sanctioned by international law and practiced by civilized nations—the product of Christianity and Western Culture. Undoubtedly, history will rectify the injustices suffered by Doenitz. Probably, it will commend his unsuccessful work during World War II. Then, he faithfully fulfilled his duty by trying to promote the success of his country's strategic, political and economic ambitions. Leadership of all kinds—in the future, will be timid and precarious if Grand Admiral Karl Doenitz does not receive from this generation and from posterity the honors and acclaim that are his just due."

Rear Admiral William Russell White, U.S.N.
Commanded U.S.S. *Vixen* in World War I
Aide to the Governor of the Virgin Islands
Ass't. Inspector of Naval Material in World War II

"My opinion will be from my personal knowledge and experience achieved during my long military service in which I have climbed up from the rank of Second Lieutenant to General in the Thai Army...Generally speaking, out of the aforesaid case (War Crimes Trials) two words could be appraised for consideration. They are 'Responsibility' and the 'Victors'...One found that Responsibility was confined at the mercy of the Might and Justice of the Victors. Their word was 'Law.' I would recall the savings 'Might Is Right' and 'There is no Justice in this World.' If the Victors were to apply *these* sayings to exercise their power, no doubt they could well put the responsibility on Grand Admiral Doenitz and caused the 'Military Tribunal' to send him to the international prison for 10 years. In summing up my opinion, it is obvious that the 'War Crimes Trials'...rested on the Might of the Victors."

General of the Army of Thailand, Luang Chati Nakrob
Director, Civil Service Commission

"I served long in submarines before World War II and served in anti-submarine warfare continuously during the war in the Atlantic, having commanded three ships, two divisions, a squadron and a force. It ever seemed to me that the various treaties entered into by the great nations prior to World War II restricting the use of submarines were wholly unrealistic. If the signatories meant what they said, there was no need to build submarines. They never could have been operated under the law. As for Admiral Doenitz, none thought of him but as a brilliant commander of submarines. In brief, I believe that no legal fault can be found in Admiral Doenitz's conduct of the war. I believe that Admiral Doenitz carried out his orders as an officer. He may have made mistakes in judgment in the employment of his forces, but not legal or morally culpable errors. I know of no order on his part which violated the basic rules of war."

Rear Admiral Colby G. Rucker, U.S.N.
Commanded U.S.S. *Owl* and other ships, Atlantic, World War II
Commander, Escort Forces, Moroccan Sea Frontier
Salvaged *U-505*

"The Nuremberg Trials constitute an impertinent violation of international law. Desiring to sentence the legitimate chiefs of the German Military Forces before a pretended Military Tribunal on the basis of principles established by the conquerors ex post factum, constitutes a rather sad precedent for the Allies. Above all: (1) the constitution of the Military Court, when considering the nature of the positions previously held by the members of the Tribunal, detracts from this high assemblage the characteristics of a *military* tribunal; (2) the Court was called together to sentence and inflict the most serious penalties, although their decisions were not supported by any international code which might have given a judicial cloak or at least a judicial semblance to the sentences; (3) to inflict the death penalty or the most severe punishments on professional officers of the highest calibre, because they had served their country in wartime, or had prepared the army, navy or air force for World War II on the orders of their own Government, constitutes a most serious and unjustified precedent in world history and in the relations between peoples; (4) the conquerors declared the war 'post factum' a war of aggression. If some of the commanders of the German Armed Forces had been guilty of crimes against humanity or had violated existing international law, then they ought to have been brought before a German court for trial, even during the occupation period, with the guaranty that the court would respect international law. The principles, however, on which the acts of the Nuremberg Tribunal were based, constitute a juridical absurdity and a very serious precedent which threatens to weaken the sense of responsibility and dignity which are the qualifications for exercising command of Armed forces in peace and in war. Judges from all over the world who have quietly and objectively studied the great tragedy of Nuremberg can judge the Nuremberg Trials as nothing but a ferocious revenge on the part of the conquerors imposed on the losing side.

"The imputations and accusations against Grand Admiral Doenitz constituted in fact the utmost absurdity...The accusation that he prepared a war of aggression was not supportable in the case of Admiral Doenitz, because before the war he was not the chief of the German Navy, but only one of the admirals under Grand Admiral Raeder. The accusation that he conducted unrestricted submarine warfare could no longer be maintained after the deposition of Fleet Admiral Chester Nimitz, U.S. Navy, who testified that the United States ever since the first day of the war conducted unrestricted submarine warfare. The court, having admitted that 'in formulating such accusation it was not able to forget the order of the English Admiralty of May 8th, 1940,' committed a juridical absurdity and a violation of facts, because the Tribunal itself was perfectly aware that in conducting the submarine war, the Allies themselves had never observed the order of the British Admiralty. The condemnation of Grand Admiral Doenitz proves once more how the verdict of the Tribunal of Nuremberg has been nothing more than a revenge with neither a judicial nor a moral basis. The sad period of imprisonment at Spandau was even extended for more than one year more, with refined cruelty, because, contrary to the legislative rules of every Country, the Allies did not include the period already spent in confinement when the admiral was awaiting his trial."

Fleet Admiral Angelo Parona,
Royal Italian Navy
Commander Submarines
Atlantic, 1940-1942
Commander-in-Chief, Adriatic, 1943-1947

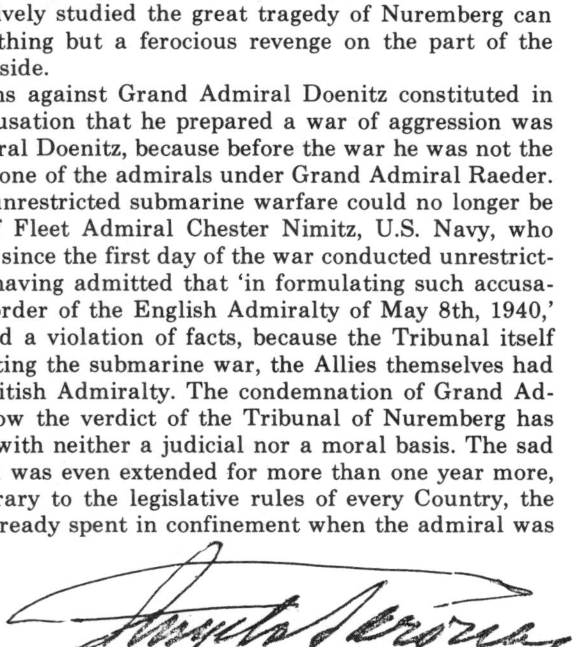

"...regarding the trial, conviction and confinement of Admiral Doenitz of the German Navy, I wish to state that I am entirely in agreement with the sentiments expressed by Admiral Dan Gallery and the editorial writer of the *Chicago Tribune*...When I first heard of these trials, including those of the Japanese high officials, they seemed wrong in principle, and I wondered whether our own high ranking officers would judge to be fitting the application of the same kind of 'justice' in the case of the defeat of the United States in war. But I suppose the concept of our defeat comes under the 'unthinkable' classification, and in any case, in the event of a nuclear war, there won't be anyone left to worry about concocting war crimes ex post facto."

Rear Admiral Winfield Scott Cunningham, U.S.N.
Commander at Wake Island, Dec., 1941
Prisoner-of-war of the Japanese, Dec. 23, 1941-1945
Commanding officer, Naval Technical Training Center 1947-1950

"It is a pleasure to congratulate you on having taken up the cudgels for Admiral Doenitz and to inform you that, from the information available, I consider unquestionably that Admiral Doenitz was most improperly and unfairly treated and that it was against normal international law to try him for the crime alleged. I consider that the crime was committed against him rather than vice versa. I hope that you will pass on to Grand Admiral Karl Doenitz my revulsion at his sentence of ten years in prison."

Brigadier General William P. Campbell, U.S.A.
Executive Ass't. to the President, Harding College
Ass't. Chief of Finance, U.S. Army, 1950-1953
Member, General Staff Corps, U.S. Army, 1949-1950
Advisor to the Peruvian Army, 1945-1947

"Admiral Doenitz was a great naval officer; our main regret should be that he was not on our side. He and a few thousand men in submarines came very nearly defeating the Allies through interdiction of sea lanes. He operated some 1,100 submarines, requiring crews of some 50,000 men. This is the equivalent of only about three division slices. I doubt if any other three divisions of men have ever achieved more in war than these did. Military effectiveness is no crime."

Rear Admiral Raymond H. Bass, U.S.N.
Commanded submarines *Plunger* and *Runner,* 1943-1946
Commander, U.S. Submarine Squadron 10, 1952-1953
Commanded, U.S.S. *Bremerton,* 1956-1959
Ass't. to General Manager, The Bendix Corp.

"I was never personally acquainted with Admiral Doenitz, but always considered his case as a flagrant example of the extremes to which the Allies went in punishing individuals...If the victor is now and in the future to have the right to execute or imprison leaders of the losing side in armed conflict, wars are apt to last longer and to lose whatever chivalric and humane practices the civilized community has previously required. I am one among many Americans who is not proud of my country's role in the 'war crimes trials.' "

Rev. Garland Evans Hopkins, M.A., LL.D. (international)
Methodist minister and author
U.S. Army chaplain in World War II
Secretary-General, World Fellowship of Muslims and Christians
Accredited non-governmental Representative to the U.N.

"You ask me my opinion on the unprecedented tribunals invented by the victors of the 1939-1945 war to try the vanquished military leaders. As an example, you cite the case of Grand-Admiral Doenitz. My opinion is simple: I think those tribunals represent a hypocritical iniquity. Iniquity, because persons can only be judged according to pre-established laws and before impartial judges. Hypocrisy, because those proceedings had no other purpose but vengeance on the vanquished while giving the masses of the peoples the impression that they were thus dispensing justice. I am thus opposed to Nuremberg and opposed to this kind of justice, because when peoples have recourse to war, the military men of each side are duty-bound to obey their respective governments and the only possible limitation on their action should be dictated by their conscience. There is no tribunal of the victors which has any right whatsoever to judge the behavior of military men on the other side for their acts committed during the war, or for their obedience to orders received. I admit that after the war the victor may neutralize and remove the heads of government of the conquered people. Even this ought to be done with humanity, and more for the purpose of avoiding future dangers if those concerned were at liberty than to punish past crimes. Furthermore this act of neutralizing ought to be considered as an arbitrary act which one must not attempt to cover hypocritically with a false verdict, a false tribunal based on false laws."

General Emile Janssens, Royal Belgian Army
Commanded 3rd Belgian Infantry Battalion in Egypt, 1943
Commanded 1st Belgian Infantry in Belgium and Holland, 1944-1945
Commander-in-chief, Belgian Congo Forces, 1954-1960

"With regard to the 'war crimes trials,' in the aftermath of World War II, I submit that it is rather unfair to try the vanquished. In my opinion their defeat is sufficient punishment. In particular, the trial of professional military, naval, and aviation officers, for the effective professional direction of the armed forces of their country in wartime, is, in my opinion, most unfair."

Sheik Hafiz Wahba
Saudi Arabian jurist and diplomat
Minister of Education, 1927-1929
Ambassador to the United Kingdom, 1930-1956
Ambassador-at-Large

"The following is what happens in the case of military and political leaders. If they are lucky in war or if they successfully carry out their diplomatic actions...then they are celebrated and honored as heroes of their people, or if they are brought to trial, they are dragged before some sort of a court and are condemned, on the basis of old or even new laws specially and *ad hoc* created for this purpose, to imprisonment or death. And that's what happened to Grand Admiral Karl Doenitz. He was on the losing side, his plans miscarried, he, like many others, had to go to jail; whether guilty or innocent evidently is of little importance in this day and age when laws are invented when expediency demands—even ex post facto—the life of the individual counts for so little and murderers become heroes."

Colonel Divisionnaire (Major General) Fritz Rihner
Commander and Chief of the Air Force and Air Defense Troops of Switzerland, 1943
Member, Swiss National Defense Commission, 1947
Holder of various aviation pilot records

"I can say that I expressed disapproval of the Nuremberg Trials at the time they occurred and I believe I was one of the few who expressed himself at the time (as did Senator Taft). I felt the same way about the Tokyo Trials. Both went far beyond the condemnation of those who had violated the laws of war and humanity. I had done much in the Navy in preparing for war against both Germany and Japan. But I realize that our really chief enemy was our 'ally?' Soviet Russia, and I know that one of the Nuremberg judges, Soviet Russia, was dripping with the blood and guilt of the Katyn Massacre. By early 1946, I realized that we would have to rearm both Germany and Japan against the real enemy (at a time when the Tokyo Trials were still going on)."

Admiral Charles M. Cooke, U.S.N.
Commander, 7th Fleet, 1945-1947
Commander, Naval Forces, Western Pacific, 1947-1948

"...I maintain that his [Grand Admiral Doenitz] sentence was unjust and that his punishment sets a dangerous precedent under which any military man might be tried for doing his duty in time of war. If his major crime was that of conducting unrestricted submarine warfare, then we are equally culpable in the employment of our submarines against the Japanese in the Pacific. Furthermore, the stigma placed on unrestricted submarine warfare becomes insignificant when we consider the effect of one atom bomb dropped on Hiroshima; and, that military mission had the blessings of our head of state and many officials in our government."

Rear Admiral D. S. Fahrney, U.S.N.
Father of guided missiles; named them and designed and developed first successful one in Sept., 1938
Head of Guided Missile Division, Navy Bureau of Aeronautics, 1940-1943 and 1945-1948
Commander, Naval Air Missile Test Center, Calif., 1948-1950

"On the general principle of war trials—they seem to me a sanctimonious way of doing your enemies in. My own feeling would be that when you win a war if you want to kill your leading enemies, do so but don't call it a trial. The concept of a victorious enemy sitting in 'judgment' on the conquered is so repugnant to any Anglo-Saxon idea of justice that it is a little ridiculous. In at least the case of one man who played a prominent part in the war trials as representing this nation, there is little doubt in my mind that he was either a Communist member or under Communist control."

William Loeb
Publisher, the *Manchester Union Leader* and the *New Hampshire Sunday News*

"The composition and the verdicts of The Nuremberg court have been severely criticized by the free world in general and in particular evaluations. These critiques have proved that what was at issue was not so much the application of basic principles of justice to punish crimes, but the vengeance of the victors over the vanquished. The definition of the crime and its punishment were fixed only *after* commission of the acts imputed. This alone radically contravenes the ancient principle of jurisprudence: *'Nulla poena sine lege, nullum crimen sine lege.'* ('No punishment without a law, no crime without a law'). For centuries, the basic legal principle that a crime could only be punished if punishment had been established in a valid law *before* the offense, has been the cornerstone of justice. The Resolution On Human Rights of the League of Nations was founded on this basic principle. Article 11 of this resolution states: 'No one may be punished for an act if at the time of this act a punishment for it was not pre-established in international law or in the laws of the country concerned. In addition, a penalty more severe than the one priorly established may not be imposed for the crime.'

"Representatives of the Soviet Union took part in the Nuremberg proceedings...At the time of the creation of the International Military Tribunal, the whole world nevertheless knew that the Soviet Union had violated, in a most flagrant manner, a great many treaties and agreements it had concluded with other countries. As an Estonian, I must point out the many treaties the Soviet Union, unilaterally, broke with Estonia, before finally robbing her entirely of freedom. Neutral investigators could ascertain that the Soviet Union had committed a terrible crime by murdering more than ten thousand Polish prisoners of war in the forest of Katyn. Tens of thousands of Estonians were murdered by the Soviet Union and many more deported to forced labor in Siberia under inhuman conditions. As for crimes against humanity, those governments which ordered the destruction of German cities, thereby destroying irreplacable cultural values and making burning torches out of women and children, should also have stood before the bar of justice. All the crimes imputed to the accused at Nuremberg had long previously been committed by the Soviet Union, but no democratic government accused them or demanded the condemnation of the criminals of the Kremlin. If one summarizes the historical record of Nuremberg, it must be declared that this court was founded on the hate of the victor for the vanquished, that this court was incompetent from the point of view of jurisdiction and justice, that its verdicts were not only illegal but also inhuman. From the point of view of jurisdiction, the Nuremberg court is also unique because no appeals could be filed against its verdicts, nor did the Allied Control Commission have the competency to mitigate the verdict rendered, which occurred in no single case."

Hon. Jaan Lattik
Lutheran pastor and dean
Estonian statesman, diplomat, historian, and author of 20 books
Minister of Education, 1925-1927
Foreign Minister, 1928-1931

"It is difficult—for a citizen of a country which was neutral during the war—to judge in a matter as delicate as the one in question. This much, though must be said, that war itself is inhumane and consequently every act of war is more or less inhumane. Where the line between 'permissible' and 'impermissible' inhumanity is to be drawn, can hardly be decided by any body. In my opinion, to be considered as a 'war criminal' would not only require that such person had clearly been trespassing this hard-to-define line, but that he had exceeded his orders and military obligations in so doing. Can this be assumed of Grand Admiral Doenitz? I will not, nor can I believe this."

Arthur Örnberg

Major General Arthur Ornberg
Royal Swedish Air Force
Chief, Flight Administration, 1936-1942

"While we and others constantly prate about 'Law and Order,' I fear that we do not always practice what we preach, for example the Berglong Case and the correspondence between Wilson and Lansing in the First World War...It seems to me a matter of whose ox is being gored. Self-righteousness seems to be of general practice, and our acts and others are justified on that ground, being somewhat sacrosanct. I am a strong believer in our Constitution and other articles of Government, but am frequently in disagreement with what those in charge thereof do under its alleged sanction. In the Nuremberg case, atavism seems to have taken hold of us and others, and the same is true of the Eichmann trial. When one invokes necessity as a basis of law or one's acts, he surely justifies Hitler et al, from their viewpoint. Many people ignore what George Washington said in his Farewell Address, that Law is Force, and we still prate about law as being something that is self-enforced and stands aside from men and their acts...Anyhow, I do not support the violation of law as it is written. Illustrations are, of course, justified to present the question. I think that when a man acts on the orders of the legitimate government, he is absolved from liability, however reprehensible the orders may be. Otherwise, we resort to barbaric actions, whatever our excuse or explanation."

Geo Washington Williams

Hon. George Washington Williams
American attorney and jurist
Counsel to the Governor of the Virgin Islands, 1921-1924
Federal District judge, 1924-1930
Anti-trust prosecutor for the F.T.C., 1938-1950

"The conviction of Admiral Raeder and the conviction of Admiral Doenitz by the so-called International Military Tribunal must be distinguished from all the other convictions recorded at Nuremberg, in which the Tribunal did no more than condemn the accused for newly created offenses which retrospectively they were held to have committed. In convicting these two defendants, the Tribunal acted not only in defiance of elementary principles of justice but also in defiance of the novel principles which the Tribunal itself had laid down for its own guidance. The Tribunal claimed in theory the right—it certainly had the power—to declare any act a war-crime. But it interpreted Article 6 of the Charter creating it, as excluding from its consideration any act committed by the victorious Powers. As a consequence any act proved to have been committed by the victorious Powers could not be declared by the Tribunal a war-crime. For this reason, the indiscriminate bombing of civilians which had indisputably been initiated by Great Britain was excluded from consideration as a war-crime by the Tribunal.

"Both Admiral Raeder and Admiral Doenitz were charged with planning and waging an aggressive war in that they had planned and directed the invasion of Norway. It was at the time common knowledge and it has since been *officially* admitted that Great Britain, concurrently with Germany, planned an attack on Norway and actually put these plans into effect a few hours before the German attack began. Full details of the British invasion plans and the first steps taken to carry them out have since been published in *The Campaign In Norway,* being Volume I of the official British History of the Second World War. In its review of this book dated the 10th December 1952, the *Times* cynically wrote:

> 'Britain was dickering with a modified version of the original scheme for securing Narvik and some troops had been actually embarked in warships, when, in the early hours of April 9th, Hitler struck. With the exception of Oslo, which had never figured in our plans, the immediate German objectives in Norway were precisely (and inevitably) the same ports whose seizure the Allies had been assiduously plotting for several months.'

"According to the principle solemnly laid down by the Tribunal itself, an act committed by one of the victorious Powers could not be pronounced a war-crime. The Tribunal however insisted on shrouding itself in a shroud of judicial ignorance. It absolutely refused to hear evidence concerning the British plans for the invasion of Norway and the first overt acts taken to initiate this invasion. It was therefore in defiance of its own principles that the Tribunal held that the planning and waging of an agressive war was a war-crime. The invasion of Norway by Germany in April 1940 was an aggressive war. Both Admiral Raeder and Admiral Doenitz had taken leading parts in this invasion. Therefore both were convicted of this newly created crime, the former being sentenced to life imprisonment and the latter to imprisonment for ten years.

"It is perhaps unnecessary to add that both Admiral Raeder and Admiral Doenitz carried out the orders of their executive government as in duty bound, in exactly the same spirit as the distinguished British and French generals and admirals carried out the orders of their executive governments in the autumn of 1956 when they planned and directed the invasion of Egypt."

F. J. P. Veale
English jurist and author

[The following contribution by the American historian, Dr. HARRY ELMER BARNES was originally written as a review of F. J. P. Veale's book, *Advance To Barbarism* (Nelson Publishing Co., 1953), but is here published for the first time.]

"Mr. Veale traces the gradual civilizing of warfare from the days of Stone Age savagery, when all opponents were massacred, to the emergence of a code of civilized warfare following 1700. The essence of this was the immunity of non-combatants unless they happened to be in the line of fire. This code was briefly challenged by President Lincoln and his generals during the Civil War, but their deviation had little effect on Old World ideals and practices. Civilized warfare even endured throughout the course of the first World War, the only notable departure being the British blockade for many months after the Armistice which resulted in the starvation of about 800,000 men, women and children.

"It was the indiscriminate bombing of civilians by the so-called strategic air forces during the second world war which culminated in the destruction of Dresden (a wholly non-military objective) in February 1945, that completely pulverized the code of civilized warfare and returned the treatment of military opponents and civilians to the level of the primary warfare that had prevailed among savages, the Assyrians, and the medieval Mongols. On the basis of the most authoritative British sources, Mr. Veale demonstrates clearly that it was the British and not the Nazis who introduced indiscriminate strategic bombing, despite the efforts of Hitler to avert this reversion to barbaric practices.

"The idea had its birth in 1936, when a 'brain wave' suggesting this innovation came to the newly formed British Bomber Command. The final decision to adopt this procedure was the result of a 'Splendid Decision' of the Bomber Command in 1940, and the first wanton attack on civilian centers was made by a fleet of British bombers on May

11, 1940. Earlier bombing by both sides had been confined to legitimate military objectives. There are no final figures on the number of civilians killed as a result of the mass-bombing, but 2,000,000 would be a very restrained figure (estimate). Despite all this, some of the more destructive, although available, instruments of warfare were held back for fear of enemy retaliation. Such were poison gas and bacterial warfare.

"The war-crimes trials, thought by many to be an effort to restore warfare to its earlier civilized status, will inevitably have the opposite effect, as has already been demonstrated by the Korean War. They set the precedent that leaders defeated in a war will be liquidated or worse by the victors. This being so, neither side in the next war can afford to hold back any death-dealing methods which might avert a defeat. Atomic warfare, chemical warfare, bacterial warfare, and whatever may be devised in the meantime, will all be thrown into the conflict. Indiscriminate bombing assured military barbarism; the war-crimes trials inevitably linked military barbarism with judicial barbarism and insured the intensification of the former.

"The war-crimes trials are the theme of the Veale book which is closest to the interest of lawyers. Veale devastatingly exposes the whole web of judicial sham which created and administered these trials. He shows that the driving force behind them, from beginning to end, was the stark Russian program of slaughtering German leaders after the war, as Stalin had already murdered about 15,000 Polish officers in 1940 in the Katyn Forest and elsewhere. But Roosevelt, and especially Churchill, demanded mock trials before the executions, and Stalin graciously conceded their point, provided that the massacre was assured. The organization and procedure in the Nuremberg Trials made certain this result, and the same was true of the Tokyo Trials.

"Veale shows that these war-crimes trials were based upon a complete disregard of sound legal precedents, principles and procedures. The court had no real jurisdiction over the accused of their offenses; it invented ex post facto crimes; it permitted the accusers to act as prosecutors, judges, jury and executioners; and it admitted to the group of prosecutors those who had been guilty of crimes as numerous and atrocious as those with which the accused were charged. Hence, it is not surprising that these trials degraded international jurisprudence as never before in human experience. The essentials on this matter are brilliantly developed by Veale. The juristic reduction ad absurdum is presented in its quintessence in Veale's final definition of a war-crime:

> 'A war-crime is an act committed by a member of a vanquished state but not a vanquished state wholly or partially absolved from war guilt for political expediency, which in the opinion of the conquerors of that state is a war-crime, but which act is not an offense which has been so flagrantly and openly committed by the conquerors themselves that mention of it would cause them embarrassment.'

"Pursuing his analysis further, Veale comes to the sound conclusion that the 'supreme international crime is to be on the losing side in a war.' The practical consequences of this fact were quickly discerned and frankly stated by British Field Marshal Bernard L. Montgomery in an address in Paris on June 9, 1948: 'The Nuremberg trials have made the waging of an unsuccessful war a crime; the generals on the defeated side were tried and then hanged.'

"Some of the leading lawyers in the Nuremberg prosecution, such as Sir Hartley Shawcross, have sought to maintain that the war-crimes trials laid down certain great and noble principles for all time which 'conferred incalculable benefits on mankind.' This contention was definitely refuted by Viscount Maugham, formerly Lord Chancellor of England, when he stated that 'the Nuremberg Tribunal never purported to lay down principles for all mankind.' The noble principles were no more than a number of 'arbitrary decisions' laid down for application to defeated Nazis. The practical results of these 'arbitrary decisions' in assuring that the next world war will probably destroy human civilization have already been pointed out. Those internationalists who are now advocating a permanent world criminal court 'along Nuremberg lines' will do well to read the Veale book. If they do so, they may curb their determination to promote the suicide of humanity.

"Veale treats with vigor the ghastly injustice involved in sentencing men like Admiral Doenitz and Admiral Raeder to brutal imprisonment in the Spandau 'bastille.' Even the British history of the Second World War admits that Churchill and his associates had planned the invasion of Norway before the German proposal to do so had been arranged and acted upon. The horrors of those years of imprisonment of men like Admiral Doenitz were in some ways even more painful and vicious than the outright execution of the defendants. The vindictive episode will remain a permanent blot on the record of the Allies."

Professor Harry Elmer Barnes, Ph.D.
American historian, sociologist, penologist, educator and author
Editor, Scripps-Howard Newspapers, 1929-1940
Consultant, War Production Board and Smaller War Plants Corp., World War II
Professor at Columbia Univ., New School For Social Research, Temple Univ., Univ. of Colorado, Univ. of Indiana, and Washington State College, 1919-1955

"At the time I read in the press about the International Court of Justice at Nuremberg and its conviction of Admiral Karl Doenitz, I became greatly agitated. I asked myself how anything like that could happen in our enlightened times. The only explanation I could think of was that the members of the Tribunal were so consumed by hatred against their adversaries in the then just ended war that they were incapable of viewing the circumstances realistically and impartially, which is the first duty of a judge. And I wondered what consequences this verdict might have on future conflicts between states. I am completely convinced that the conviction of Admiral Doenitz was a nefarious, illegal outrage, and I fully support the quotations by Rear Admiral Dan V. Gallery, U. S. Navy, concerning the conviction of Admiral Doenitz. It is probably not possible to give Admiral Doenitz a complete redress now, but it should be comforting and edifying for him to know that his colleagues in various nations give him their sympathies."

Major General Karl E. Beskow, Royal Swedish Army
Commanded various divisions of infantry

"I am pleased of the opportunity to add my voice to such a distinguished list of citizens of the Western World who deplore the fact that professional military men were brought to trial for 'war crimes' after World War II. I agree thoroughly with Rear Admiral Gallery, U. S. Navy, and with the views expressed in the *Chicago Daily Tribune* in the issue of October 6, 1956. As a professional naval officer for 35 years, the trial of Grand Admiral Karl Doenitz was particularly against all my beliefs and feelings. You are to be complimented for your efforts in your present undertaking."

Vice Admiral Ephraim R. McLean, Jr., U.S.N.
Commander, Destroyer Divisions and Squadrons, World War II
Commanding Officer, U.S.S. *Columbus,* 1948-1950
Commander, Cruiser Division 2, 1955-1956

"I believe the trials were a travesty on Justice and violated all concepts of the Anglo-Saxon elimination of Ex Post Facto prosecutions. Additionally, the stage is set for the prosecution and eventual conviction and execution of the leaders of any loser in the future. Such leaders are convicted in advance merely through their actions in carrying out the orders of their governments, a refusal to do so would and should, be interpreted as at the least insubordination, if not outright treason. The military leader of the future is therefore caught between two fires. He can obey the dictates of his own government and face trial as a *war criminal,* or he can, if defeat appears imminent, disobey these orders and face trial, if returned to his country, as a mutineer or worse. These trials had no basis in international law as recognized at the outbreak of the war, nor by any international pronouncement by all belligerents during the war. They were revengeful and willful, designed as a sop to public panic at the outbreak of hostilities. I have these feelings and you are welcome to use them."

Vice Admiral Theodore D. Ruddock, Jr., U.S.N.
Ass't. Chief, Bureau of Ordnance, 1941-1943
Commander, Battleship Division 4, 1944
Superintendent, Naval Gun Factory, 1946-1948

"Although I fought, as an Infantry officer, in both World War I and World War II against the Germans and consequently had no charitable feelings toward them, I formed the opinion in 1946 that the U.S. Government had made a major error in agreeing to or participating in the War Crimes Trials before the International Military Tribunal. In February of 1946 I was assigned, first as Deputy and later as Commander, of the Nuremberg-Furth Enclave and remained on that assignment for a number of months. During that period I had occasion to visit the court-room in the Palace of Justice repeatedly and to observe the Tribunal proceedings.

"It was my opinion then and it is my opinion now, that if the U.S. Government had felt it necessary to bring *any* German military commander before a court, that commander should have been placed before a United States Military Court-Martial only. The defendant to have exactly the same rights as American military personnel appearing before a General Court. Undoubtedly history will record our participation in the International Military Tribunal as a serious mistake and that we allowed the Trials to be conducted as they were a more serious mistake."

Samuel T. Williams

Lieutenant General Samuel T. Williams, U.S.A.
Commanding General, 25th Infantry Division, 9th and 16th Army Corps, 1952-1954
Commanding General, 4th U.S. Army, 1954-1955
Commanding General, Military Advisory & Assistance Group, Vietnam, 1955-1960

"I have never at any time sympathized in any way with the procedure followed at Nuremberg, which in my opinion was in violation of American concepts of justice. Those trials were not military in any sense, and the defendants were not, in my opinion, tried by an impartial tribunal. As regards Admiral Doenitz, as I see it, he was simply a naval officer pursuing the policy of his Government that he had been directed to carry out. A most dangerous precedent was established at Nuremberg, which I trust that our soldiers and sailors will never have occasion to rue."

Harry J. Lemley

Honorable Harry J. Lemley, LL.D.
United States District Judge
(Eastern and Western District of Arkansas), 1939-1958

"The phrase, 'in war, the laws are silent' is unfortunately still very true in our world today. The individual moral outlook rarely has any final decisive effect in measurements of military force. And the expression 'in politics and diplomacy, all means are permitted,' is considered to be good practice in peacetime as well. This is evidenced by the impudence, unscrupulousness and lying which thrive to a certain extent in our times. But there nevertheless are general moral concepts, international conventions and principles of honor which, in the name of decency we cannot take casually even in wartime...The verdicts on Grand Admirals Raeder and Doenitz were based on the fact that the Nuremberg Tribunal was not an objective court of law. If they really had wanted to administer justice with respect to naval warfare during the second World War, the war-criminal prosecution should have been conducted by the Hague Court, reinforced by the required number of neutral experts. Then there would have been certain quarantees that the verdicts could be accepted without justified challenge. But a court where only the final victors sat, both as accusers and judges, was both theoretically and practically incapable of issuing impartial decisions. In the presence of the macaber spectacle at Nuremburg, it was difficult to shake off the impression that, above the door to the hearing room there was an invisible, but well-known device: *Vae Victis* (woe to the vanquished)...one could only observe that the moral weight of the court was seriously shaken, and that among the great powers accusing and judging there was one which had been guilty of horrible atrocities and mass deportations of people from occupied countries, and which previously, during the same war, had been condemned by an at least theoretically objective court, for unprovoked wars of aggression, and consequently, was excluded from the League of Nations.

"The two Grand Admirals were not politically involved and they demonstrably had no part in any atrocities. As honorable navy officers...they were enrolled in a legal military organization, which the court should have exonerated from collective responsibility for presumed offenses. Nor could any personal initiative or any orders that might have violated international principles of naval warfare be attributed to them [the admirals], in spite of the accusers' zealous and ill-willed attempts.

"It is certainly more than probable that Raeder took the initiative in the attack on Norway and Denmark in order to broaden the basic range of U-boat warfare, and forestall the British. But he certainly did not take the initiative in the general world madness that was then raging, and of which the occupations of Norway and Denmark were but a detail...*None* of the general or detailed points of the charges touched Grand Admiral Doenitz. He merely did his duty as a sworn officer according to the code of honor which is standard for all naval forces. And every honorable man should admit that Doenitz had no possibility of counteracting or sabotaging Hitler's policies at a time when he stood at the pinnacle of his power. Since Doenitz, in spite of this, was sentenced under point 1 of the accusation for war crimes, breach of humanity and breach of the peace, this must be classified as simple legal quibbling and hypocritical moral pathos. An acquittal in this case would certainly have been greeted with satisfaction by objectively thinking naval officers with a sense of duty, everywhere in the world.

"The Nuremberg trials, in my opinion, were, in certain respects, a dictate, which could not be altered by the defense attorneys because they often were deprived of the right to present aggravating counter-evidence. This was particularly applicable to the case of Doenitz. A copy in miniature of this debatable procedure is represented by the war responsibility case in Helsingfors [Finland] of a later date, when a victorious power enforced a piece of legislation with retroactive effect so that the accused could be sentenced."

Uno Fagernäs

Major General Uno Fagernas, Army of Finland
Regimental and Brigade Commander, Lake Ladoga campaign, 1939-1940
Commanded Divisions and a Finnish Army, 1941-1944
Commander of Military Forces, 1945-1954

"Of all those who appeared as defendants before the Nuremberg Tribunal, my sympathy did go out to Admiral Doenitz. When I search for a reason I think it was principally because I shared his interests in the sea and the naval profession...I also felt that it was unjust to order him before that 'court' for actions which were required, by virtue of his office. As commander of the German Naval Forces it was his duty to conduct a successful sea campaign in support of his country which was at war. Such campaigns inherently involve taking life. Unhappily our own sea commanders were faced with planning and directing similar operations in order to win our objectives. I reconcile the actions of Admiral Doenitz by thinking of him in a position similar to that of our own war time chief of Naval Operations, Admiral King. My feeling for Admiral King is respect and admiration for a job well done. On the other hand, my feeling for Admiral Doenitz is respect for trying to do his job well, but I am thankful that he did not succeed in his mission. To denounce for criminal guilt in malicious killing would seem inappropriate for either man..."

John F. Greenslade

Rear Admiral John F. Greenslade, U.S.N.
Commanding Officer, U.S.S. *Kitkun Bay,* 1945-1946
Office of the Chief of Naval Operations, 1947
Commander, Formosa Straits Patrol, 1950-1952

KING SIMEON II

"His Majesty fully agrees with the points of view expressed in your statement, and has more than once considered unjust some of the rash sentences handed out by the 'International Military Tribunal' at Nuremberg. His Majesty the King has read with great interest Grand Admiral Doenitz's book, finding it to be a valuable contribution to history and a decisive step in clearing the German Navy from black legends which were, and sometimes still are, spread by those interested in seeing Germany crushed once and for all. His Majesty still remembers that his late Father had a very high opinion of the Grand Admiral, which He also shares...the cause of truth and justice is particularly close to the heart of our King, due to the injustice that Bulgaria has been submitted to since World War II."

G. Guentcheff

Colonel George Guentcheff, Chief of Chancery, for His Majesty Simeon II, King of the Bulgarians.

[To Grand Admiral Doenitz]

"It gives me great pleasure to be able at last to tell you how glad I am that you have been liberated from imprisonment in Spandau as a 'war criminal.' I shared Senator Robert A. Taft's feeling of opposition to the whole idea of trying and imprisoning the leaders of the forces against which our country had fought. As was admirably expressed in the very titles of books and articles that were published over here, you and your colleagues suffered from 'victor's justice,' which is bound to be injustice, by the very nature of the case. It follows without question that, if the tide of victory had flowed the other way, the commanders of our armed forces would have been the victims of similar trials and similar injustice...It is my hope that you may use the great influence which you will recover in your freedom to make Germany a leader in the cause of permanent world peace."

Frederick J. Libby

Frederick J. Libby, Executive Secretary
National Council for Prevention of War

"...With respect to war crime trials in general, I have questioned for some years the ethics involved in bringing to trial a professional military man of any nation for performing his military tasks, just so long as he made such effort as was possible under the conditions confronting him at the time, to conform to the generally accepted principles of international law. In my opinion, it is highly important that the ethics involved in this matter be analyzed after a suitable period of time has elapsed since World War II to permit proper perspective. Then only can the violent views engendered in the heat of conflict be tempered by time to the point where the subject may be properly evaluated...With reference to the Doenitz case in particular, in his capacity as commander of the German navy, it seems that he carried out the orders of his government, and waged unrestricted submarine warfare. This, to the undersigned, in the light of known facts of the waging of unrestricted submarine warfare by opposing navies in World War II, does not in itself qualify him as a 'war criminal.' Therefore, his trial on this charge seems unjustified. With regard to unrestricted submarine warfare, war as we know it is an all out effort to destroy the ability of the enemy to wage war. Unrestricted submarine warfare was one of the most effective means of accomplishing that objective. The quickest method of bringing the conflict to a successful conclusion was sought and adopted by both sides. Because we were successful and the enemy was not seems no reason in itself to consider the enemy's attempt to do likewise a crime. In conclusion, I have felt gravely concerned that...we may have gone too far in imposing penalties on those in the military profession in very responsible positions who did no more than attempt to fulfill their lifetime training in performing military missions in accord with lawful orders directly laid down by their superiors in authority. While we consider this historical reappraisal of the dangerous precedent set at Nuremberg, we must ever be aware of the fact that in our world today we are dealing with the Soviets, and others of like uncivilized philosophy, who need no precedent to exterminate any whom they choose whether rulers, military personnel or civilians."

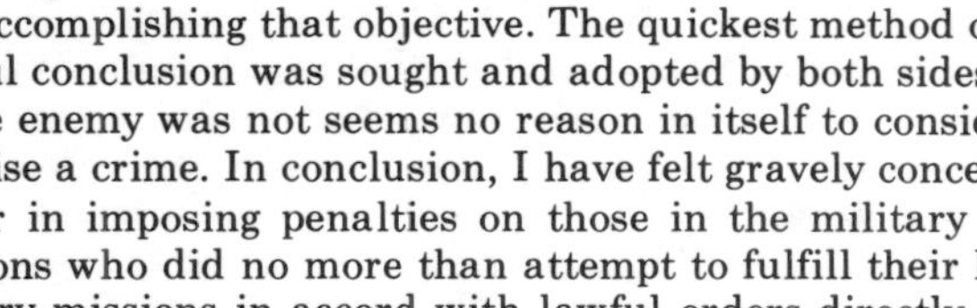

Rear Admiral Joseph M. Worthington, U.S.N.
Commanding Officer, U.S.S. *Benham,* 1941-1942
Commander, Destroyer Squadron 57, 1945
Commanding Officer, U.S.S. *Rochester,* 1948-1949

"It is an extremely bad precedent to rope in servicemen of defeated countries for discharging their duty in compliance with their Government's orders. True, that if they do anything against the Geneva Convention or against the customs of war, they should be held liable for it. But that, I suggest, is much better done by the Governments that employ them and not by victors who are out looking for blood and vengeance. I believe that the war crimes trials of servicemen that took place after the last War have set a very bad precedent for the future; and those countries that have done so, may well have cause to regret it in the long run."

Field Marshal Mohammad Ayub Khan, H.P., H.J.
President of Pakistan

"You place me in your debt for giving me this opportunity to express my opinion regarding the so-called 'war crimes trials.' This has been a subject which has troubled me no end and has caused me to give study and thought to the animus and basic injustice involved in these farcical excursions into international 'jurisprudence.' I include in this category the German, Japanese and Eichmann pseudo trials. There never has existed any basis in international or national law which could give any right or privilege to any nation or group of nations or peoples to bring to trial or to judge any person for waging war under orders from high command or otherwise. Many attempts have been made from time to time to 'humanize' war procedures and all have failed in the net result. It is obvious that the fundamental reason for this continuing failure is that the belligerents in any war try to win with any and all means at their then command. War has always been one of the colossal mistakes which have plagued the human race throughout time. And yet we still talk of national honor which must be upheld at all costs even in mass murder and destruction. These ridiculous 'war crimes' trials are just another manifestation of man's incapabilities to live by reason, not by force."

Brigadier General Eugene Sharp Bibb, U.S.A., LL.D.
Combat veteran of Mexican Punitive Expedition (1916), World War I and World War II
Lawyer (since 1912) and member of the Bar of the U.S. Supreme Court
Radio commentator, lecturer, and author

"The spirit which led the British and American people to look on complacently whilst their authorities were committing the monstrous injustice of holding the Nuremberg Trials, was nothing new; for it is latent in every savage beast; and, in civilized Man, is only kept in check by the nobility and chivalry which comes of superior cultivation and high standards of good taste. The spirit in question consists in the lust for vengeance and the bitter resentment provoked by wounded vanity.

"In 1918, this same lust for vengeance and merciless resentment were caused in the Allies by the fact that, throughout World War I, they had suffered military and naval reverses far more severe and humiliating than they had ever expected, that they had been forced to call more than half of the rest of the world to their aid in order to escape defeat, and that their self-esteem was accordingly profoundly wounded. In the behaviour of the Allied Occupation troops and the fulfillment of the Armistice terms by the Allied officials in Germany, every sign of this spirit of revenge and bitter resentment reached its fullest expression—so much so that the American, Herbert Hoover, who was a prominent and exceptionally humane witness of all that happened, was compelled to declare, 'The Allies are sowing hatred for the future, they are piling up agony, not for the Germans, but for themselves...In after years, the mine the Allies have planted will blow up in the faces of these world peace-makers. (*Memoirs of Herbert Hoover,* 1952, Chap. XXXIX). Nor was the Allied attitude to the German military and naval personnel and their leaders, both during and after the conflict, either fair or even consonant with the chivalry of former times, or with Wilson's 14 points. For instance, it was only King George V's opposition to the Cabinet's plan to impose differential treatment upon the crews of the German submarines, which ultimately caused this foolish and inhuman policy to be dropped. 'In the King's opinion,' Lord Stamfordham wrote to the Prime Minister, 'they have but obeyed orders—brutal and inhuman though these orders may be.' Again, when in June 1919, the Supreme Council of the (Peace) Conference decided to bring the Kaiser to trial, George V wisely intervened and warned the authorities against the difficulty of imparting to any tribunal composed only of judges from the Allied countries, who would also be the accusers, the faintest semblance of fair play (Harold Nicolson: *King George V,* 1952, Chapters VII and XX). Much the same exchange of views took place between the King and his Ministers when the Allies insisted upon delivering a number of German generals and superior officers up to trial as 'war criminals' *(Ibid).* Would that we had King George's counsels after World War II!!...

"World War II led to even greater humiliation of the Allies than they had suffered in World War I. It is only necessary to mention the titanic rout of the British and French Armies which culminated in the flight of the former from Dunkirk, in order to make this clear. Consequently, in the matter of chivalry, justice, and fair-play, the English record is even blacker than it was after World War I and the savagery and inhumanity that was displayed was far less restrained...From the looting and sadistic ill-treatment of the defenceless population by the Allied troops and control officials—Englishmen, Frenchmen, Russians and Americans—to the despicable display of troglodytic beastliness in the Nuremberg Trials, where Englishmen, Frenchmen and Americans sank to the level of Russian prosecutors in a 'great Purge' trial, and committed the extra infamy of pretending that the proceedings were 'legal' and 'just'.

"At least when the ancients 'liquidated' the military or other leaders of their defeated enemy, they marched a Caractacus or a Vercingetorix through the streets of Rome, they never aggravated the iniquity by trying to make it appear the outcome of a just and *bona fide* legal process. The world had yet to witness that advance in 'civilized' conduct which enabled an English High Court judge, sitting beside a judicial colleague from Red Square, Moscow, to condemn men like Keitel and Doenitz either to death or imprisonment after the wholly Allied tribunal had gone through the motions of giving them a 'fair' trial...As to the Nuremberg trials themselves, I must let the late Very Rev. Dean Inge have the reader's attention...'I disliked the Nuremberg trials,' says the Dean, 'for three reasons. First, trials of the vanquished by the victors are never satisfactory and are generally unfair. Secondly, the execution of the political and military leaders of a beaten side by the victors sets a most dangerous precedent. Thirdly, one of the judges—Russia—ought certainly to have been in the dock and not on the bench' (Foreword to *Advance to Barbarism* by F.J.P. Veale). Lord Norwich comments similarly on the latter point. 'Could we,' he asks, 'as the allies of Marshal Stalin, go into court with a clear conscience and clean hands?'—We certainly could not! But wounded Anglo-Saxon vanity did not pause to ask or answer such awkward questions.

"Only one more distinguished Englishman shall be quoted, and, for the alert reader, this should suffice. In the [House of] Lords (5. 5. 49), Lord Hankey declared that, 'there was something cynical and revolting in the spectacle of British, French, and American judges sitting on the Bench with a colleague representing a country which before, during, and since the trials, had perpetrated half the political crimes in the calendar.' "

Anthony M. Ludovici
English Army officer (World War I)
Secretary to, and biographer of, Auguste Rodin
Philosopher and author of 33 works, 1909-1960

"I totally condemn judicial proceedings—resting upon new laws created for the purpose—against the losers of a war, and instigated by the dictate of the victors."

Major General Nils Stenbeck, Royal Swedish Army
Chief, 5th Infantry Regiment, 1934-1937
Deputy Commander, 2nd Military District, 1942-1945
Military Governor of Stockholm, 1945-1950

"Very few German officers committed actions by their own free will during World War II of such a nature that they, because of such actions, could be regarded as war criminals. Following a war, it is not only justified but highly desirable to try to find out who committed excesses or breaches of international laws, statutes, or agreements, as well as to punish those guilty of such acts. But those who judge in such proceedings must be impartial and stand absolutely above any question of partisanship. It is evident that the Nuremberg trials did not answer these demands. On the contrary, those trials must be considered instead as an act of revenge against the conquered, with the victors functioning both as accusers and judges. A great many of their verdicts against the German officers were, without doubt, neither right not just. Besides, the Nuremberg tribunal was one-sided, as it only examined and condemned personnel of the conquered. But even among the forces of the victorious powers evil deeds were committed, cruelties and offenses against humanity, without any consequences for those responsible. Only two examples: no Russian has, insofar as one knows, been held responsible for the massacres of Polish officers, although it has been fully proved that it was Russia, *not* Germany, behind that outrageous crime. No doubt Stalin gave the order for this himself, but he went free from any accusation. Even the senseless and highly culture-destroying terror acts against, for example, Luebeck and Dresden, carried out by Allied pilots, should have been investigated and brought before a proper court of justice."

Major General H. Bratt, Royal Swedish Army
Commanded several divisions during World War II
Commander, 3rd Military District, 1942-1946

"Generally speaking, I never felt that the Nuremberg Trials reflected any credit on the allies, and I am afraid that history will not look upon them as a legitimate legal procedure. Particularly the principle of trying military personnel who were defending their country seems to me to create a very bad precedent."

Major General Edward P. Curtis, U.S.A.F., LL.D.
Combat pilot, World War I
Chief of Staff, Strategic Air Force, Europe, World War II
Vice President and Director, Eastman Kodak Company
Special Assistant (on aviation facilities planning) to President Eisenhower

"I have the honor to give you my views on the case of the German Admiral Doenitz. There is validity in the opinion of many senior officers belonging to a nation which first used the atomic bomb intentionally against a civilian population, that both sides conducted an indiscriminate campaign in the last world war. Therefore, Admiral Doenitz is no war criminal...I particularly consider the verdict of ten years confinement, rendered against Admiral Doenitz at Nuremberg, as indiscriminating and unjust."

Lieutenant General Baron van Voorst tot Voorst, Royal Netherlands Army
Delegate to the Disarmament Conference, 1932
Commander, Field Army and Fortress Holland, 1937
Commander, Netherlands Field Army, 1940

"I am much interested to learn that so many officers and others whose opinions carry weight now share the views which I myself held from the beginning. I have always maintained, and I have written to this effect, that the war crimes trials were wholly illegal from the point of view of international law. My own experience in the Belsen trial made it clear to me that in 1945, passions and vengeance prevailed over law and justice."

Sincerely yours

Herbert A. Smith, D.C.L.
Professor of International Law, University of London, 1928-1946
Member, British Mission to the U.S., World War I
Professor of Jurisprudence and International Law, various universities, England and Canada
Author of many legal works, including *The Law and Custom of the Sea* (1948)

"Your timely effort to bring the entire subject of World War II 'war crime trials' into historical perspective merits national applause. Their appalling miscarriages of justice, illustrated by the sentencing of Grand Admiral Karl Doenitz to 10 years in an 'international prison' by the 'International Military Tribunal' at Nuremberg, reveal the tragic relapse by civilized nations into the barbarism that occurred during the Second Great War. They represent a reversion to primary warfare, traceable to Stalin's 1943 proposal at Teheran for the mass murder by firing squads, as fast as captured, of 'all of Germany's war criminals,' at least 50,000.

"Many thoughtful professional officers of the armed forces deplored from the start, and still deplore, the establishment of the Nuremberg precedent for evil. Unfortunately, they were not in positions to avert that notorious affair or to prevent ensuing punitive procedures of victors over the vanquished. Subsequently published revelations of the gross hypocrisy of the operations of some of the 'war crime' tribunals and their prosecuting teams, bound neither by the technical rules of evidence nor the principles of justice embodied in the U.S. Constitution, surpassed the worst fears. Their lawless actions reflected a spirit of blind revenge that is foreign to Western civilization, and this has again been illustrated since 1959 in Cuba. Experienced officers who have studied the history of 'war crime' trials and their vindictive punishments trust that the ordeal of Admiral Doenitz was not in vain. They hope that it served to give him a profound insight into the entire subject and that his experiences, coupled with his background as a naval officer of distinction, will serve to place him in a position of leadership in what may be a difficult task of disavowing Western relapse into barbarism represented by Nuremberg and to bring about a return to the principles of civilized warfare, especially with respect to the treatment of prisoners of war...It cannot be emphasized too strongly that unless the dangerous precedents of Nuremberg and other post-war trials are formally repudiated and the restraints of law re-imposed, the ground work has been laid for the ultimate destruction of civilization through brutal and ruthless conduct of warfare."

Captain Miles P. DuVal, Jr., U.S.N.

Commanding Officer, U.S.S. *Dupont* (1933-1935), *Antares* (1939-1940), and *Dade* (1944-1946)

Expert and author on the Panama Canal; directed marine operations, Panama Canal (1941-1944) and developed the Terminal Lake-Third Locks Plan.

"A dispassionate study of the procedure followed by the International Military Tribunal of Nuremberg in the judgment of the so-called 'war criminals' must necessarily come to the conclusion that it produced lamentable errors in its technical-juridical [legal] and procedural aspects; but above all, that which was transcendental and serious in the procedure rests in the scope which it *pretended* to give to Penal Law, violating principles and precedents, as well as establishing a most grave precedent by incorporating political considerations into juridicial problematics. At Nuremberg it cannot be said that the International Community *sat in judgment,* since solely the victors of the second World War were present...Orlando characterized the juridical aspect of the war-crimes proceedings contemplated at Versailles as a 'real procedural monster because of its pretensions to judge conduct both as judge and (interested) party.'

"On the 8th of August, 1945, the London Agreement or the so-called 'Declaration of Moscow' made specific the principles constituting an International Military Tribunal which was to judge the 'major war criminals.' If we analyze the 'Declaration of Moscow' of October 3, 1943, the origin of the Nuremberg Tribunal, it cannot be denied that political considerations far outweighed any juridical ones. The 'major war criminals' were accorded a trial and punishment completely devoid of any legal foundation. Attempts have been made to show that Article 6 of the Military Tribunal of Nuremberg *established the crime.* However, if there is any indefinite and vague article, it is precisely that one...As anyone who reads the article can see, it fails to establish the type of crimes imputed to the 'major war criminals.' As the criminologist Jiminez de Asua states: 'In this Article 6 an *enumeration* is made which is by no means clear, and which totally confuses some factors with others as to what constitutes crimes of aggression, i.e., war of aggression...' An attentive reading of paragraphs a, b, and c of Article 6 will show us that in not one of them is reference made to such acts or alleged conduct. It offers nothing more than a confused account naming crimes, which does not satisfy a legal definition of them. To say 'aggression, conspiracies, deportation, execution, despoliation, assassinations, maltreatments, devastation, etc.' is not to describe actions or punishable omissions classifiable as crimes, but on the contrary, is at most, an enumeration of crimes or a *nomenclature* of them. In accordance with the principles which guide Penal Law, the deficiency or insufficiency of type, or its absence, is equivalent to the specification of punishment corresponding to each type of crime. Categorically, in Article 6 of the Declaration, the punishment corresponding to each crime was not indicated, as is prescribed by penal science...This article wretchedly confuses the legal imperative of imposition of punishment with a 'law,' fixing in addition, a penalty, that of 'death,' and indeterminedly, 'whatever other penalty'...the same Tribunal might consider just.

"In jurisprudence it is incontrovertible that nobody can be judged except by a Tribunal legally established previous to the commission of the acts imputed...*'Nemo Judex sine lege previa.'* This principle includes the postulate of the irretroactivity of the law, excepting the application of the new law insofar as it is favorable to the accused. Therefore, this principle conflicts with the creation of extraordinary tribunals, created *'ad-hoc,'* all the worse if these tribunals are constituted by members designated specially and posteriorly to the commission of the acts...judicial proceedings which emanate from an incompetent judge or tribunal are non-existent in law. On the other hand, within the rigorous juridical proceedings is the necessity of completely proving the culpability of the accused; intuitive belief is not sufficient. There must be solid evidence that the acts were committed, that the accused participated in them, the imputation that they were executed freely and consciously, and that the acts in question were codified in law as crimes [prior to their commission] and had a corresponding established penalty.

"Possibly it was thought at Nuremberg that Military Law was the most expeditious, nevertheless its [the International Military Tribunal] composition does not qualify it as such. In Articles 3 and 8 of the Charter of London a serious juridical and legal error was committed, since in the first of them the right of appeal for plaintiffs and defendants alike was excluded. Furthermore, each signatory was able to replace its members or alternates on the Tribunal for reasons of ill-health or other valid reasons, without specifying what these might be and without further limitation than that of the duration of the proceedings...

"The famous Mexican jurist Leyva stated, when studying the Nuremberg Trials: '...there was no clear and precise definition of each crime to avoid extensive interpretations which turn the judge into an arbitrary subjectivist and a legislator for each concrete case. This is invariably to be condemned in law...' Not even the major apologists for the Charter of London have dared fully and completely to justify the International Military Tribunal.

"Doctor Antonio Quintano Ripolles, Prosecutor of the High Court of Bilbao and ex-Judge of the International Tribunals of the Saar and Cairo, states, with consummate accuracy: '...The 3 principles (no crime without a law, no penalty without a law, and no incrimination *post factum*), for a long time considered axiomatic and even sacrosanct in the juridical and political consciousness of Western Civilization, to which they seemed indissolubly linked, have suffered most brutal blows in the jurisprudence of Nuremberg and also in that of Tokyo, which, as is natural, have not served to enhance their prestige. So certain is this, and so much has criticism grown, that in the time intervening between the two proceedings, the conduct of the judges has been seen to vary; thus while at Nuremberg, in 1946, the resolutions were unanimous, in Tokyo on the other hand, in November of 1948, the condemning sentences were achieved only by a majority, the French, Philippine, and Dutch judges reserving their veto, precisely because of the scruple of the absence of previous typification...' The London Charter, as we have already established, ignored juridical postulates which constitute the very essence of the guarantees which are basic and fundamental to human life and freedom, axioms such as: *'Nullum crimen, nulla poena'* [no defined crime, no punishment], the right to challenge members of the court, the impossibility of acting simultaneously as judge and party, etc., etc."

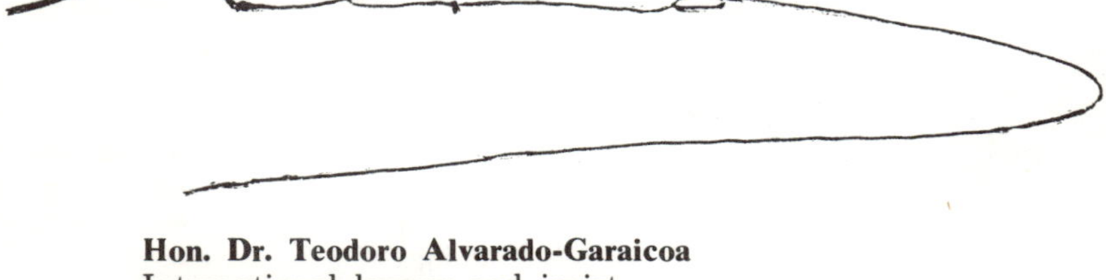

Hon. Dr. Teodoro Alvarado-Garaicoa
International lawyer and jurist
Foreign Minister of Ecuador, 1952-1953
Minister-counsellor to the U.S.A., 1948, and the U.N.
Minister of the Superior Court of Justice of Ecuador

"Anybody who was a victim of the iniquitous Nuremberg Trials has my deep sympathy. I am only surprised that so many reputable men in both our countries were found willing to take part in such a travesty of justice. Admiral Doenitz was a distinguished member of a fine profession, against which I had the honour to fight in World War I. Naturally you would not expect me to treat the charges brought against the admiral otherwise than with suspicion. The Nuremberg Trials leave an indelible blot upon the reputations of all countries which took part in them. I have been studying the Harry Dexter White papers, published in 1955 by your government, where I found my views as to the origin of the trials confirmed."

Admiral Sir Barry Domvile, R.N., K.B.E., C.B., C.M.G.
Chief of Staff, Mediterranean, 1922-1925
Director of Naval Intelligence, 1927-1930
Commander, 3rd Cruiser Squadron, 1931-1932
President, Royal Naval College, and War College, 1932-1934

Frank L. Beals
American author and educator
Ass't. Sup't. of Schools, Chicago, 1935-1946
Wrote 25 books, 1914-1954

"You have asked for my opinion of the so-called 'war crimes trials' of career officers at the termination of World War II. My feeling is that those who conducted the trials were the greater criminals. They made a mockery of law and justice. That members of the highest courts and leaders in the legal profession conducted the trials makes one wonder if there is such a thing as justice before the law, or if justice is only a word, and whether it is a useful word for which vengeance might not well be substituted. There can be no excuse for the punishment meted out to those professional soldiers and sailors who performed the duties assigned them and there can be no excuse for their having been tried. May I congratulate you on the fine work that you are doing."

"...the military career has its glories, and its sacrifices. The professional soldier is one of those individuals whose main mission in life is to serve their country regardless of the obstacles that must be overcome and the ordeals which the unrestricted fulfillment of their duty imposes on them. In the Second World War, Admiral Doenitz without doubt kept his oath. As a good commander, he employed all his knowledge and skill to lead his navy to victory. He followed established routine. If there were excesses, improprieties of his officers, he cannot, in good conscience, be held responsible. Who can, in such an atmosphere, stop or contain the impulses of men of the sea, who are always in imminent danger of losing their lives, before the threat of a mere depth bomb? Will it ever be possible to limit the action or effect of missiles with nuclear explosives to military targets, without affecting peaceful elements round about? The soldier is well acquainted with adverse circumstances. Defeated, in the conqueror's hands, he cannot expect kindness. History is full of examples...For the great soldiers and sailors the war does not always end with the cessation of hostilities. Bitter trials may arise: the cold vengenance of the victor or unjust appraisal by its leaders, even against their peers."

Joao Valdetaro de Amorim e Mello.

Marshal Joao Valdetaro de Amorim e Mello, Army of Brazil
Chief of Military Cabinet of President Dutra, 1948-1950
Minister of Public Works, Cabinet of President Dutra, 1950-1951
Director of Army Engineering, 1954-1955
First Sub-Chief of Staff, Brazilian Army, 1955-1957
Commandant, 1st Military Region, Rio de Janiero, 1958

"In my book *Sea Devils,* I wrote the following: 'I preserve the most cordial recollections of the hospitality of the German Submarine Headquarters and of the personality of Admiral Doenitz. My good wishes often go out to that honourable and gallant seaman in his prison at Spandau, where, after being sentenced to 10 years' imprisonment by the Nuremberg Tribunal, he is now atoning for misdeeds attributed to him by the victors, the chief of which, though not acknowledged by the hypocritical participators in that tragic judicial farce, was that of having fought on the side of the vanquished.' This was in 1950. Today I can only express again the same thought and the same feeling adding my best wishes for gallant Admiral Doenitz who in the meantime, has been released from Spandau after 10 years' imprisonment."

Valerio Borghese

Prince J. Valerio Borghese
Commander, Motor Torpedo Boats, Royal Italian Navy

"I devoted some thought to the matter of the Nuremberg Trials prior to their taking place. While I am not a lawyer, I have read some law, and for this reason I devoted a lot of thought to the question of what legal precedent there might be for such a trial. I had a discussion on this very subject with Mr. Justice Jackson in London, when he was on his way to attend the 'Nuremberg Trials'...Mr. Jackson frankly conceded that there was no precedent to go by, and furthermore, I had the distinct impression that he agreed with my opinion that these trials would establish some sort of new laws and precedents...To me, the thing that is important is first—whether or not there could have been any benefit to the majority of the world's population in these trials. Secondly—whether justice was done to the individual being tried. Under the first consideration above, I doubt that there can be any definite benefit to the majority of the world's population in the future. Under the second point, if this action is to be taken as an accepted legal precedent in the future for a victorious nation, then any commander, no matter how far down the line of succession, may look forward to a war crimes trial in the event the war is lost. This will probably mean that he will be inclined to fight to the death of himself, and possibly his command, rather than surrender. Of course, this could mean that we will generate military commanders of unlimited determination to win, but they will probably accept a fatalistic philosophy. They dare not consider surrendering—for the penalty of surrender is likely to be death—or worse—a lifetime in prison. In this event, their judgment and strategy will be affected accordingly. To bring the matter near home and considering our own constitutional principles, it seems to me that there is a triple jeopardy involved. (1) If the commander did not carry out the directives he received, he would be court-martialed and relieved. (2) If he did not, with high patriotic principle, defend his country in the best manner possible by a fight to a decision, or a strategic retreat to reorganize and fight under better circumstances, he would fail as an officer and would suffer dishonor within his own nation. (3) No matter who loses a war, and no matter how senseless such a war is, the professional military commander has no alternative to death in the event he loses such a war, regardless of whether such a war is right or wrong in the views of the rest of the world...The principle that I would be concerned with is the overall precedent concerning the fact that the winning nations considered they had a right to try the commanders of the losing nation. If they could do it at the 'Nuremberg Trials' without regard to authorization or precedent in international law, then the next winning nation, or group of nations, can do anything they wish that seems to further their interest at such a time."

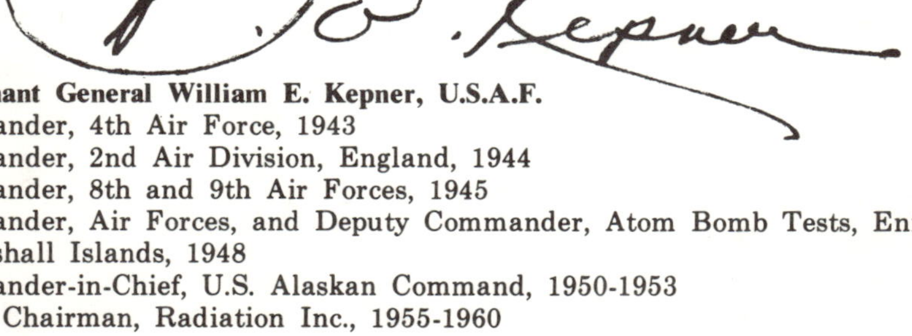

Lieutenant General William E. Kepner, U.S.A.F.
Commander, 4th Air Force, 1943
Commander, 2nd Air Division, England, 1944
Commander, 8th and 9th Air Forces, 1945
Commander, Air Forces, and Deputy Commander, Atom Bomb Tests, Eniwetok, Marshall Islands, 1948
Commander-in-Chief, U.S. Alaskan Command, 1950-1953
Board Chairman, Radiation Inc., 1955-1960

"I consider the 'war crimes trials' of professional military men were inexcusable and outrageous. They set a precedent which I fear many of the younger men who took part in them will live to regret. All military men eventually will regret them. At the time of the trials, I believed them wrong. Twelve years later, I feel more strongly that they were wrong. Americans should be ashamed of the farcical trials and terrible punishment of Japanese and German military leaders. I am of this opinion today, Oct. 19, 1974, more strongly than ever."

Very truly yours

Major General Alden H. Waitt, U.S.A.
Ass't. Chief, Operations, Chemical Warfare Service, 1941-1945
Chief, Chemical Corps, U.S. Army, 1945-1949

"Accusations by English scribblers of 'barbarism' on the part of German or other troops invariably provoke my indignation by their arrant hypocrisy. Accident of fate has brought it about that much of my military and civil career was occupied with the suppression, or attempted suppression, of armed rebellion or severe civil commotion, and I have seen or investigated enough atrocities committed by British and Irish troops and police in three countries to fill several books. Experience taught me that although in many cases these excesses were due to laxness or sheer bloody-mindedness on the part of individual commanders, in many other cases (and always so in Palestine) there was connivance on the part of the Government concerned and condonation on the part of Whitehall.

"May I conclude by tendering to you my respectful congratulations on what you are doing to try to redress the monstrous injustice done to a man whose moral courage and singleness of heart ought to have elicited the applause of all thinking civilized men. When Hitler died, every German knew the end was near. It would presumably have been easy for Admiral Doenitz to have declined to accept leadership of this defeated nation. And yet he bravely accepted it, probably in the full knowledge of what this would mean to him...Indeed the occasion is opportune for the open and unqualified affirmation of what can be heard whenever two or three Englishmen are discussing the Nuremberg affair, namely that to charge as criminals the admirals and generals of a defeated enemy is an innovation in our national history of which we may live to be profoundly sorry and ashamed."

A. T. O. Lees.

Aubrey T. O. Lees
English Colonial Administrator and Army officer
Served in Ireland during the Revolution (1920-1922), in Iraq (1922-1925), and for ten years in Palestine.

"I think the Nuremberg trials are a black page in the history of the world ... I discussed the legality of these trials with some of the lawyers and some of the judges who participated therein. They did not attempt to justify their action on any legal ground, but rested their position on the fact that in their opinion, the parties convicted were guilty ... This action is contrary to the fundamental laws under which this country has lived for many hundreds of years, and I think cannot be justified by any line of reasoning. I think the Israeli trial of Adolph Eichmann is exactly in the same category as the Nuremberg trials. As a lawyer, it has always been my view that a crime must be defined before you can be guilty of committing it. That has not occurred in either of the trials I refer to herein."

Edgar N. Eisenhower
American attorney
Brother of President Dwight D. Eisenhower

"I fought the Germans in 1914-1917, and was twice wounded, when I had the honor to serve in the Russian Imperial Army, originally in the Imperial Cavalry and temporarily (in 1915) in the Army Infantry. I fought also in the White Armies during the Civil War, and held the rank of Colonel. When I read about the Nuremberg Trials, especially about the case of Grand Admiral Karl Doenitz, I took it as an insult to the whole military profession of the world. The modern pseudo-christian 'democracies' could learn moral lessons from a pagan Julius Caesar or from the Mahometan Mongolian conquerors. These, in the dark ages of the past, proved to be finer gentlemen and better jurists than some of those who now pretend to be such, for in our modern era of 'advanced culture,' generals had better win wars otherwise they are hanged. I studied international law (1902-1905) at the Imperial University of Moscow, and I also remember that the 'International Military Tribunal' at Nuremberg had no authorization or precedent in international law. I am glad to know that Admiral Doenitz was finally released...but until now no official apologies for the Nuremberg *mistrials* have been presented to its victims."

Serge S. Boutourline, Sr.
Colonel, Russian Imperial Army

"You have my compliments on your project to re-expose the terrible blot on civilized warfare caused by the War Crimes Trials. From the beginning of this travesty on justice, I could not conceive of the mentality which would even censure an officer for doing his sworn duty and nothing more. To sentence such an officer to death or imprisonment was a reversion to barbarism. It is inconceivable that the United States would participate in it. As to Admiral Doenitz in particular, I have always admired and respected him, as I have Admiral Nimitz. He was not tried and convicted; he was just crucified. I hope you will let him know that civilized Americans with even a spark of chivalry abhor his treatment and wish him well."

Major General Jack W. Heard, U.S.A.
Commanded Flying Fields at Kelly (Texas),
Scott Field (Illinois), Payne Field (Missouri), 1917-1940
Commanding General, 13th Cavalry, Fort Knox
Commanding General, 5th Armored Division, 1942
Director, War Dept. Manpower Board, 1944

"No matter how many reasons of a moral or legal nature, which might be advanced in justification of the punishment of the war criminals (reasons such as international reaction against them, the political conditions created in conquered and occupied countries, the precedent for the judging of future criminals, the voluntary submission on the part of the victors to the rule of justice, and various other reasons propounded by defenders of the judgement of Nuremberg), it is certainly the case that neither those reasons nor any others are sufficient to offset, much less to destroy, the legal and moral arguments in opposition to the system of Nuremberg and Tokyo. In my opinion, this system not only infringed against justice and Christian civilization, but also committed a serious error, the root of which is to be found even more in the characteristics and procedures than in the constitution of the International Tribunal. In fact, the International Tribunal of Nuremberg lacked all the guarantees of independence and impartiality inherent in every legal Tribunal, since it was formed exclusively by judges of the victorious countries, one of those judges being the representative of the Soviet Union, which had committed in Poland the same aggression, in the same year, and with identical imperialist intentions as the accused Germany, her actual ally at the time of carrying out the aggression. And not only this, but many other acts of which the conquered were accused, had also been committed by the conquerors. One also tends to overlook the internal situation in Germany, which was fighting for her very existence, and the absolute control which Hitler exercised over the high officials, the armed forces, and the people, which made it impossible for anybody to oppose his desires or disobey his orders.

"Concretely, in the case of Admiral Doenitz, all these arguments against the judgement of Nuremberg acquire a more sharply defined character. Admiral Doenitz was sentenced on October 1, 1946 to ten years imprisonment for a finding of guilty under Article 6 of the Statutes of the Tribunal, crimes against peace and war-crimes. The first of these charges included the preparation and conduct of aggressive war. Doenitz, nevertheless, was considered innocent of planning or starting the war, since the Tribunal judged that he was an officer of the line who had restricted himself to carrying out his professional duties. On the other hand, he was found guilty of the second charge, that of carrying out the war of aggression. His condemnation was also based on the fact that in October of 1939 Doenitz had made a few theoretical proposals concerning submarine bases in Norway, and that upon succeeding Hitler in the Chancellory of the Reich, he had ordered continuation of the fight against the Soviet Union [Editors' Note: As Admiral Doenitz testified, this was necessary to enable operational units of the German Armed Forces to effect the rescue of hordes of refugees fleeing Russian-occupied areas.] But the most serious accusation made against Admiral Doenitz was having waged unrestricted submarine warfare, violating the London Protocol of 1936...The tribunal decided that the Protocol was decisive, and declared that if the submarine commandant could not take care of the rescuing of personnel of the merchant ship, it ought not to sink it either, and ought to let it pass in front of its periscope without causing it harm. If the conclusion had ended here, the trial would have had as a practical consequence the declarations of illegality of the use of submarine arms in the destruction of merchant shipping. But they formulated new considerations which implied the exhoneration of penal responsibility by virtue of the famous trial argument, *'Tu Quoque'* ('you too').

"In view of all the facts proved and in particular of an order of the British Admiralty of May 8, 1940, in which it was announced that in the Skaagerak all ships sailing at night would be sunk, and bearing in mind the statements of the North American Admiral Nimitz to the Nuremberg Tribunal in which he declared that in the Pacific Ocean the U.S. had waged unrestricted submarine warfare, the condemnation of Nuremberg could hardly be based on the fact that Admiral Doenitz had violated prevailing international law for submarine warfare The German admiral was declared *guilty* by the Nuremberg Tribunal for having violated the Protocol of 1936, but he was not *sentenced* for the said cause in consideration of the fact that the submarines, especially the British and North American, had acted in a similar manner. Admiral Doenitz was condemned for other reasons already cited...What results from this? Even if the *Tu Quoque* argument was rigorously excluded from the debates, or at least was not accepted as exempting by the sentencing tribunal, there can be no doubt that it had such an extraordinary influence over the said tribunal that it may allow us to reach the conclusion that, 'A crime ceases to be punishable when the victorious parties are liable for the same acts as the conquered.'

"But it is clear that in not sentencing Admiral Doenitz for the sole fact that he was previously considered as culpable under criminal law and its having been thus for reasons of extreme generality and vagueness, and without a previous legal declaration of punability, the injustice of the sentence stands out all the more. And the ink was not even dry on the signatures confirming the sentence when the most total disauthorization was formulated by the Assembly of the United Nations itself which, in the Declaration of the Rights of Man of Dec. 10, 1948, held that no person can be judged without there being in effect all the guarantees necessary for his defense, and that there cannot be imposed on anyone a greater penalty than that applicable at the time the penal offense was committed. There can be no doubt, in the light of these declarations, that the sentences of Nuremberg openly violated the Rights of Man as proclaimed by the Assembly of the United Nations. The accused were not judged by an impartial authority, nor was a previously existing penal law applied to them, nor were there provided to them the necessary guarantees for their defense.

"The sentences of Nuremberg will not serve even to prevent, in a future war, other cruelties or excessive violence. As Field Marshal Montgomery has said, the judgments at Nuremberg have made a crime of defeat, and in future wars the defeated admirals and generals will first be judged and afterwards hanged by the victors. Does this mean that international conscience and morality are to remain indifferent to atrocities and violent acts which may be unnecessary in a war and, in short, to actual crimes? No! All that we want—those of us who find in the judgments of Nuremberg a series of injustices and mistakes, as much of a juridical as a moral nature—is that the authors of such crimes, when they may in fact exist, be judged with impartiality and with every kind of guarantees. Men, above their national obligations, have others of a human and international nature, the infraction of which implicitly carries a responsibility. But as an illustrious Spanish jurist has said, this responsibility is limited by the doctrine of obedience owed, or of *force majeur,* so deeply rooted in Spanish tradition and based on *natural law,* superior both to national and international law."

Hon. Raimundo Fernandez-Cuesta Y Merelo
Spanish jurist, statesman and diplomat
Minister of the Navy, Inspector General of the Legal Corps, 1957-
Minister of Agriculture (1938-1939), Minister of Justice (1945-1951)
President of the Council of State (1945)
Ambassador to Brazil (1939-1942) and Italy
Member of the National Council, and the Royal Academy of Jurisprudence and Legislation
Author, *Maritime Law and Legislation*

"The fact that the Allies have established a legal principle by which they gave themselves, at their own discretion, judicial rights over their defeated opponents, was not compatible with justice. As far as the particular case of Admiral Doenitz is concerned...this supreme commander conducted the naval war only within the recognized limits of professional activity."

Lieutenant General G. Dromazos, Royal Hellenic Army

“I wish to present to Grand Admiral Karl Doenitz my heartfelt greetings and my sentiments of admiration for a man such as he, who knew how to fulfill his duties to and with his fatherland and who heroically endured and survived, as a defenseless prisoner, the vengeance of the powerful conquering powers. I want him to know that those of us who, for professional reasons, were in a better position to judge his case, we rejoice in his liberty and we hope that one day the illegal verdict which condemned him as a ‘war criminal’ will be revoked by a competent tribunal, and that thus justice be reestablished and his name be vindicated.

“As for my ideas on the ‘war crimes judgments,’ it is necessary to begin by defining: 1. What is meant by war crimes, 2. What punishments correspond to said crimes, 3. What tribunals ought to judge them, and 4. What should the procedure be to carry out the judgment. The aforementioned points should have been established prior to the judgments carried out in Nuremberg, if they had wanted to do real justice, since no law can be applied retroactively. Moreover they should have been defined in laws of an international character and validity, accepted by the nations which took part in said judgments [victors and vanquished]. Nothing of this sort occurred, and the definition of the above mentioned points and the proceedings themselves were exclusively at the mercy of the conquering countries. Before the Second World War, nations had made laudable efforts to alleviate war, attempting to bring to wars a certain Christian spirit to make them less ferocious than in primitive times. Some norms were established and accepted by all the nations, especially with respect to the manner in which non-belligerents and prisoners of war were to be treated. Unfortunately, the Second World War marked a retrogression of centuries in this respect, setting a most regrettable precedent like the one set at Nuremberg, in which the conquerors declared themselves judges, arbitrarily defined the crimes, imposed punishments and constituted themselves as hangmen and jailkeepers. What made all this worse was that the ‘crimes’ of which they accused the conquered were also committed by them [the conquerors].

“It is unnecessary to comment at length to establish that the ‘judgments of Nuremberg’ constituted the most flagrant injustice, and with respect to Grand Admiral Doenitz the injustice is more readily apparent, since as a professional of the armed forces of his country, and especially as Commander of the Navy, he did nothing more than carry out orders and sacred obligations. It is indeed very serious to think that so many years after the end of hostilities, and an organization like the U.N. being in existence, of which the nations which were belligerents form a part, and whose principal mission is to establish a lasting peace in the world, they have not as yet tried to correct past errors, causing justice to be re-established no matter who transgressed it. It would be desirable if there came forth from the aforementioned organization the decision to revise the judgments which were carried out under the influence of the passions which sparked the war, naming for this end a tribunal of nations which were not belligerents.”

General Luis F. Lesmes
General of the Army of the Republic of Colombia
Head, National Committee on Radio Communications

"I was most interested in the memorandum in regard to the 'war crimes trials' of military officers, and specifically in the case of Grand Admiral Karl Doenitz of the German Navy. I would like to go on record as expressing vigorous opposition to the philosophy which generated these war trials. To me they represent a complete travesty of justice, have absolutely no basis in law, and are an insult to anyone in the military service of any country whose sole motivation is patriotism and dedication to the interests of his country. They represent the most vicious type of war or post-war hysteria. The world will indeed be in a sorry shape if patriotism and dedication to the service of one's country is ever again to be regarded as a crime."

Vice Admiral Ralph E. Wilson, U.S.N.
Naval Liason Officer, Guadalcanal, 1943
Operations Officer, 3rd Fleet, Pacific, 1944
Deputy Commander, Military Sea Transportation Service, 1951
Commander, Cruiser Division 5, 1953
Deputy Chief of Naval Operations, 1957-1960
Chairman, Federal Maritime Board, 1961

"During the Nuremberg Trials, I felt profound indignation. To judge members of the government and chiefs of the Armed Forces of conquered Germany as war criminals, condemning among others, Foreign Minister von Ribbentrop to death, and Admiral Doenitz to ten years imprisonment—apart from the sadistic manner in which they were incarcerated during the long ordeal—was, without room for doubt, a return to barbarism. It is my most profound hope that this horrible precedent will not be repeated, and that its sad memory will pass into oblivion, in homage to the civilization which we thought we had attained."

Brigadier General Enrique Nunez Morgado
Air Force of the Republic of Chile

[To Grand Admiral Doenitz]
"I served in the U.S. Navy in combat zones in World Wars I and II. The German Naval Forces were efficient, honorable, and gallant foes whom we highly respected. Between the World Wars, and since the last one, I have known a number of German naval officers, and hold them in strong friendship and comradeship. The professional military of all nations, of course, view the Nuremberg 'trials' of military officers as disgraceful—a 'blot' upon the history of the victor nations, and a wholly unwarranted libel upon the military profession.

"I am fully cognizant of your outstanding career and your splendid command of the German submarine forces in the last war. For you, sir, I have the highest admiration, esteem, and respect. May I extend to you my heartiest best wishes for many happy and productive years in retirement, knowing, as you must, that your wartime foes and your post-war 'comrades-in-arms' so highly admire you."

Vice Admiral T. G. W. Settle, U.S.N.
Holder, world flight altitude record, 1933
Commander, Airships (Blimps), Pacific Fleet, 1943-1944
Commanded U.S.S. *Portland* (heavy cruiser), 1944-1945
Vice Chief of Naval Material, 1950
Commander, Atomic Test Joint Task Force 131, 1950-1951
Commander, Amphibious Forces, Pacific Fleet, 1954-1956

"It was Admiral Doenitz who, from the beginning of the Second World War, opposed the carrying out of 'Operation Giselle,' a lightning war stroke involving the occupation of Spain and Portugal, the Canary and Azores Islands, in addition to Gibraltar, 'for destroying,' as Hitler himself announced, 'this flank of the Anglo-Saxon offensive and to substantially smooth out the position of Germany in the Mediterranean.' It was then that Doenitz forced his opinion, that such an operation should not and must not be carried out without the consent of Spain. It cannot be forgotten that this isolated gesture of Karl Doenitz, alone among the men of the Third Reich, fits in a gentlemanly manner into the legal framework for regulating war, and marks him as entitled to the respect of those laws which are applied both to conquerors and the defeated...

"Concretely considering the ten-year sentence against Admiral Doenitz handed down by the so-called 'International Military Tribunal' convened at Nuremberg, the following adverse comment springs out: such a sentence not only lacks juridical basis, but also has no precedent in the history of cultured nations. Admiral Doenitz acted in the capacity of a professional military officer in the service of his country, just as other senior commanders would have done—and did—under similar circumstances. Admiral Doenitz maintained, in his activities, a standard of strict conformance with the obligations of a professional officer, carrying out the specific directives of his superiors in rank during World War II. He could by no means disobey, avoid, discuss or protest the orders received. His war activities were specifically confined to fighting the naval forces of the hostile countries, disabling or destroying their vessels, interrupting their supply routes, attacking their bases, and generally destroying their capacity to make war. Such was the task of Admiral Doenitz, which he fulfilled over all the seas on the map. And whenever his submariners encountered a hostile vessel, a tanker or supply ship, they acted, just as the Allies acted in establishing a blockade of Germany regardless of the fate of millions of civilians ruthlessly left to starve...

"The judgments and sentences of the so-called 'International Military Tribunal' have provided a lesson of deep meaning which the soldiers and statesmen of World War III will not forget. Future warriors will go into the fray with a fierce fury, since complete annihilation of the enemy will be the aim of the strife. Men of future wars will know that surrender is impossible because it means hanging or dishonor. All these men will carry with them the bitter memory of the massacres of Nuremberg and Tokyo."

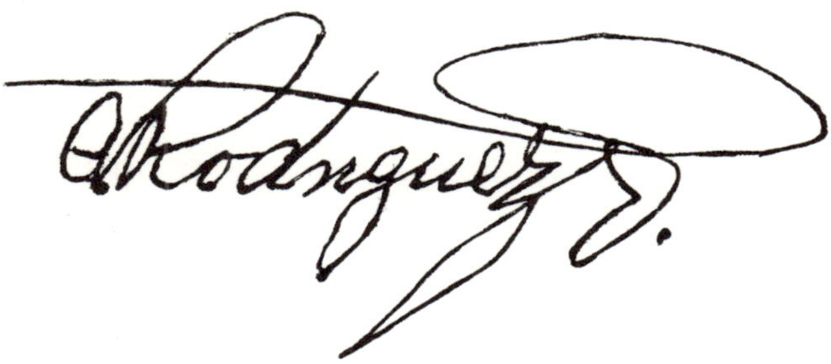

General Amadeo Rodriguez V., Army of the Republic of Colombia
Civil and Military Commander, The Amazons, 1932
Consul General of Colombia at Barcelona, 1955
Deputy to the Assembly of Cundinamarca
Member of the Legislature, and the Bolivarian Society

"Admiral Doenitz should not have been condemned for having waged unrestricted submarine warfare. No other kind is possible and, besides, that decision was the concern of the head of state."

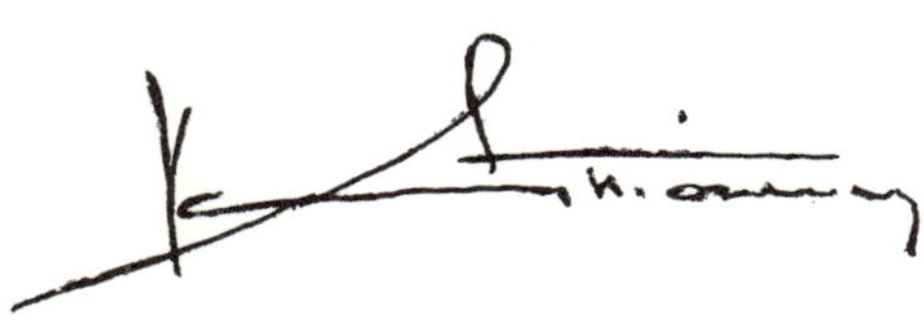

Lieutenant General V. Sottiaux, Royal Army of Belgium
Colonel of artillery in 1940
Prisoner of war, 1940-1945
Major General in charge of Military Conscription, 1946-1949

“Beginning in March, 1946, while the Nuremberg trials began and took place, I published in *Civilta Cattolica* four very long critical articles, soon translated into German, French, English and Dutch. These translations were privately distributed by the parties involved. The American and Dutch translators encountered difficulties with the publishers, due to the post-war atmosphere. A short comment which I wrote on the verdict of guilt was published by the journal *Politica Estera.* These writings, revised and somewhat enlarged, were brought out in book form, the third edition of which appeared at Rome in 1948, *Crimini di guerra e delitti contro l'umanita.* I discussed the complex aspects of international law, penal and procedural matters, etc., also taking into exact account the specific acts and documents, but according to the most basic ethical and juridical principles, with ample substantiation of the *severely critical conclusions,* which I believe to have been among the first to formulate and to demonstrate. It has seemed to me that the lawfulness [legality] of the so-called International Tribunal was certainly to be ruled out, and hence the ability of their sentences to form valid precedents for the future, to mark progress in the course of international justice and thus to make a contribution to peace among peoples. And this on the basis of strictly juridical, rigorously technical arguments...”

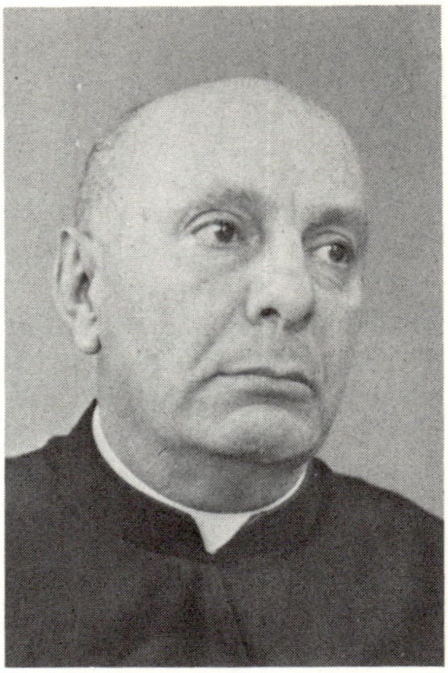

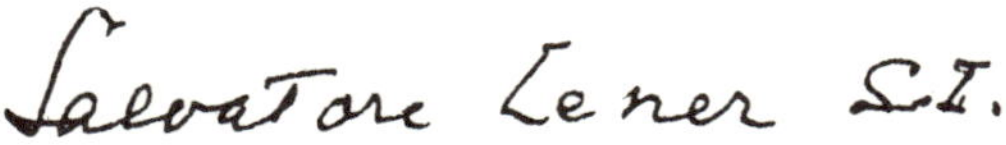

P. Salvatore Lener, S.J.
Lawyer, and priest of the Society of Jesus
Assistant in Trial Law, University of Rome
Professor of International Law, Lateran
Pontifical University
Journalist on staff of *La Civilta Cattolica*

“To me it is evident that men in Armed Forces are instruments for executing the orders of their governments, which make decisions and determine policies. If they fail in their duties and their responsibilities, they are charged with severest crimes and punished accordingly. This has been the state of affairs: an instrument of execution is not criminal...Remnants of our primitive instincts should give way to understanding and love for mankind because the progress of science and technology, with much improved means of transportation and communication, is making our world too small. It is time for the wise and the peace-loving elements to get together and resolve not only to absolve the honor of a few who have been wronged, but to...reach the lofty goal of Universal Peace...”

Major General Shoaullah Ala'i
Imperial Army of Iran

"Being myself a military man, I still cannot understand how the International Military Tribunal at Nuremberg could convict and punish such a man as Admiral Karl Doenitz. For what? For the 'crime' of fighting, as a professional officer, in the service of his country? Or for effective professional direction of the wartime navy of his country? Or for conduct of 'unrestricted submarine warfare'? But almost any Russian, British, French or even American career military or naval officer also could be convicted for such 'crimes.' Why, if a defeated officer had committed it, it must be a crime, but if victors—the prosecution—has committed it, it could not be a crime! Do we recognize the very old, but also very wrong, principle, 'Might Makes Right'? But where is the Justice? The Nuremberg 'war crimes trials' of professional military men were and still are a very dangerous precedent for all countries, including the United States of America, especially for the future."

General Stasys Rastikis, Republic of Lithuania
Former Commander-in-Chief of the Lithuanian Army

"As a former soldier and veteran of World War I, my feelings were outraged by the Nuremberg Trials at which honorable men were treated as common criminals for having served their country in time of war. This infamous 'trial' will always remain as a black page in the records of the 'allied" governments that participated in it. There are millions of Americans, like myself, who are ashamed of the fact that the United States Government was one of these participants."

Bela Hubbard, Ph.D.
American petroleum geologist and author

"As a veteran of the Greek Army who has participated in all the war operations in which Greece has been involved since 1918, I am convinced that the duty of all military leaders of a country at war is the attainment of victory. The safety of the Fatherland is the main thought which rules the wartime strategy and methods that military leaders have to use, even if these are considered very cruel. Of course, inhuman actions are to be condemned when it is certain that they do not serve the war purposes directly or indirectly, and are not used by the enemy. Therefore, in this spirit I should express my views on the case of Grand Admiral Karl Doenitz..."

Lieutenant General Solon Ghikas
Chief of Staff, Cavalry, 1940-1941
Commanded Army School in Palestine, 1942-1944
Military Attache in the U.S., 1946-1948
Commanded 42nd Brigade, 7th and 8th Divisions, 1949
Commander, 3rd Army Corps, 1950-1951
Chief of Army General Staff, 1954-1956
Minister of Communications and Public Works

"In his brilliant and forthright dissenting judgment in the so-called Tokyo War Crimes Trial, Mr. Justice Radha Binod Pal of India observed that 'when time shall have softened passion and prejudice, when reason shall have stripped the mask from misrepresentation, then justice, holding evenly her scales, will require much of past censure and praise to change place.' This observation applies, with equal validity, to professional military and naval officers, like Grand Admiral Karl Doenitz, tried at the Nuremberg War Crimes Trials on the novel and somewhat dubious charge of 'conspiring to wage,' or waging, 'aggressive war.'

"With the benefit of hindsight and the dampening of post-war passions, few, if any, will now hesitate to concede that it was not justice but the heady wine of victory and the irrefutable logic of defeat which provided the blatantly contrived justification for the conviction of and imposition of harsh sentences on professional officers, like Grand Admiral Karl Doenitz, who had, in the line of duty, efficiently and effectively directed their Armed Forces. If the War had not been lost, they would have been hailed as national heroes and no Military Tribunal, set up by the victors, would have branded them as war criminals.

"Both the victor and the vanquished had been equally 'guilty' of unrestricted submarine warfare and of indiscriminate bombing of civilian targets. Grand Admiral Karl Doenitz did not, by any standard, commit the mass slaughter inherent in the dropping of the atom bomb on Hiroshima and Nagasaki. The Nazis set out to reverse the 'Diktat' of Versailles and to establish the supremacy of the 'Herrenvolk' but Doenitz was by no means part of the inner political hierarchy around the Fuehrer. The professional soldier has a strong sense of obedience to the established political authority. This is particularly so among the Germans...

"A generally acceptable definition of 'aggression' has yet to be found and often it is difficult to draw a line between aggression and self-defence. So long as the concept of the nation-state lasts—and it will be some generations before the concept of world citizenship and of obedience to a higher international law takes root—the professional soldier will fight for his country, right or wrong, and give allegiance to his Government till death...

"The Nazi phenomenon arose from the desire of the German nation to avenge the defeat of 1918 and to find a place in the sun for the most dynamic of European nations. It was a continuation of the struggle between the 'have-nots' and the 'haves' of the great European Powers who, over a period of two centuries or more, established their political and economic stranglehold over vast areas of the globe. No one can pretend that political intrigue and unprovoked aggression—and, in some cases, genocide—had no part in the building up of their far-flung empires...

"Scientific progress has outstripped the development of human values. We are living in the Atomic Age and the Conquest of Space. Time and distance have been annihilated. Any future War—atomic, thermonuclear, chemical, bacteriological, or ecological—unless effectively curbed by the World Community would be tantamount to human suicide. Old traditional values have been eroded, and humanity is floating rudderless to destruction. The time has come for a return to the eternal path of basic human values. A cosmopolitan culture in which there is no racial arrogance, no domination of one people over another, and from which want and poverty have been eliminated, is the need of the hour. As the great philosopher-statesman, Radhakrishnan put it: 'We cannot allow ourselves to be destroyed by forces which we have the knowledge to create but not the wisdom to control.'

"The problem is not one of punishing the defeated enemy for war crimes, but that of eliminating war as an instrument of national, racial or regional aggrandizement."

Hon. Major General Khub Chand
Indian statesman and diplomat
Acting High Commissioner for India in Pakistan, 1950-1952
Ambassador to Italy and Albania, 1957-1960
High Commissioner in Ghana and Sierra Leone, Commissioner in Nigeria, and Ambassador to Liberia, Guinea, and Mali, 1960-1962
Ambassador to Sweden and Finland, 1962-1966
Ambassador to Lebanon, Jordan and Kuwait; High Commissioner in Cyprus, 1966-1967
Ambassador to the Federal Republic of Germany, 1967-1970
Vice-President, Indian Council of World Affairs, 1974

"...I do not under any circumstances go along with punishing officers who have simply carried out the orders of superiors under the circumstances where the penalty for not doing so was obviously to be done away with...I cannot, in conscience, hold anyone responsible for things they have no way of controlling. Authority and responsibility must go together, and if one is to be held responsible to the point of trial and conviction and imprisonment, then one must be demonstrated to have had full authority to do or not do that of which he is convicted. Obviously, at least to me, Grand Admiral Doenitz was not in any position where the things that went on that were directly contrary to the Geneva Convention were under his control, and therefore he was not actively involved. In my opinion, he should not have come under conviction."

Major General John B. Medaris, U.S.A.
Ordnance Officer, 1st Army, Europe, World War II
Chief, U.S.A. Mission to Argentina, 1948-1952
Commanding General, Ballistic Missile Agency, 1956-1958
Commanding General, U. S. Army Ordnance Missile Command, 1958-1960
Ordained Priest of the Episcopal Church, 1970
Associate Rector, Episcopal Church of the Good Shepherd

"As Cadets at West Point many years ago we were taught the General Appleby definition of discipline, which was said to be: 'the instant and willing obedience to all orders, or in the absence of orders to what you think those orders would have been.' I presume that the professional soldiers of other countries, whom later we were to meet in battle, were similarly indoctrinated. War is not a game of sportsmanship with rules enforced by referees; it is a deadly and usually last resort to the preservation of national security; it affords no choice to the professional soldier but to carry out his orders.

"I have always thought that the idea behind the war crimes trials was a great mistake. They could serve no purpose but to gratify an unreasoning desire for revenge and bring injustice upon the professional military and naval leaders against whom they were to be directed. Even as I sorrow that so many like Admiral Doenitz were wrongly punished, it pains me more to think of a military court such as was convened after the Japanese surrender to try General Yamashita and condemn him to execution. Such actions were unworthy of a great Nation that had always been magnanimous in victory."

Brigadier General Herbert D. Vogel, U.S.A., Dr.-Ing., M.S., C.E.
World War II service in Southwest Pacific
Lieutenant Governor, The Panama Canal, 1949-1952
Division Engineer, U. S. Army Corps of Engineers, 1952-1954
Chairman of the Board, Tennessee Valley Authority, 1954-1962
Engineer Advisor, The World Bank, 1963-1967

"The Nuremberg Trials justly deserve the epithet *infamous*. I think it is the first time in the history of this country that we have applied the doctrine of 'ex post facto crime.' The whole affair was as unprecedented as it was wicked. It constitutes and ineradicable blot on the honor of my country. Admiral Doenitz was a brave and capable commander, and served his native land, as all men should. He deserves to be accorded the honor due every loyal and brave patriot."

Hon. Archibald S. Coody
American jurist and author
Public official for 38 years

"I deplore the 'War Guilt Trials!

"To apprehend, arraign and try an individual for the wanton killing—murder, if you please—of prisoners of war, for example, is one thing. To do likewise to individuals who waged war in the uniform of their nation and under the orders or directives of their superiors, is another and quite different thing. I believe the former is fully justified. I believe the latter is unjustified and repugnant to the code of enlightened governments.

"Until such distant date, if this ever transpires, as nations can and will agree on a world political organization with judicial tribunals whose jurisdiction is acknowledged and whose judgments are accepted, I think trials in the second category described above, are steps backwards to the distant past when the fate of a defeated people was determined at the whim of the victor.

"I concur with the substance of your views as stated in your memorandum dealing specifically with the case of Grand Admiral Karl Doenitz, and you have my permission to include, not only this statement, but also the above."

General Matthew B. Ridgway, U.S.A.

Commanded 82nd Infantry Division, 82nd Airborne Division, and 18th Airborne Corps in Europe, World War II

Commander Mediterranean Theatre of Operations and Deputy Supreme Allied Commander Mediterranean, 1945-1946

Commander-in-Chief, Caribbean Command, 1948-1949

Commander, 8th Army in Korea, 1950-1951

Commander-in-Chief, Far East and Supreme Commander, Allied Powers in Japan. 1951-1952

Supreme Allied Commander in Europe, 1952-1953

Chief of Staff, U. S. Army, 1953-1955

Chairman, Board of Trustees, Mellon Institute of Industrial Research, 1955-1960

"There are no war crimes. The crime is the war! This was already obvious after World War I when the Netherlands, where the former Kaiser Wilhelm II had taken refuge, refused to surrender him to the Allies. During this war, while the Allies were contending that they were defending civilization, Lloyd-George had proclaimed that the Kaiser would be shown through the United Kingdom in an iron cage! Later, the Supreme Court of Leipzig acquitted the German chiefs who had been singled out as war criminals. The only evident crimes during a war are those committed against civilians...

"The fundamental aim of the Soviets, at the end of the last war [World War II], was to single out war criminals. They knew they were deepening the cleavage between the Occidental powers that the war had separated. This led to the Nuremberg trials...there were no war criminals among the mass of German generals and admirals. They were responsible only for having lost the war. *Vae Victis.* The only real justification of a war is to be the winner! If the Japanese had won the war, under the same principle they would have attempted to hang those in America who were responsible for the atomic bombing of Hiroshima.

"The exaggerations of the Nuremberg Tribunal were proved by the prosecution of Gustav Krupp, whose sole responsibility was to have manufactured war weapons. How can one justify today the life imprisonment of Rudolf Hess, who sought to put an end to the war? And the execution of Field Marshal Keitel, who signed the Armistice of May 1945? The ten-year imprisonment of Grand Admiral Doenitz was a flagrant injustice. And the present effort of Keith Thompson and many other fair Americans to get the historical record straight in the troubled world of today, compels my personal esteem and admiration. I think this feeling should be shared by all those who still believe in 'historic' justice."

Roger Peyrefitte
French author of more than 22 books
In French diplomatic service, 1931-1940, 1943-1945, 1962-

"The so-called 'War Crimes Trials' were merely another form of subservience to Godless Communism, and said subservience has been going on ever since. They meant to establish a precedent while public feelings were still running high, and a justice of the U.S. Supreme Court allowed himself to be used for that purpose. Acts of war were made crimes retroactively. This precedent has been used many times since, notably in Cuba."

Rear Admiral E. D. McEathron, U.S.N.
Commanded U.S.S. *Grebe* during Pearl Harbor attack
Commanded Mine Squadron 10, Pacific, World War II
On Staff, Commander Mine Force Pacific, 1945-1946

"The Nuremberg Trials took place in the emotional aftermath of the war. Their implications especially as regards the position of soldiers, sailors, airmen and civil servants in any future war were never considered, except perhaps, by a few of the more thinking. To the politicians, of course, the expediencies of the moment were paramount, and one cannot expect much more of these people. There were many of us, however, experienced in actual combat and subject to the pressures and disciplines of war, who wondered at what would have been the position if we had been on the losing side, or in view of the precedent set by these trials, what might be our position in some future war.

"For there is little doubt that these trials were purely political shows, designed to appease the wrath of the masses who had suffered during the war, and that they had no justification in international law as it existed at that time. In fact, they were 'kangaroo courts' much on the level of the vigilante posse and its lynch law. Victors in past ages were perhaps more direct. They paraded the conquered and then executed or threw them to the lions in the circus. In the twentieth century the same procedure was covered over by legalistic forms but the result was the same, though less honest.

"However culpable the politicians might be who initiate and direct a war, and however just it might be that, in case of defeat, a like nemesis befalls them, it is with the servants of the state that I am concerned; those who by oath are bound to serve as directed by their political masters, who in a democracy are ultimately the people.

"The case of Grand Admiral Doenitz therefore was one of paramount importance, and it would seem that his real 'crime' was that he assumed the mantle of Hitler when that fell unsought upon his shoulders, and then tried to salvage what he could of his country. One cannot seriously consider that war crimes were committed by him in the pursuance of unrestricted war at sea, for this was the tactic and strategy of all belligerents, and just as reprehensible as the bombing of civilian populations by both sides. The principle of a War Crime Tribunal, a witch hunt after a war by the winning side, is a most dangerous precedent and will certainly be used by any aggressive Communist state which wishes to remove, by these quasi-legal methods, those leading figures in a subdued country, who might successfully oppose their occupation.

"The Western Nations should avoid this danger and restore the confidence of their servants by a declaration that these trials were a mistake, and would never be resorted to again. Otherwise, the morale, self-confidence, and efficiency of their servants will be severely strained in any future war, for they will be looking over their shoulders at a time when their thoughts should be solely on doing their duty as outlined by their masters, who should indeed bear the sole and full responsibility for the actions of their servants."

Brigadier Andrew Skeen, I.C.D., O.B.E., P.S.C.T., M.P.
Rhodesian soldier and statesman
Service with British Regular Army, 1926-1947
Director, Combined Operations India, 1944
Deputy Director, Prisoners of War Dept., London, 1945-1946
Member of Rhodesian Parliament, 1966-1974
Rhodesian High Commissioner (Ambassador) to England, 1965

17/ July 1975

"I strongly endorse the view expressed in your memorandum regarding the 'trial' of Grand Admiral Doenitz. This survey is of great importance for the reassurance of all permanent service officers of today and the future, who must comply with the orders of higher authority. I consider it my duty and am happy to add my name to those of my many friends and brother Admirals in the Royal Navy and the United States Navy who agree with the views you express."

Vice Admiral John A. Collins, K.B.E., C.B., Royal Australian Navy
Commanded H.M.A.S. *Sydney,* 1939-1941, and *Shropshire,* 1943-1944
Commodore Commanding China Force, 1942
Chief of Naval Staff, 1948-1955
Australian High Commissioner in New Zealand, 1956-1962

"In the conduct of modern war today, the responsibilities of a senior military officer inevitably overlap into many other areas beyond the duties he was trained and brought up to face. In addition, and particularly in defeat, he often has to bear the brunt of the mistaken decisions made by his political masters, decisions in the formulation of which he had no say, with which he may not have agreed but yet which fell to his duty to execute. Mr. Keith Thompson's volume on the Doenitz Case clarifies for the future how this particular military dilemma might be viewed and handled, thus filling a very vital gap in the assessment of the aftermath of war."

General Joyanto Nath Chaudhuri, O.B.E., Indian Army
With Indian 7th Cavalry, Middle East and Burma, 1939-1945
Military Governor of Hyderabad, 1948-1949
Commander, Goa Operation, 1962
Chief of Staff, Indian Army, 1962-1966
Ambassador to Canada, 1966-1969
Vice President, International Institute of Strategic Studies
Chairman and Managing Director, Andrew Yule & Co., Ltd., 1973

"It was most gratifying to learn that you have taken the initiative of conducting an international survey of the 'War Crimes Trials' of World War II, dealing with the naval cases and in particular, with the trial of Grand Admiral Karl Doenitz.

"I am glad to learn that this survey was highly critical of the 'trials' and strongly in defense of the professional naval officers of all countries who must comply with the orders of higher authority. In this respect, I may recall that as a young lawyer immediately after the Second World War, I could hardly understand the manner in which the Nuremberg Tribunal conducted the trials against some of the military and naval officers who acted in performing their professional functions under the order of higher authority; and that in the absence of any precedent in International Law which neither defines war crimes nor permits ad hoc definitions. I must add immediately that I believe that International Law must reach the stage where crimes against peace in general and war crimes well-specified, should be defined and punished by competent international courts.

"It was along this line that I expressed my views as my country's delegate before the Legal Committee of the United Nations when some related questions were being discussed. It is therefore, hardly necessary to say that I find myself in general agreement...I am convinced that this symposium of opinions will contribute further to the recognition of the rightness of this cause.

"In conclusion may I express the hope that this lauded effort will prevent the precedent established at Nuremberg from having an undue impact on the future of the international criminal laws."

Honorable Jalal Abdoh, LL.D.
Iranian diplomat and jurist
Public Prosecutor, 1940-1944; Parliamentary Deputy, 1944-1948
Member, Administrative Tribunal, U.N., 1949-1953
Head, Iranian Delegation to Bandong Conference, 1955
Permanent Representative and Ambassador to U.N., 1955-1959
Iranian Minister of Foreign Affairs, 1959
U.N. Plebiscite Commissioner, Cameroons, 1959-1961
Ambassador to India, 1965-1968, and to Italy, 1968-1972
President, International Law Association, Iran, since 1973
Member, Permanent Court of Arbitration, U.N., since 1946

"I disapprove of everything which was done in that counterfeit court in which the victorious side in the war arrogated to itself the roles of accusing party, indicting party, and judge against individuals pre-selected from the losing side in the war. No trial ought to be held contrary to the fundamental norms of procedural penal law dictated and established by the consensus of men of good will.

"There is a basic rule for a fair and valid judgment, based on human rights, namely: Nobody may be judged by a court interested in the condemnation of the accused. Therefore, no court set up by the victors of a war has sufficient moral capacity for judging persons pre-selected as scapegoats among the losers of the war. The victor has hatred towards the defeated who were provoked to fight him, and usually he committed the same crimes as his adversary. If the victor would hang his own war criminals, together with those of the defeated nations, then one could speak of justice, However, even so, it would be usurping the role that should fall to a super-national or world state. Without the existence of a world state, of a world penal code, of a world code of penal procedure, of a super-national judiciary power, and of an army capable of imposing discipline and obedience to the Law on recalcitrant nations, *the term 'war crime' has no legal meaning.* Acts of war are acts of defiance of the law, of disobedience to reason, and today a warring people kills multitudes of civilians (in the majority, women and children) and destroys irreplaceable property acquired by generation after generation. And today's weapons are so atrocious, so ingeniously invented to destroy and to burn, that Dante would regard the verses of his *Inferno* as inadequate to express the indescribable torments that such weapons bring about.

"A nation which spreads over another a sheet of inevitably deadly gases or eradicates entire cities from the earth by the explosion of atomic bombs, does not have the right to judge anyone for war crimes; it has already committed the greatest atrocity, equal to no other atrocity; it has killed—amidst unspeakable torments—hundreds of thousands of innocent people.

"Let us consider the existence of a world state and a world penal code, and then the designation 'War Crime' takes on legal meaning: a 'War Crime' would be any act of major atrocity, of unnecessary cruelty, of patent inhumanity, *prohibited by the world penal code.* And such offense may have been committed both by officials or soldiers of a victorious side and by officials or soldiers of a defeated side. However, even so, defendants would have the right to justify their acts before a world court which would judge them impartially, invoking, in their favor, the same causes impeditive of condemnation that a criminally indicted citizen can invoke in his own national courts. He would have the right: (a) to deny the allegations; (b) to contest or invalidate the evidence brought against him; (c) to allege and prove the bias of the judge; (d) to prove that he acted in lawful defense of his country (or of his troops) with the requisites of lawful defense which the world penal code would establish; (e) to prove that he acted in a state of necessity, i.e. that he practiced a considerably *lesser* evil in order to avoid a considerably *greater* evil; (f) to prove that he acted in compliance with an order from higher authority to which he could not refuse obedience, because it was invested with the requisites established by law.

"When a group of victorious nations seizes and condemns for war crimes individuals pre-selected among the leaders and mentors of the defeated nations, *this is not a judgment—it is a reprisal.*"

Hon. Lydio Machado Bandeira de Mello, Dr. Juris.
Brazilian educator and jurist
Professor of Criminal Law, Univ. of Minas Gerais, 1952-1971; Professor of Comparative Criminal Law, 1959-1971
Author of more than 40 works, 1935-1974, on law and philosophy

"I was opposed to the war trials that were conducted in Germany and Japan following World War II. I felt then and still do that they were as barbaric as anything out of ancient history. Heaven forbid that America ever lose a major war. If it does we can expect to see our leaders of that time tried and executed as criminals just as the Germans and Japanese were, and that regardless of whether the United States actually perpetrated the war."

Hon. Meldrim Thomson, Jr.
Governor of New Hampshire
Attorney and publisher of legal textbooks

"I consider that this important question is of much interest from the historical, juridical and military point of view, and that its impartial clarification is very fitting, although it is late as a *fait accompli,* but not as concerns the necessity of defending the principles of international justice, protecting them against procedures which seek to disregard them. I also think that it is plausible, as an exercise of professional morality, to rectify or condemn the deeds which were not in conformity with the application of prior established norms of justice in judging those who were considered as 'war criminals.' One of the principal objectives of this procedure would be that of preventing the establishment of unfavorable precedents in the history of nations against the respect of the individual and his inalienable rights."

Rear Admiral Julio C. Ayala, Colombian Navy
Ambassador of the Republic of Colombia to Sweden

"Thank you for the opportunity you gave me in your letter of July 3rd, to comment on the War Crimes Trials of career military officers. I was deeply shocked when I learned that this Country in concert with its allies intended to bring to trial some career military officers for so-called war crimes, when it appeared to me that, on the surface, they were merely carrying out orders from higher authority. I remarked at the time that 'there, but by the Grace of God, go I.' I conjectured that the same thing could happen to my sons if they were to become career military officers, and this Country would have the misfortune to be the loser in some future war during their life time. I am satisfied that the persons who advocated the trials of career military officers were sincere at the time in their convictions, but I can always hope that they have long since had a change of heart, although this cannot change the position this Country took at that time."

Mitchell D. Matthews

Rear Admiral Mitchell D. Matthews, U.S.N.
Commander, Destroyer Squadron 14, 1949-1950
Commander, Mine Division 60, 1945
Commander, Destroyer Division 34, 1944
Commanding Officer, U.S.S. *Butler,* 1942-1944

"My brief comments on the subject relate to two aspects: (1) Whether the convictions of the accused by the International Military Tribunal at Nuremberg were supported by the international law; (2) Whether the conviction of the Grand Admiral Karl Doenitz of the German Navy was valid. Article 6 of the Charter establishing the international military tribunal for the trial of the war criminals authorized the tribunal to try three categories of crimes, namely: (1) Crimes against peace; (2) War crimes (crimes against the rules and customs of war) and (3) Crimes against humanity. The charges against the accused before the said tribunal were that they in pursuance of their common plan *conspired and waged wars of aggression* in violation of international treaties, agreements or assurances. The objects of the conspiracy were (1) to abrogate and overthrow the treaty of Versailles and its restrictions on military re-armaments; (2) to acquire territories lost by Germany in the First World War; and (3) to acquire still further territories in continental Europe at the expense of neighboring and other countries. The defendants raised the following points in their defense: (1) There could be no punishment for a crime without a pre-existing law, *nullum crimen sine lege, nulla poena sine lege;* (2) ex post facto punishment is opposed to the law of all civilized nations; (3) no sovereign power had made aggressive wars a crime at the time of the commission of the alleged criminal acts; (4) the aggressive war had not been defined by any law, nor any penalty prescribed, nor any court created for the trial and punishment of offenders accused of such crimes; (5) they were only acting under the orders of Hitler and they were bound to carry out his orders.

"The Tribunal rejected the said pleas. It held that the first maxim was only a principle of justice and was not a limitation of sovereignty, that the defendants knew the treaties signed by Germany outlawing recourse to war, particularly that embodied in the pact of Paris, that as Germany in resorting to war broke the said pact, and that as the said pact was legal in international law, those who were parties to the plan to wage the said war had committed an international crime.

"In my view the judgement is assailable. It was mainly based upon the pact of Paris. But a close scrutiny of that pact discloses that it was merely a record of a common understanding between the signatories and that it did not constitute the declaration of war as an international crime so as to make each individual participant in the war liable for an international crime. Indeed that pact was not acted upon in the context of war waged between some of the signatories and therefore remained a dead letter. If that pact had not the force of internation law, as I said it had not, the whole conviction based upon the breach of that law was bad.

"The aforesaid two fundamental principles of criminal jurisprudence that there can be no punishment of a crime without a pre-existing law and that ex post facto punishment was opposed to the law of all civilized nations are as much the integral parts of international law as they are of national law. As there was no law at the time the alleged acts were committed declaring the waging of war or a conspiracy to wage a war as war crimes, the said principles of justice would preclude the Tribunal from relying upon the charter for convicting the defendants for war crimes.

"That apart, it is not possible to hold definitely who was the aggressor in a conflict between the two groups of countries. In the context of a war the concept of aggressor may only mean the leader of a losing party. If the Allies lost the war, Germany could have with equal plausibility named the Allies as aggressors. In the olden days the conqueror slaughtered the leaders of a defeated country and pillaged and plundered the properties of the people of the said country. The Nuremberg trial is only an institutionalization of the said act of vindictive retaliation. The aggressors destroyed the defeated leaders through the legal process of a Tribunal in disregard of all principles of natural justice. The Judges were nominated by the victorious countries. The defeated leaders were convicted for offences that were not in existence at the time they waged the war. The whole trial was one sided and contrary to principles of natural justice.

"Be that as it may, I am of the view that Grand Admiral Karl Doenitz of the German Navy was illegally convicted of the offences. He was a subordinate officer and was acting under the orders of Hitler. If he did not act he would have been court martialled. By no stretch of imagination could it be said that he was a member of the conspiracy to wage the aggressive war against the Allies, nor was there any clear evidence to hold that he acted viciously on his own contrary to the orders issued to him.

"At the same time it is necessary to have a judicial tribunal to decide the war crimes on the basis of clear and precise concepts of international law. The United Nations shall bring about an international treaty clearly defining the incidents of a war crime and the judicial procedure for enforcing the said law. It shall constitute an international Tribunal comprised of Judges from all the neutral states so that both the victor as well as the vanquished can be tried by the said Tribunal for the breach of the international law of war crimes. While I therefore agree that the Nuremberg trial did not comply with the requirements of law, I am strongly of the view that it is necessary to have an independent international Tribunal, which could objectively go into the war crimes irrespective of the fact they were committed by the vanquished or the victorious on the basis of a clear and precise international law of war crimes."

Hon. K. Subba Rao, LL.D.
Judge, Madras High Court, 1948-1954
Chief Justice, Andhra High Court, 1954-1956, and Andhra Pradesh High Court, 1956-1958
Justice, Supreme Court of India, 1958-1967
Chief Justice of India, 1966-1967

"I commend your efforts to highlight the implications of such trials, and the inadequacy of international law regarding the responsibilities of service chiefs and senior commanders in the execution of the orders and directives of the government, and in the discharge of their duties. It is extremely difficult if not impossible to define as to when a service chief should assess the morality or justifications of the orders and directives of the duly constituted government.

"The weapons systems and the methods of employing them are constantly changing and, at the moment, the world is faced with the probable use of nuclear weapons. Yet there is no international code on limitations to their employment. Any attempt to *legalize* punishment of service chiefs of a defeated nation without a previously agreed upon international code would not be fair. There are, however, precedents where the winners have punished the defeated according to the whims and notions of the men in power at the time."

Lieutenant General Prem Singh Gyani, O.B.E., Indian Army
Commanded field regiment, Burma Theatre, 1944-1946
G.O.C., infantry division, 1959
Commander, U.N. Emergency Force, Gaza, 1959-1964
Commander, U.N. Cyprus Force, 1964
President, Birla Institute of Technology, 1963-1967
Member, Punjabi University Syndicate, 1971-1973

"I agree with the view that soldiers, sailors and airmen are the military servants of the governments which they serve both in peace and in war and as such follow out the instructions of their governments. Modern war is a savage business—destroy the enemy or be destroyed. Therefore it cannot be waged without hatred of the enemy. Although combatant soldiers, sailors and airmen are quick to lose their hatred of a beaten enemy, the non-combatants of a nation are much slower to forget. This is particularly so when the homeland has been devastated by enemy bombardment and the loss of human life and the misery entailed thereby. If the war ends in victory for the nation there is a demand for vengeance, not only against the political heads of the defeated, but also their senior military servants. This is a human characteristic even though it is not humane.

"The only solution would be to abolish war as an instrument of national policy applied to all nations. But throughout history, force of arms has been the final arbitrament in the settlement of international and national disputes when all peaceful means have failed to achieve a settlement. Therefore it is impossible for me to believe that war can ever be abolished as an instrument of national policy. Cases where nations or coalitions of nations have been magnanimous in victory are very rare indeed. One can but deplore this in the aftermath."

Major General Chris Vokes, C.B., C.B.E., D.S.O.
Commanding General, 1st and 2nd Canadian Infantry, Italy, 1942-1944
Commanding General, 4th Canadian Armored Division, 1944-1945
Commanding General, Canadian Occupation Force, Germany, 1945-1946
G.O.C., Central Command, Canadian Army, 1946-1950
G.O.C., Western Command, Canadian Army, 1951-1959

"I do feel in agreement with the point of view expressed in the memorandum on the Doenitz case; i.e. that the war crimes trials were not in accordance with then existing international law and the customs of war."

Lieutenant General E. L. M. Burns, C.C., D.S.O., O.B.E., M.C.
Canadian Army officer, statesman, and author
Deputy Minister, Dept. of Veteran Affairs, 1950-1954
Chief of Staff, U.N. Truce Supervision Organization, Palestine, 1954-1956
Commander, U.N. Emergency Force, 1956-1959
Canadian Representative, Disarmament Conferences, 1960-1968

"It should be noted at the outset that international law is a highly controversial subject, and one in which disputes can rarely be settled. Since the international community possesses neither a legislative authority nor a system of courts of general and compulsory jurisdiction, international 'law' is something less than law in the domestic sense of the term. The rules of this so-called law can only be inferred from the practice of nations, which varies considerably. Differences of opinion on the subject are thus frequent. However, it is my impression that, prior to the first world war, certain principles were generally agreed upon both by the more important powers and the great majority of authoritative writers.

"First, international law governed sovereign states. It neither gave rights nor imposed duties on the individual citizen. The highest obligation of the individual was to his own state, and his highest duty was obedience to the public authority of that state. Secondly, the individual was not held legally responsible for political decisions of his government in the international sphere. This was true even in regard to the high political officers who actually made the decisions. It was doubly true as regards the private citizen and likewise doubly true as to the personnel, both commissioned and enlisted, who carried out any military operations which might result from such political decisions. Thirdly, war as such was not contrary to international law. On the contrary, it was a recognized institution, and an elaborate body of rules to regulate its conduct had grown up, based both upon usage and specific treaties. A given state might undertake by treaty not to engage in war against other given states, and such treaties were often made (and often violated). As far as the individual was concerned his own government's judgment of the binding force of such treaties in given situations was conclusive, and it was never dreamed that he might expose himself to criminal liability under any circumstances by obeying orders from those lawfully in military or political authority over him. It was likewise never dreamed that military personnel carrying out explicit orders relating to the conduct of military operations would be subject to the judgment, years later, of a tribunal (composed of officials of the late enemy state and hostile in attitude), as to the necessity and propriety of such orders.

"Due to the unprecedented scale of the first world war, and the extent to which it affected the lives of entire populations, a great deal of emotional tension and hostility was built up. This in turn resulted in pressure on the victorious governments to wreak vengeance on individual rulers, statesmen and soldiers of the defeated nations, without regard to previously recognized rules of international law. At that time, circumstances prevented this program of revenge from being carried out. In the period between the two world wars, most informed opinion regarded this as fortunate, and dismissed the proposals to 'Hang the Kaiser' and their like as regrettable excesses resulting from war hysteria.

"History repeated itself after the second world war. In fact, the demand for revenge was far greater, due to the even greater scale of the war in part, but due more to the politically revolutionary character which the struggle took in many areas. There was undeniably a breakdown in the observance of traditional rules of warfare, particularly with regard to civilian populations. It was thought immediately after the end of hostilities that the measures complained of had been largely resorted to by the Axis powers, but subsequent information indicates that certain of our principal allies were guilty of equal or worse excesses. Also, it is doubtless true that new weapons and tactics made observance of the traditional rules difficult, especially where air or submarine warfare was involved.

"The circumstances that had prevented proceedings against individual soldiers and statesmen of the defeated countries were absent at the conclusion of the second world war. The major allied powers yielded to the pressure of certain of their citizens and instituted a program of proceedings patterned after criminal trials. In order to justify such proceedings, they evolved many new theories of 'law.' The soundness of such theories from the technical viewpoint of the lawyer was doubtful, and the wisdom of the program from the standpoint of the statesman appeared even more doubtful. Considerable criticism from responsible opinion was heard at the time, and the events of the subsequent years have tended to confirm this criticism.

"The Nuremberg trials, which were the best known and may be taken as typical, grouped the alleged crimes of the defendants into four categories: (a) Waging aggressive war, (b) Conspiracy to wage aggressive war, (c) Crimes against humanity, and (d) Violations of the laws of war. The first two are closely related, differing as to technicalities of proof. They both assume that there is such a thing as 'aggressive' war which can be legally distinguished from other kinds of war. Of the four categories, only the last had any substance under international law as it had generally been understood prior to the time of the trials.

"Prosecutions for violations of the laws of war represented the major exception to the principle that an individual would not be held legally responsible for consequences of military operations in which he was engaged. Such prosecutions can be justified for the reason that all major powers had accepted in principle the existence of such rules, and most had subscribed to multilateral treaties such as the Geneva Convention setting them out in detail. The rules could, as a result, be regarded as a portion of the domestic law of the countries concerned. An officer or soldier violating them, or ordering his subordinates to violate them, could thus be considered to have violated the laws of his own country.

"The prosecutions were carried out, and various persons were condemned to death or imprisonment. They have duly suffered the infliction of the penalties adjudged. Emotions have somewhat cooled on the issue in the intervening period. It remains to consider whether the precedent is a sound and desirable one. It is the viewpoint of the writer that the answer should be 'no'. The grounds for this view are numerous.

"First, the precedent cannot do other than gravely handicap the process of ending any war and the restoration of international peace and friendship. Formerly, a government engaged in a losing war had every motive to make peace on terms at the earliest possible moment. Under the new rules, however, the strongest possible motive exists for continuing the war to the bitter end. Substantial numbers of the population may find themselves subject to trial and branded as criminals by the occupying forces. (Entire organizations, it should be remembered, were condemned at Nuremberg). The officers of government who must actually make the decisions, being the likeliest candidates for the noose, are those with the strongest reasons for continuing the struggle.

"Secondly, it is impossible as a practical matter to secure an impartial tribunal. Nationals of the victorious powers cannot and will not do other than reflect the positions of their own governments as to the true version of facts and as to the proper law. It is also impossible to avoid the effect of ex post facto law. Since the proceedings can be depended on to lack these basic elements of any civilized system of criminal law, it is unlikely that the vanquished nations or even the fair-minded elements of the victor nations will come to accept them as representing justice.

"Thirdly, it places an impossible burden on the government and on the higher military officers of a warring state. It is their duty to do all in their power to win. It is also their duty to obey their lawful superiors. They are rightly subject to punishment for failure in this respect. To impose on them liability for carrying out an order which an enemy tribunal may later adjudge unlawful is to punish them for doing what may and probably will appear at the time to be the duty they have sworn to do.

"Finally, to engage in measures which, however cloaked in legality, are in fact no more than vengeance and reprisal is to promote the breakdown of the rules which have in recent centuries governed the conduct of warfare among civilized states, and to reinstate the law of the jungle. As a practical matter, the late war crimes trials will be taken by those involved in warfare as establishing only the principle that many of those on the losing side will suffer death or imprisonment. That leads to the thought that one had better not lose, which in turn leads to the conclusion that any method of warfare is justifiable if it brings victory. One must dissent from the view that this is progress.

"The conclusion drawn is, therefore, that the result of the program for the trial of 'war criminals' was not to advance the cause of civilization or the elimination of warfare among nations, but instead to increase the probability of unlimited warfare and to raise problems of a sort not yet fully apparent."

Lieutenant General A. D. Bruce, U.S.A., LL.D.
Chancellor of the University of Houston
Organized, built, and commanded Tank Destroyer Center, 1941
Commanding General, 77th Division, Pacific, World War II
First Governor of Hokkaido, Japan
Deputy Commander, 4th Army, 1947
Commandant, Armed Forces Staff College

"Although it is a glaring fact that the case of Grand Admiral Karl Doenitz, condemned by the co-called 'International Military Tribunal' as a war criminal, is perhaps the most notorious, it is my opinion that because of the very nature of the trials themselves, no distinctions should be made between this case and the others when judging the trials of the 'war criminals'; what must be done is not the judging of one isolated case, but instead, the entire nefarious precedent established at Nuremberg must be condemned in the most energetic manner possible. With that aberration of an 'International Military Tribunal' constituted by the victors, the doors have been opened to barbarism. The victor has domain over the life of the vanquished. In effect, if at Nuremberg a man like Doenitz was condemned, solely and exclusively for exercising his military function in the form which his patriotism and professional knowledge dictated to him as the most efficacious for his country, who would be surprised if in a future contest the victor should consider it more convenient to condemn to death not only the political leaders and military chiefs but also those who followed their orders?

"As far as 'unrestricted warfare' is concerned, does another kind of submarine warfare exist? The bombardment of cities, wasn't this also 'unrestricted,' and the dropping of the 'A' bombs, was this perhaps 'restricted'? Indeed, who ever had the idea of informing the enemy, before dropping bombs on a city, for the purpose of safeguarding the lives of its inhabitants? War is a hard and cruel thing. The duty of military professionals is to obtain victory by their arms by whatever means and in the least time possible."

Rear Admiral Felix Vargas Prada
Navy of the Republic of Peru

"I have your letter about your book concerning Grand Admiral Karl Doenitz at Nuremberg. I thought at the time and still think that the Nuremberg trials were unprincipled. Law was created *expost facto* to suit the passion and clamor of the time. The concept of *expost facto* law is not congenial to the Anglo-American viewpoint on law. Before criminal penalties can be imposed there must be fair warning that the conduct which one undertook was criminal.

"There has never been a code of International Law governing aggressive wars. So a punishment within the scope of domestic laws would have been impermissible, and I think that a nation must practice abroad what it practices and preaches at home if it is to take its place among the nations of the world and still be true to its own ideals.

"Scholars have searched frantically for little pieces of evidence of whether there was ever an International Law and have pieced together fragments that in their minds justify the conclusion that aggressive war is an international crime—but the reasoning in those cases is shaped to the urgent necessity to find an *expost facto* justification for what was done."

William O. Douglas, LL.D.
Professor of Law at Yale University, 1928-1939
Associate Justice, Supreme Court of the U.S., 1939-1975
Author of 27 books, 1940-1974

INDEX

M

N

O

P

R

S

T

V

W

Y